THE CLASSIC FARMERS' BULLETIN ANTHOLOGY
ON GROWING A SMALL-SCALE FRUIT AND VEGETABLE GARDEN FOR THE BACKYARD OR HOMESTEAD

ORIGINAL USDA TIPS AND TRADITIONAL METHODS
IN SUSTAINABLE GARDENING

BY **U.S. DEPARTMENT OF AGRICULTURE**

<u>COLLECTS USDA FARMERS BULLETINS:</u>
818, 1673, 1733, & 255

LEGACY EDITION
CLASSIC HOMESTEADERS AND FARMERS LIBRARY
BOOK 3

Doublebit Press
Eugene, OR

New content, introduction, and annotations
Copyright © 2020 by Doublebit Press. All rights reserved.
Doublebit Press is an imprint of Eagle Nest Press
www.doublebitpress.com | Eugene, OR, USA

Original content under the public domain. Originally published by the U.S. Department of Agriculture: FB 818 The Small Vegetable Garden (1917); FB 1673 The Farm Garden (1931); FB 1733 Planning a Subsistence Homestead (1934); FB 255 The Home Vegetable Garden (1906)

This title, along with other Doublebit Press books including the Classic Homesteaders and Farmers Library, are available at a volume discount for youth groups, outdoors clubs, or reading groups.

Doublebit Press Legacy Edition ISBNs
Hardcover: 978-1-64389-127-9
Paperback: 978-1-64389-128-6

Disclaimer: Because of its age and historic context, this book could contain content on present-day inappropriate methods, activities, outdated medical information, unsafe chemical and mechanical processes, or culturally and racially insensitive content. Doublebit Press, or its employees, authors, and other affiliates, assume no liability for any actions performed by readers or any damages that might be related to information contained in this book. This text has been published for historical study and for personal literary enrichment toward the goal of preserving the American handcraft and outdoors recreation tradition, timeless trade skills, and traditional artisanal knowledge.

First Doublebit Press Legacy Edition Printing, 2020
Printed in the United States of America
when purchased at retail in the USA

INTRODUCTION
Classic Homesteaders and Farmers Library

The old experts of artisanal trades, country and homestead knowledge, and the woods and mountains taught timeless principles and skills for centuries. Through their timeless books, the old experts offered rich descriptions of how the world works and encouraged learning through personal experiences *by doing*. Over the last 125 years, manufacturing, farming, and construction have substantially changed. Of course, many things have gotten simpler as equipment and technology have improved. In addition, some activities of pre-digital times are now no longer in vogue, or are even outright considered inappropriate or illegal. However, despite many of the positive changes in manufacturing and crafting methods that have occurred over the years, *there are many other skills and much knowledge that have been forgotten.*

By publishing the reprint series of the old USDA *Farmers' Bulletin*, it is our goal at Doublebit Press to do what we can to preserve and share the works from forgotten teachers that form the cornerstone of the history of the American artisans and traditional crafts. So much farm, homestead, and handcraft knowledge was passed to each generation through experience and hard work. An original mission of the US Department of Agriculture was to optimize farm outputs and increase the quality of life on farms through handcrafts, construction, and old-time farm tricks, tips, and skills. In their *Farmers' Bulletin* series, the USDA captured and passed on knowledge that applied to far more than just farmers!

Through remastered reprint editions of timeless classics, perhaps we can regain some of this lost knowledge for future generations. Today's interest in mastery of old handcraft skills, homestead self-sufficiency, and artisanal character has renewed an interest in the old arts. Luckily, the USDA's *Farmers' Bulletin* series contains thousands of pamphlets dedicated to teaching, improving life, and ensuring self-sufficiency to thrive in both the city and on a farm.

This book is an important contribution traditional handcraft and country skills literature and has important historical and collector value toward preserving the American handcraft and outdoors tradition. The knowledge it holds is an invaluable reference for practicing skills and hand craft methods. Its chapters thoroughly discuss some of the essential building blocks of knowledge that are fundamental but may have been forgotten as equipment gets fancier and technology gets smarter. In short, this anthology of *Farmers' Bulletin* pamphlets was chosen for Legacy Edition printing because much of the basic skills and knowledge it contains has been forgotten or put to the wayside in trade for more modern conveniences and methods.

With technology playing a major role in everyday life, sometimes we need to take a step back in time to find those basic building blocks used for gaining mastery – the things that we have luckily not completely lost and has been recorded in books over the last two centuries. These skills aren't forgotten, they've just been shelved. *It's time to unshelve them once again and reclaim the lost knowledge of self-sufficiency.*

Based on this commitment to preserving our outdoors and handcraft artisanal heritage, we have taken great pride in publishing this book as a complete original work. We hope it is worthy of both study and collection by outdoors folk in the modern era of outdoors and traditional skills life.

Unlike many other photocopy reproductions of classic books that are common on the market, this Legacy Edition does not simply place poor photography of old texts on our pages and use error-prone optical scanning or computer-generated text. We want our work to speak for itself, and reflect the quality demanded by our customers who spend their hard-earned money. With this in mind, each Legacy Edition book that has been chosen for publication is carefully remastered from original print books, *with the Doublebit Legacy Edition printed and laid out in the exact way that it was presented at its original publication.* We provide a beautiful, memorable experience that is as true to the original text as best as possible, but with the aid of modern technology to make as beautiful a reading experience as possible for books that can be over a century old.

Because of its age and because it is presented in its original form, the book may contain misspellings, inking errors from print plates, and other printing blemishes that were common for the age. However, these are exactly the things that we feel give the book its character, which we preserved in this Legacy Edition. During digitization, we ensured that each illustration in the text was clean and sharp with the least amount of loss from being copied and digitized as possible. Full-page plate illustrations are presented as they were found, often including the extra blank page that was often behind a plate. For the covers, we use the original cover design to give the book its original feel. We are sure you'll appreciate the fine touches and attention to detail that your Legacy Edition has to offer.

For traditional handcrafters and classic artisanal enthusiasts who demand the best from their equipment, this Doublebit Press Legacy Edition reprint was made with you in mind. Both important and minor details have equally both been accounted for by our publishing staff, down to the cover, font, layout, and images. It is the goal of Doublebit Legacy Edition series to be worthy of collection in any outdoorsperson's library and that can be passed to future generations.

Every book selected to be in this series offers unique views and instruction on important skills, advice, tips, tidbits, anecdotes, stories, and experiences that will enrich the repertoire of any person who enjoys escaping a bit from today's modern technology-based, cookie-cutter, and highly industrialized skills. Instead, folks seeking to make things with their hands like the old days may find great value from these resurrected instructional manuals from the past. These books were not simply written to be shelved in a library – they contain our history and forgotten methods to make things with real character and energy with a *human* component.

Therefore, to learn the most basic building blocks of a craft leads to mastery of all its aspects. We hope this book helps you along this path with its rich descriptions and illustrations!

About the USDA Farmers' Bulletin Series

Back in the early 1900s, the US Department of Agriculture (USDA) began publication of small pamphlets that were meant to improve the outputs of America's farms, promote self-sufficiency, and help farmers and farming communities thrive. This publication series continued for decades, and volumes were always available when someone wanted to learn more about a specific skill or topic that could come in handy on the homestead.

Each of the 2,000+ volumes specializes in one specific topic, be it growing a certain crop, raising a particular animal, or building a type of farm structure. Each of the pamphlets captured the best knowledge available at that time, which often represented decades or centuries of old farmer knowledge, which we know, is incredibly useful and reliable!

As we continue to blaze paths into the digital frontier, many of these lost "farmers' tips" have become more useful than ever, particularly to folks looking to start homesteads and small-scale farms, as well as those who just want to live more sustainably, simply, and consciously in light of today's factory processed world. The *Farmers' Bulletin* is also highly useful for people who live in cities, as they contain much information for community gardens, urban and rooftop farming, and sustainable living tips.

Unfortunately, many of these print volumes of the *Farmers' Bulletin* are now out of print. Indeed, because these texts are in the public domain, they are easily found and are available on the Internet. However, many of these books that are easily found on the web are often low-resolution photocopies, complete with scribble marks or other distracting spots. For the first time, high-quality, professionally restored *Farmers' Bulletin* reissues are being made by Doublebit Press to increase access to the timeless knowledge that each contains.

This Doublebit Press Legacy Edition republishes this tradition of handcrafted quality and artisanal work. We hope that this deluxe printed edition of this book will help you gain mastery in your craft, as it is presented in the exact form that it was originally published. Even today, the knowledge contained within its pages are timeless and have much to teach!

Finally, as works of art, the USDA *Farmers' Bulletin* issues contain beautiful illustrations and line art that are a sign of simpler, yet authentic times when quality mattered and craftsmanship was king. This collectible volume makes a great addition to the bookshelf of any handcrafter, maker, artisan, farmer, homesteader, or outdoors enthusiast!

Enjoy some old-time, vintage charm when the government actually encouraged you to be self-sufficient with these beautifully illustrated and classic instruction manuals by the USDA!

THE SMALL VEGETABLE GARDEN

SUGGESTIONS FOR UTILIZING LIMITED AREAS

FARMERS' BULLETIN 818
UNITED STATES DEPARTMENT OF AGRICULTURE

Prepared under the Direction of the Bureau of Plant Industry
WM. A. TAYLOR, Chief

Washington, D. C.   April, 1917

BY THE exercise of care and forethought in planning succession crops and rotations and by the utilization of every foot of available space it is possible to grow considerable quantities of vegetables on limited areas and so supplement the family food supply. The principal factors in accomplishing this are the use of seed boxes and hotbeds to give plants an early start in spring before seeds may be planted outdoors, the use of outside seed beds to carry plants for main-season crops while early crops are occupying the garden space, and the planting of late or succession crops as soon as earlier plants have been removed.

In order that gardening may be carried on successfully in such an intensive way it is especially important that soil of good texture be available, and that it be well supplied with humus and plant food. It is essential also, as in all gardening, that sufficient moisture be present, that the garden be kept free of weeds, and that the soil be cultivated frequently and well.

In the following pages specific suggestions are made for planning an intensive garden enterprise, for preparing the soil and maintaining its fertility, and for planting and growing the crops.

THE SMALL VEGETABLE GARDEN.

CONTENTS.

	Page.		Page.
Essentials of gardening	3	Gardener's planting table	18
Planning the small garden	4	Cultivation	24
Choosing crops	8	Irrigation	25
Aids to earliness (hotbed, seed box, cold frame)	9	Protecting plants from diseases and pests	25
		Cultural suggestions for the commoner vegetables	28
Tools	12		
Preparing the soil	14	Vegetables for winter use	42
Planting vegetables in the open	16	Fruits in the small garden	44

ESSENTIALS OF GARDENING.

THE primary needs for successful vegetable gardening on a small scale are the same as those for gardening on a large scale. On limited plots, however, greater emphasis must be placed on intensive culture and carefully arranged rotations so that every available foot of space may be made to produce the maximum yield.

The essentials of all gardening are soil of suitable texture containing available plant food, water to dissolve the plant food so that the plant rootlets may make use of it, seeds or plants which will produce the desired crops, sunshine and warmth to bring about germination and plant development, and cultivation. Much also depends upon the gardener and the care he bestows on his enterprise.

Other factors—location and exposure—can not always receive much consideration in gardening small plots since there is ordinarily little room for choice. Such spaces are located usually in yards, or the choice of location is restricted in other ways by the necessity that the spaces be accessible to dwellings. When a possibility for the exercise of choice does exist, however, several considerations should be kept in mind by the gardener. It should be recognized that frost is less likely to injure vegetables planted on high ground than those planted in low places or valleys into which the heavier cold air commonly settles; that crops will mature more rapidly on land that has a sunny, southern exposure than on other plots; that the garden should be fairly level, but well drained; and that a warm, sandy loam will produce an earlier crop than a heavier soil that retains more water and less heat.

The soil is the storehouse of plant food and should, therefore, have a relatively open texture so that the rootlets of vegetables may extend themselves readily in their search for sustenance. A high proportion of humus or rotted vegetable material is desirable in the soil, since it produces an open texture, adds nitrogen, insures the presence of beneficial bacteria, aids in unlocking plant food from mineral particles, and increases the moisture-retaining properties of the soil.

About 50 per cent of ordinary earth is not soil at all, but consists of air and water. Water makes the soluble plant food that is present in the soil freely available, while the air in the soil makes possible bacterial development and facilitates chemical action, which makes additional plant food available.

IMPORTANCE OF A GOOD SEED BED.

The cultivation of crops is important because the stirring and loosening of the soil directly conserves moisture to some extent, kills weeds, which draw moisture and plant food at the expense of the crops, and incorporates air into the soil.

Too much emphasis can not be laid on the preparation of a good seed bed. A seed bed of fine tilth—made such by deep plowing, careful harrowing, and fining of the soil—is the foundation of good gardening. It is essential for the proper germination of seeds and growth of young plants. The soil must be friable and free from clods. A clod locks up plant food and prevents its utilization by the plant. Good soil and fine tilth furnish best conditions for root development. Upon the fine, hairy, fibrous, feeding roots, which are possible only in well-tilled soil, the plant depends for its stockiness and growth.

The careful gardener will regard his whole garden as a seed bed and will cultivate and fertilize it accordingly.

FERTILIZERS.

Fertilizers, the plant foods for the garden, should be carefully selected. Nitrogen, which stimulates leaf growth, is best supplied by turning under rich, well-rotted, or composted manure or rotting vegetable matter. Sheep manure and poultry droppings will hurry plants along more rapidly than most chemical fertilizers. These substances, as well as bone meal, also a valuable fertilizer, usually may be obtained from seed stores.

PLANNING THE SMALL GARDEN.

With a little forethought a comparatively small tract of land may be made to supply the average family with fresh vegetables throughout the growing season. Most owners of small gardens are content to raise a single crop on each plot of land at their disposal. It is quite possible, however, to grow two or three crops of some vegetables in one season, and if these are properly selected the home-grown produce should be both better and cheaper than any that can be purchased on the market.

Just what vegetables are to be grown depends, of course, upon the individual tastes of the family. In general the aim of the home gardener should be to raise vegetables in which freshness is an important quality. Peas, string beans, Lima beans, asparagus, and sweet corn, for example, lose much if they are not cooked almost immediately after they are picked. On the other hand, as good

FIG. 1.—A back-yard vegetable garden which gives evidence of having received the care and attention that are essential to success in small-scale gardening.

potatoes usually can be bought as can be grown. Moreover, potatoes occupy a large area in proportion to their yield and consume in a back yard or small garden valuable space which, in most cases, could be put to much more profitable use. This may be true also, in some cases, of corn, cucumbers, squashes, and melons.

It will pay the home gardener to grow certain specialties of which he may be fond, and which may be troublesome or expensive to purchase. Okra is an example of this class, and little beds of parsley, chives, or other herbs take up very little room and provide the housewife with additions for her table, which are most welcome if they can be picked at the right moment without trouble.

THE GARDEN DIAGRAM.

If the small garden plot, however, is to be made to bring the maximum returns in economy and pleasure to the owner, every available foot of it must be made to work continuously. This can be accomplished only by careful planning, and it is recommended, therefore, that a complete lay-out for the garden be drawn up in advance. A typical plan of this character is shown in figure 1. This plan, of course, will be of use chiefly as an example, and in most cases a different arrangement will be necessary to meet the conditions surrounding individual garden spaces. On the plan the gardener may indicate the approximate date when each of his projected crops is to be planted. No more space should be allotted to each than is needed to furnish a sufficient quantity of the vegetable for family consumption or for other known needs. In many cases, also, space should be left between the rows for the interplanting of later crops and for easy cultivation. Plants which make a high growth and cause heavy shade should not be located where they will interfere with sun-loving small plants. It is well also to separate perennials, such as rhubarb and asparagus, which are not cultivated, from plants which must be tilled.

THE DIAGRAM AS A RECORD.

If a garden is planned in this way and the scheme carried out, the plan should be kept for use the following year, with notes of the success or failure of the different items in it. For example, if too much or too little of any vegetable was grown, this fact should be recorded. It is not desirable, however, to follow too closely the same plan in succeeding years. The same kind of vegetables should not be grown twice, if this can be avoided, in the same part of the garden. The danger of attack by diseases and insects is heightened when vegetables of the same kind follow each other repeatedly in a given space, such as a row or bed. If a radically different kind of plant is grown in a space, on the other hand, disease spores and insects, though present in the soil, probably will not attack the second crop.

In making a diagram of the garden it is well to use a tough paper, such as heavy wrapping paper, which will stand repeated handling and use out of doors. A fairly large scale should be adopted, so that full notes can be kept in the spaces representing rows. If the garden is fairly large or abnormally long, the diagram may be made in separate sections for the sake of convenience.

A BACK-YARD GARDEN.

The garden shown in the diagram (fig. 2) was a city back yard 25 by 70 feet in dimensions near New York City. It happened

THE SMALL VEGETABLE GARDEN. 7

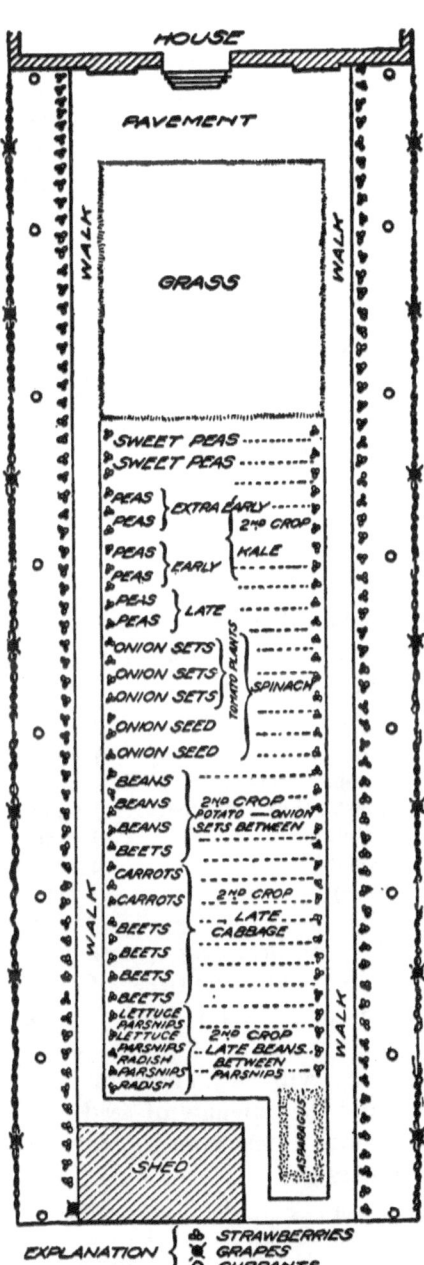

Fig. 2.—A typical back-yard garden plan, showing a possible arrangement for permanent and annual plants.

to be bounded on two sides by a board fence, and advantage was taken of this fact to plant and train grape vines. Strawberry plants were set alongside the flagstone walks and currant bushes between the walks and the fence. In the space between the bushes and the strawberries low-growing vegetables, such as bush beans, peppers, eggplants, and the like, were set out. In a space about 12 feet wide between the walks low-growing, quick-maturing varieties of early vegetables were planted in such a way that later-maturing varieties could be put out at proper intervals between them. The early plantings consisted of radishes, early beets, lettuce, carrots, and a few parsnips. The beets gave way later to a few late cabbage plants. The sunniest portion of the yard was turned over to tomatoes, of which there were about a dozen plants trained to a single stem and set about 18 inches apart in each direction. Early and late peas were put out in the least sunny portions of the yard. Later, in the fall, spinach, kale, and potato-onion sets were planted in order to provide a supply of green succulents for the winter and early spring.

IMPORTANCE OF SUNLIGHT.

In making the garden plan the gardener should recognize that no amount of fertilizer, watering, and cultivation will make up for the absence of sunlight in a garden. Careful consideration should be given to how many hours a day any part of the yard is in shadow from buildings, fences, or trees. If a successful garden is to be maintained, the greater portion of the plot must have at least five hours of sunlight a day. As a rule foliage crops, such as lettuce, spinach, and kale, do fairly well in partial shade, but even these need sunshine two or three hours a day. Plants which must ripen fruits, such as tomatoes and eggplant, should have the sunniest locations.

CHOOSING CROPS.

Vegetable seed should be ordered in advance of the time for planting in the open, so that they will be on hand for planting in flats or frames and also for use outdoors as soon as the weather and the condition of the soil make planting possible. Before ordering seed it is a good idea to look over the garden plot, decide on the best location for each vegetable, and determine how much seed will be required for the space available for each variety. The garden plan may then be drawn.

SEED FOR A FAMILY OF FOUR.

The following are the approximate quantities of seed that should be purchased for a garden which is to supply vegetables for successive plantings throughout the season for a family of four:

Beans, snap	1 pint.	Parsnips	½ ounce.
Beans, pole Lima	½ pint.	Salsify	1 ounce.
Beans, bush Lima	½ pint.	Squash, summer	½ ounce.
Cabbage, early	½ ounce.	Squash, Hubbard type	½ ounce.
Carrot	1 ounce.	Cauliflower	1 packet.
Celery	1 ounce.	Eggplant	1 packet.
Cucumber	½ ounce.	Parsley	1 packet.
Kale, or Swiss chard	½ ounce.		

For most of the vegetables listed the plantings may consist of the entire quantities mentioned. Relatively small quantities of cauliflower, eggplant, and parsley will be sufficient for most families, however.

The following vegetables undoubtedly will be planted in larger amounts than those just mentioned, and the amounts of seed given will be a guide for ordinary requirements. Some families may need more of the various vegetables and others less:

Beet	2 ounces.	Radish	1 ounce.
Cabbage, late	½ ounce.	Spinach	½ pound in spring and ½ pound in fall
Corn, sweet	1 pint.		
Lettuce	½ ounce.		
Muskmelon	1 ounce.	Tomatoes, late	¼ ounce.
Onion sets	2 quarts.	Turnips	1 ounce.
Peas, garden	2 to 4 quarts.		

The entire supply of seeds of string bean, bush Lima bean, sweet corn, lettuce, peas, and radish should not be planted at one time, but successive plantings two to three weeks apart should be made so that a fresh supply of the vegetables may be had throughout the season.

Of early Irish potatoes 1 peck to ½ bushel will be required, and of late potatoes ½ bushel to 1 bushel, or more, depending upon the amount of ground available for this purpose. If abundant space is available, it may be well to grow enough Irish potatoes to last throughout the winter.

If the family wishes to raise vegetables to supply current needs and also to supply a surplus for canning, the amounts indicated above should be increased considerably.[1]

AIDS TO EARLINESS.

The hotbed, the "flat" or seed box, and the cold frame are the gardener's greatest aids in raising early crops. The hotbed and the flat enable him to plant seed and produce seedlings long before most of the seeds may be planted out of doors and before those which have been planted in the plot have begun to germinate. The cold frame enables him to get the seedlings produced in the hotbed gradually accustomed to outdoor conditions and to raise these into strong, sturdy planting stock by the time the garden is ready for them. Resetting from a hotbed into a cold frame, or from one flat into another, or into pots, gives most plants a better root system and makes them stockier and more valuable for transplanting into the open ground. Besides being used in hardening plants that have been

FIG. 3.—A hill of beans started in a berry box in the house long before the seeds may be planted in the open garden.

---

[1] The home gardener should find useful Farmers' Bulletins 359, Canning Vegetables in the Home; 521, Canning Tomatoes, Home and Club Work; 255, Home Vegetable Garden; and 647, Home Garden in the South. The latter is designed particularly for use in the warmer climates, but contains many suggestions that can be adapted readily by home gardeners in the North. The Department of Agriculture will supply these bulletins free on application as long as its stock for free distribution lasts.

started in the hotbed, the cold frame is utilized in mild climates instead of a hotbed for starting plants before seeds can be planted safely in the open. In the extreme South the cold frame is much more extensively used than the hotbed, but each has its place in garden economy.

Still another method of giving plants an early start is used extensively for beans, cucumbers, melons, sweet corn, and other warmth-loving plants. This consists in planting enough seeds for a "hill" in berry boxes filled with soil. (Fig. 3.) The boxes are kept in the house or in greenhouses until the garden soil becomes warm, by which time the plants should have reached a considerable degree of development. The bottoms of the boxes are then cut away and the remaining frame is sunk with the plants in their permanent location in the garden.

STARTING EARLY VEGETABLES IN THE HOUSE.

The flat or seed box (fig. 4) which is kept in the house is perhaps the most practical device for use by the home gardener for starting early vegetables. By its use earlier crops of tomatoes, cabbage, cauliflower, Brussels sprouts, peppers, eggplant, and lettuce can be had with little outlay for equipment. Early potatoes sometimes are forced in the same way. Seeds

FIG. 4.—Flat or seed box for use in starting plants in the house.

so planted germinate and are ready for transplanting by the time it is safe to sow the same kind of seed in the open ground. When danger of frost is over and the soil is dry enough to work, therefore, the early garden may be started with seedlings well above the surface. Transplanting, if properly done, instead of injuring seems to help such plants to develop a strong root system.

HOW TO MAKE AND USE A SEED BOX.

Any sort of wooden box filled with good soil answers the purpose, but the following specific suggestions for a box of convenient size may be useful. Construct a box 3 to 4 inches deep, 12 to 14 inches wide, and 20 to 24 inches long. A layer of about 1 inch of gravel or cinders should be placed in the bottom of the box. It should then be filled nearly full with rich garden soil or soil enriched with decayed leaves or manure. The rich soil beneath the family woodpile or around decaying logs is splendid for this purpose. The soil should be pressed down firmly with a small piece of board and rows made one-fourth to one-half inch deep and 2 inches apart crosswise of the box. The seed should be distributed 8 or 10 to the inch in the rows and be covered. The soil should be watered and the box set in a warm place in the light. The best location is just inside a sunny window. Water enough must be given from time to time to cause the seeds to germinate and grow thriftily, but not enough to leak through the box. If a piece of glass is used to cover the box, it will hold the moisture in the soil and hasten the germination of the seeds.

When the plants are from an inch to an inch and a half high they should be thinned to 1 or 2 inches apart in the row, so as to give them space enough to make a strong stocky growth. If it is desired to keep the plants which are thinned out, they may be set 2 inches apart each way in boxes similar to the seed box. When the weather becomes mild the box of plants should be set out of doors part of the time so that the plants will "harden off" in preparation for transplanting to the garden later. A good watering should be given just before the plants are taken out of the box for transplanting, so that a large ball of earth will stick to the roots of each one.

THE HOTBED.

Locate the hotbed in some sheltered but not shaded spot which has a southern exposure. The most convenient size is a box-like structure 6 feet wide and any multiple of 3 feet long, so that standard 3 by 6 foot hotbed sash may be used. The frame should be 12 inches high in the back and 8 inches in the front. This slope is for the purpose of securing a better angle for the sun's rays and should be faced toward the south.

The hotbed not only must collect any heat it can from the sun, but also must generate heat of its own from fermentation in fresh manure. Fresh horse manure, free from stable litter, is best for generating heat.

If the hotbed is to be an annual affair, make an excavation 18 inches to 2 feet deep, about 2 feet greater in length and width than the frame carrying the sash. Line the excavation with plank or with a brick or concrete wall. A drain to carry off surplus water is essential. This may consist of either tile or pipe extending to a low portion of the garden or a trench partially filled with coarse stones covered with a layer of hay or sod and then filled level with soil.

After a sufficient amount of fresh horse manure has been accumulated fill the hotbed pit, and while it is being filled tramp the manure as firmly and as evenly as possible. When the ground level is reached, place the frame in position and bank the sides and ends with manure. Place about 3 inches of good garden loam on top of the manure inside the frame and cover it with the sash. After the heat has reached its maximum and has subsided to between 80° and 90° F. it will be safe to plant the seeds. Select the plumpest, freshest seeds obtainable. Use standard varieties, and get them from reliable seed houses.

Keep the bed partially dark until the seeds germinate.

After germination, however, the plants will need all the light possible, exclusive of the direct rays of the sun, to keep them growing rapidly. This is a crisis in plant life, and ventilating and watering with great care are of prime importance. Too close planting and too much heat and water cause the plants to become spindling. Water the plants on clear days, in the morning, and ventilate immediately to dry the foliage and to prevent mildew.

FIG. 5.—Cold frame open for ventilating plants.

THE COLD FRAME.

The cold frame (fig. 5), so useful in hardening plants started in the hotbed and for starting plants in mild climates, is constructed in much the same way as the hotbed, except that no manure is used, and the frame may be covered either with glass sash or with canvas. A cold frame may be built on the surface of the ground, but a more permanent structure suitable for holding plants over winter will require a pit 18 to 24 inches deep. The cold frame should be filled with a good potting soil. The plants should have more ventilation in the cold frame, but should not receive so much water. It is best to keep the soil rather dry.

In transplanting, remember that plants usually thrive better if transplanted into ground that has been freshly cultivated. Transplanting to the open field is best done in cool, cloudy weather and in the afternoon. This prevents the sun's rays from causing the plant to lose too much moisture through evaporation. In transplanting the gardener will find a child's express wagon an excellent trolley tray for bedding out his seedlings.

TOOLS.

The necessary tools for preparing and caring for the small garden are few. A spade or garden fork for digging, a hoe, a steel-tooth rake, a trowel, and a dibble or pointed stick complete the list of essentials. The gardener will find it convenient, however, to possess some additional implements. (Fig. 6.) If tree roots underlie any portion of the garden plot and must be cut away, a hatchet, ax, or mattock will be a real necessity. If the soil of the plot has become compacted, as where walks have existed, a pick may be needed for digging. Perhaps in such cases it will be most economical to fill both cutting and digging needs by purchasing a pick-ax which has a pick point at one end of the head and a cutting blade at the other. Apparatus for watering plants also should be included. This may be a watering pot of generous proportions or, where running water is available, a

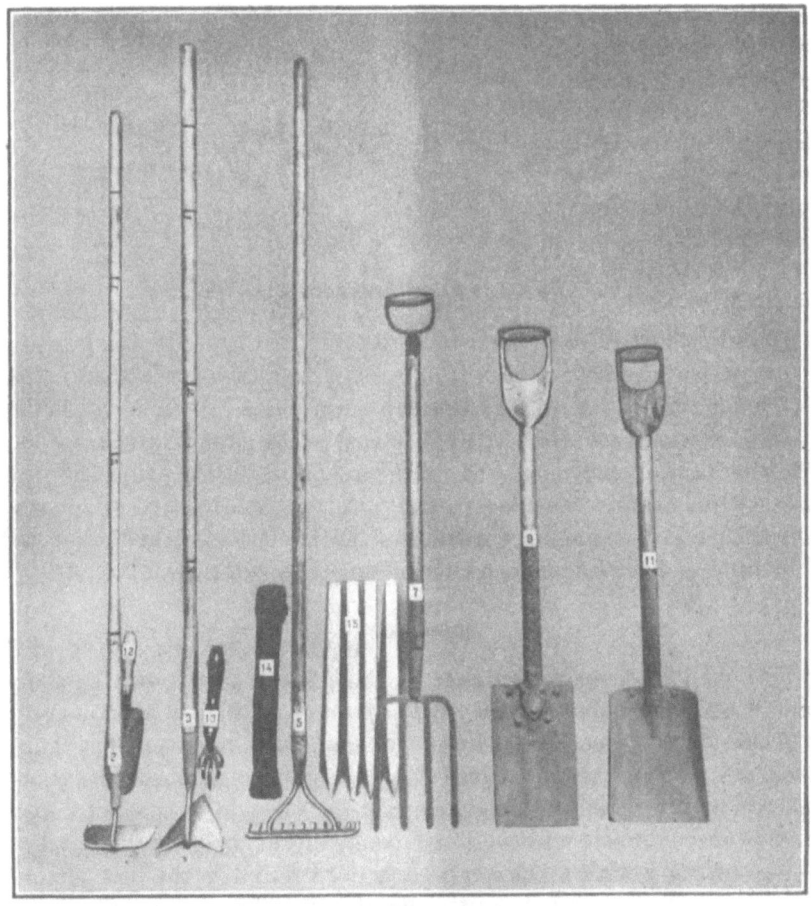

FIG. 6.—A set of garden tools, including the essential implements and a few others. (2) Hoe, (3) heart-shaped furrow hoe, (5) steel-tooth rake, (7) fork, (9) spade, (11) shovel, (12) trowel, (13) scratch weeder, (14) line, (15) stakes. Note that the handles of some of the longer implements are marked off in feet and half feet for convenience in measuring.

hose. In order that rows may be made straight and uniform a substantial line or cord should be provided.

A most convenient implement for use in the home garden, especially where the plot is fairly large, is a hand cultivator or wheel hoe. (Fig. 7.) This implement is a miniature cultivator or plow, with adjustable blades, mounted on a wheel or wheels, and is pushed along by hand. Attachments make possible either the turning of small furrows, the stirring of the soil, or the removal of weeds. Much time and labor may be saved by such a device.

Among the other implements which may be useful in the home garden but which are not essential are planting and cultivating hoes of special shapes, a combination hoe and rake, a wheelbarrow, a shovel, hand weeding tools, and other small implements for special uses (fig. 8).

FIG. 7.—Wheel hoe.

PREPARING THE SOIL.

A simple test to determine when garden soil is ready for plowing or working is to take a handful of earth from the surface and close the fingers tightly on it. If the earth compacted in this way is dry enough for cultivation, it will fall apart when the hand is opened. This test is applicable only to comparatively heavy soils, but it is these which receive the most injury if they are worked when wet. On such soils overzealous gardeners not only waste their time but frequently do actual damage by attempting to work them too early.

BREAKING.

The kind of preparation that must be given to the small garden and the amount of work that will be required will depend largely, of course, on the condition of the plot and the use to which it has been put. If the ground selected for the garden has been firmed by much tramping, as is often the case in back yards, it can not be got into proper condition without the expenditure of considerable labor. When plowing with a team can be practiced that is the best method for giving the ground its initial breaking. The surface, of course, should be harrowed as soon as possible after plowing.

If the plot can not be plowed, the gardener must resort to the use of a garden fork or spade or, in the case of very hard spots, a mattock. The soil should be well loosened to the depth of the spade or fork. If heavy clay is encountered at this depth, it should not be turned up to the surface, but the slices of soil should be kept in their normal position. As soon as each spade or fork full of earth is loosened, it should be broken up by blows with the back of the implement. Later the freshly dug surface should be fined and smoothed with a steel-tooth rake. It is not sufficient that the surface be made fine; the soil should be well pulverized to the depth of the digging. Any sod or plant growth on the garden plot should be turned under to rot and form humus. In turning under sod with a spade or fork it is well to reverse each segment so that foliage will be down and roots up.

Fig. 8.—Small hand tools for the garden. From left to right they are: Hand weeder, dibble, onion hoe, trowel, and scratch or claw weeder.

The first digging of a plot of ground which has not before been cultivated is likely to be a laborious task, and may even take away the enthusiasm of the would-be gardener. After this portion of the work is done, however, the fining of the soil, planting, and cultivation are not arduous. It may be well in many cases for the gardener to employ some one to break his ground, whether this be done with plow, spade, or fork.

IMPROVING SOIL TEXTURE.

It is desirable that the soil of the garden be as open and light as possible. Where a natural loam exists in the plot good texture can be given by digging and cultivating. Where the soil is heavy, containing much clay, however, other steps are necessary. If clean sand is available this may be mixed with the soil. Well-sifted coal ashes which, unlike wood ashes, have no fertilizing value, are useful in lightening the soil. Care should be taken that no coarse cinders or pieces of partly burned coal are added to the soil with the ashes.

Lime added to the soil also will tend to lighten it and will, at the same time, correct acidity. A thin coat of air-slaked lime should be spread on the ground and worked in well. Lime is not a plant food, but its function in gardening is important none the less. By correcting acidity it makes possible the development of countless soil bacteria which aid in unlocking plant food from the mineral particles of the soil and in making these substances available for the plants. In acid soils these helpful organisms do not thrive, and in their absence vegetables do not grow at their best.

FERTILIZERS.

After the soil has been got into good mechanical condition, it usually is desirable to apply some form of fertilizer. Barnyard or stable manure, which furnishes both plant food and humus, undoubtedly is the best, and applications of from 20 to 30 tons to the acre are satisfactory. This is roughly equivalent to from 400 to 600 pounds, or several wheelbarrow loads, for each plot 20 by 20 feet. The manure should be distributed evenly over the surface, and later worked in with a hoe and rake.

Frequently it is advisable also to apply commercial fertilizer. An application of 1,000 to 1,500 pounds to the acre, or 10 to 15 pounds per plot 20 feet square, usually is sufficient. In order to supply potash, if this is needed, unleached wood ashes may be distributed over the garden at the rate of 1,000 pounds to the acre, or 10 pounds to each plot 20 feet square. Wet or leached ashes have less fertilizer value. Double the quantity of these should be used. In order to start the plants in the spring, applications of 100 pounds to the acre of nitrate of soda, or 1 pound to each 20-foot square, may be used. By far the best way to use nitrate of soda in the small garden, however, is to dissolve a teaspoonful of the chemical in a gallon of water and use the solution for watering young plants. It is important to remember that no form of commercial fertilizer will yield good results unless the soil is well supplied with humus.

Reference already has been made to the use of prepared sheep manure as a fertilizer. When this plant food can be obtained at a reasonable price, it is perhaps the safest concentrated fertilizer for use by the home gardener. It will not pay to broadcast prepared sheep manure. Small quantities should be applied under the drill when the seeds are planted or the plants set out. Later applications may be worked in with a trowel around the plants.

PLANTING VEGETABLES IN THE OPEN.

WHEN TO PLANT.

Vegetables may be divided into two classes—" cold temperature " and " warm temperature " vegetables. When peach and plum trees are in blossom, or, where these trees do not occur, when silver maples put forth leaves, or catkins appear on willows and poplars, it is time to sow in the open ground the seeds of lettuce, spinach, kale, endive, radish, parsley, beets, turnips, cabbage, cauliflower, Brussels sprouts, carrots, round-seeded peas, and onions. The wrinkled peas should not be planted until later, as they are more likely to rot in cool ground than are the smooth varieties. When the apple trees bloom, or when the dogwood and white oak buds unfold, it is time to plant the heat-loving vegetables such as cucumbers, beans, sweet corn, okra, pumpkin, and squash. This is an old approximation for planting dates, but has been found in most cases to be satisfactory.

Planting times may be fixed in still another way on the basis of the occurrence of frost. Frost ordinarily will kill tender growths of vegetables, but young plants of a few kinds will survive light frosts. Among the latter, which may be called Group I, are cabbage, lettuce, Irish potatoes, early peas (smooth seeded), onion seeds and sets, parsnips, salsify, beets, radishes, and such salad plants as kale, spinach, and mustard.

A "second early" group of vegetables, which may be called Group II, may be planted as soon as danger of frost is over. In this group are included lettuce plants and seeds, radishes, wrinkled peas, carrots, and early sweet corn.

A week or 10 days after the seeds and plants of Group II are placed in the ground, string beans and late sweet corn, constituting Group III, may be planted.

A group of plants, which may be called Group IV, should be planted only after the ground has begun to warm up. In this group are cucumbers, melons, squashes, pumpkins, Lima beans, and tomato, eggplant, and pepper plants.

Detailed suggestions for planting are given in a table on pages 18 and 19

DEPTHS OF PLANTING.

No general rule can be given with regard to the depth for planting seeds, since different varieties of vegetables and different soils necessitate different practices. The smaller the seeds, usually, the shallower the planting should be. In heavy clay or moist soils the covering should be lighter than in sandy or dry soils.

GARDENER'S PLANTING TABLE.

Quantity of seeds or number of plants required for a row 100 feet in length, with distances to plant, times for planting, and period required for production of crop.

[Brackets indicate that a late or second crop may be planted the same season.]

Kind of vegetable.	Seeds or plants required for 100 feet of row.	Distance for plants to stand— Rows apart. Horse cultivation.	Distance for plants to stand— Rows apart. Hand cultivation.	Distance for plants to stand— Plants apart in rows.	Depth of planting.	Time of planting in open ground. South.	Time of planting in open ground. North.	Ready for use after planting.
Artichoke, globe	½ ounce	3 to 4 ft	2 to 3 ft	2 to 3 ft	1 to 2 in	Spring	Spring	15 months.
Artichoke, Jerusalem	2 qts. tubers	3 to 4 ft	1 to 2 ft	1 to 2 ft	2 to 3 in	Spring	Spring	6 to 8 months.
Asparagus, seed	1 ounce	30 to 36 in	1 to 2 ft	3 to 5 in	1 to 2 in	Autumn or early spring	Early spring	3 to 4 years.
Asparagus, plants	60 to 80 plants	3 to 5 ft	12 to 24 in	15 to 20 in	3 to 5 in	Autumn or early spring	Early spring	1 to 3 years.
Beans, bush	1 pint	30 to 36 in	18 to 24 in	5 or 8 to ft	½ to 2 in	February to April. [August to September.]	April to July	40 to 65 day.
Beans, pole	½ pint	3 to 4 ft	3 to 4 ft	3 to 4 ft	1 to 2 in	Late spring	May and June	50 to 80 days.
Beets	2 ounces	24 to 36 in	12 to 18 in	5 or 6 to ft	1 to 2 in	February to April. [August to September.]	April to August	60 to 80 days.
Brussels sprouts	¼ ounce	30 to 36 in	24 to 30 in	16 to 24 in	½ in	January to July	May and June	90 to 120 days.
Cabbage, early	¼ ounce	30 to 36 in	24 to 30 in	12 to 18 in	½ in	October to December	March and April. (Start in hotbed during February.)	90 to 130 days
Cabbage, late	¼ ounce	30 to 40 in	24 to 36 in	16 to 24 in	½ in	June and July	May and June	90 to 130 days
Cardoon	½ ounce	3 ft	2 ft	12 to 18 in	1 to 2 in	Early spring	April and May	5 to 6 months.
Carrot	1 ounce	30 to 36 in	18 to 24 in	6 or 7 to ft	½ in	March and April. [September.]	April to June	75 to 110 days.
Cauliflower	¼ ounce	30 to 36 in	24 to 30 in	14 to 18 in	½ in	January and February. [June.]	April to June. (Start in hotbed during February or March.)	100 to 130 days.
Celeriac	¼ ounce	30 to 36 in	18 to 24 in	4 or 5 to ft	⅛ in	Late spring	May and June. (Start in cold frame during April.)	100 to 150 days.
Celery	¼ ounce	3 to 6 ft	18 to 36 in	4 to 8 in	⅛ in	August to October	May and June. (Start in hotbed or cold frame during March or April.)	120 to 150 days.
Chervil	1 ounce	30 to 36 in	18 to 24 in	3 or 4 to ft	1 in	Autumn	Autumn	1 year.
Chicory	¼ ounce	30 to 36 in	18 to 24 in	4 or 5 to ft	½ in	March and April	May and June	5 to 6 months.
Citron	1 ounce	8 to 10 ft	8 to 10 ft	8 to 10 ft	1 to 2 in	March and April	May and June	100 to 130 days.
Collards	¼ ounce	30 to 36 in	24 to 30 in	14 to 18 in	½ in	May and June	Late spring	100 to 120 days.
Corn salad	2 ounces	30 in	12 to 18 in	5 or 6 to ft	½ to 1 in	January and February. [September and October.]	March to September	60 days.
Corn, sweet	½ pint	36 to 42 in	30 to 36 in	30 to 36 in	1 to 2 in	February to April	May to July	60 to 100 days.
Cress, upland	½ ounce	30 in	12 to 18 in	4 or 5 to ft	½ to 1 in	January and February. [Autumn.]	March to May. [September]	30 to 40 days.

Cress, water	½ ounce	Broadcast			On surface	Early spring	April to September	60 to 70 days.
Cucumber	½ ounce	4 to 6 ft	4 to 6 ft	4 to 6 ft	1 to 2 in	February and March. [September.]	April to July	60 to 80 days.
Dandelion	¼ ounce	30 in	18 to 24 in	8 to 12 in	⅛ in	Early spring or autumn	Early spring	6 to 12 months.
Eggplant	½ ounce	30 to 36 in	24 to 30 in	18 to 24 in	½ to 1 in	February to April	April and May. (Start in hotbed during March.)	100 to 140 days.
Endive	1 ounce	30 in	18 in	8 to 12 in	½ to 1 in	February to April	April. [July]	90 to 180 days.
Horse-radish	70 roots	30 to 40 in	24 to 30 in	14 to 20 in	3 to 4 in	Early spring	Early spring	1 to 2 years.
Kale, or borecole	¼ ounce	30 to 36 in	18 to 24 in	18 to 24 in	½ in	October to February	August and September. [March and April.]	90 to 120 days.
Kohl-rabi	¼ ounce	30 to 36 in	18 to 24 in	4 to 8 in	½ in	September to March	March to May	60 to 80 days.
Leek	½ ounce	30 to 36 in	14 to 20 in	4 to 8 in	1 in	May to September	March to May	120 to 180 days.
Lettuce	½ ounce	30 in	12 to 18 in	4 to 6 in	½ in	September to March	March to September	60 to 90 days.
Melon, muskmelon	½ ounce	6 to 8 ft	6 to 8 ft	Hills 6 ft	1 to 2 in	February to April	April to June. (Start early plants in hotbed during March.)	120 to 150 days.
Melon, watermelon	1 ounce	8 to 12 ft	8 to 12 ft	Hills 10 ft	1 to 2 in	March to May	May and June	100 to 120 days.
Mustard	¼ ounce	30 to 36 in	12 to 18 in	4 or 5 to ft	¼ in	Autumn or early spring	March to May. [September]	60 to 90 days.
New Zealand spinach	1 ounce	36 in	24 to 36 in	12 to 18 in	1 to 2 in	Early spring	Early spring	60 to 100 days.
Okra, or gumbo	2 ounces	4 to 5 ft	3 to 4 ft	24 to 30 in	1 to 2 in	February to April	May and June	90 to 140 days.
Onion, seed	1 ounce	24 to 36 in	12 to 18 in	4 or 5 to ft	½ to 1 in	October to March	April and May	130 to 150 days.
Onion, sets	1 quart of sets	24 to 36 in	12 to 18 in	4 or 5 to ft	1 to 2 in	Early spring	Autumn and February to May.	90 to 120 days.
Parsley	¼ ounce	24 to 36 in	12 to 18 in	3 to 6 in	⅛ in	September to May	September and early spring	90 to 120 days.
Parsnip	½ ounce	30 to 36 in	18 to 24 in	5 or 6 to ft	½ to 1 in		April and May	125 to 160 days.
Peas	1 to 2 pints	3 to 4 ft	30 to 36 in	15 to ft	2 to 3 in	September to April	March to June	40 to 80 days.
Pepper	⅛ ounce	30 to 36 in	18 to 24 in	15 to 18 in	½ in	Early spring	May and June. (Start early plants in hotbed during March.)	100 to 140 days.
Physalis	½ ounce	30 to 36 in	18 to 24 in	18 to 24 in	½ in	March to May	May and June	130 to 160 days.
Potato, Irish	5 lbs. (or 9 bu. per acre).	30 to 36 in	24 to 36 in	14 to 18 in	4 in	January to April	March to June	80 to 140 days.
Potato, sweet	3 lbs. (or 75 slips).	3 to 5 ft	3 to 5 ft	14 in	3 in	April and May	May and June. (Start plants in hotbed during April.)	140 to 160 days.
Pumpkin	½ ounce	8 to 12 ft	8 to 12 ft	Hills 8 to 12 ft.	1 to 2 in	April and May	May to July	100 to 140 days.
Radish	1 ounce	24 to 36 in	12 to 18 in	8 to 12 to ft	½ to 1 in	September to April	March to September	20 to 40 days.
Rhubarb, seed	½ ounce	36 in	30 to 36 in	6 to 8 in	½ to 1 in		Early spring	2 to 4 years.
Rhubarb, plants	33 plants	3 to 5 ft	3 to 5 ft	3 ft	2 to 3 in		Autumn or early spring	1 to 3 years.
Rutabaga	¼ ounce	30 to 36 in	18 to 24 in	6 to 8 in	½ to 1 in	August and September	May and June	60 to 80 days.
Salsify	1 ounce	30 to 36 in	18 to 24 in	2 to 4 in	½ to 1 in		Early spring	120 to 180 days.
Spinach	1 ounce	30 to 36 in	12 to 18 in	7 or 8 to ft	1 to 2 in	September to February	September or very early spring.	30 to 60 days.
Squash, bush	½ ounce	3 to 4 ft	3 to 4 ft	Hills 3 to 4 ft.	1 to 2 in	Spring	April to June	60 to 80 days.
Squash, late	½ ounce	7 to 10 ft	7 to 10 ft	Hills 7 to 9 ft.	1 to 2 in	Spring	April to June	120 to 160 days.
Tomato	⅛ ounce	3 to 5 ft	3 to 4 ft	3 ft	½ to 1 in	December to March	May and June. (Start early plants in hotbed during February and March.)	100 to 140 days.
Turnip	½ ounce	24 to 36 in	18 to 24 in	6 or 7 to ft	¼ to ½ in	August to October	April. [July]	60 to 80 days.
Vegetable marrow	½ ounce	8 to 12 ft	8 to 12 ft	Hills 8 to 9 ft.	1 to 2 in	Spring	April to June	110 to 140 days.

SEED BEDS.

The gardener may find it desirable to reserve a small area of his garden for a seed bed in which some of the second crops for his rotations may be grown while the ground in which they are to develop is still occupied. In this way also advantage is taken of the fact that transplanting makes for stockiness. In seed-bed culture much the same practices are in force as in growing plantlets in flats and frames. The rows of seeds, however, are not spaced so closely in the outdoor seed beds as in the boxes and frames. When the plantlets crowd they may be thinned out or transplanted to another part of the seed bed. Late cabbage, lettuce, Brussels sprouts, cauliflower, etc., are plants that in many cases may be treated conveniently in this way.

FIG. 9.—Use of a rake handle and line in opening a furrow for planting.

PLANTING PRACTICES.

In planting many kinds of seeds in the garden thick sowings are made to insure a good stand, and the superfluous plants later are pulled up. Straight rows or drills should be used in all cases. The use of a line will make accuracy possible. The line is stretched between stakes at the ends of the row, and with this as a guide the furrow is then opened. This may be done with the end of a hoe or rake handle (fig. 9), with the corner of a hoe, or the point of a special furrow hoe, with a hand plow, or with the edge of a board pressed into the loosened soil. Small seeds may be shaken out of the packet by hand in a thin stream while the packet is held close to the bottom of the furrow. Larger seeds, like peas and beans, may be dropped from the hand. Mechanical planters, built like wheel hoes, may be purchased if the size of the garden justifies their use.

DRILLS, ROWS, AND HILLS.

Small plants which are to be left almost touching each other, as is the case with onions and carrots, are said to be grown in drills. Plants grown at fixed distances, as cabbages or potatoes, are in rows. When plants are grown at distances of several feet apart in both directions they are said to be in hills. Furrows are opened for planting in both drills and rows. Hills, however, may be opened with a spade or trowel. An excellent method of using fertilizer is to apply it in the drills, rows, or hills before planting. In such cases the fertilizer should be mixed carefully with the soil in the bottom of the opening before the seeds are deposited.

FINAL PLANTING TOUCHES.

In planting the gardener should keep in mind that to germinate and develop properly into sturdy plants the seed must be firmly imbedded in well-fined, moist soil. The condition of the soil beneath the seeds is most important, since it is in this soil that the rootlets on emerging must find sustenance. Air spaces or cracks may cause the rootlets to shrivel. It is well, therefore, especially if the soil is at all dry, to force the seeds gently into the soil, compacting it slightly. This may be done with the back of a hoe in the case of small seeds, or with the ball of the foot when large seeds such as beans and peas are being planted. The seeds should then be covered immediately with soil. This should be very slightly compacted over the seeds with the back of the hoe. If weather conditions are such that there is a tendency for the soil to bake over the drills and rows before the plants appear, it is well to rake very lightly with a steel-tooth rake. It may be necessary, also, to work the ground at the sides of the rows as the plants are breaking through the surface. This should be done very carefully to avoid injury to the tender shoots.

SETTING OUT PLANTS.

Plants grown in flats, hotbeds, or cold frames should be "hardened off" as has already been suggested, before they are to be planted out of doors. Another preliminary step, if the plants are too tall or succulent, is to trim away about one-half of the large leaves. Several hours before transplanting the plants should be watered thoroughly, so that the soil will be moist enough to stick to the roots in balls of considerable bulk. After staking out rows and marking planting positions, lift the plants out with a trowel, keeping as much soil as possible on the roots. Cut or tear the plants apart when their roots are intertwined.

If the ground is moist, merely open a hole with a trowel or dibble, insert the earth-incased roots of a plant, draw soil up to the stalk and firm with knuckles and the balls of thumbs. If the soil is at all dry, pour about a pint of water into each hole before the plant is set. The surface about each plant should be raked carefully when all the plants are set.

Transplanting (fig. 10) should be done if possible in cloudy weather or late in the afternoon. If the weather is especially bright it may be necessary for a day or two to shade the plants with news-

FIG. 10.—Transplanting stimulates branching root growth. Celery plants on the left were transplanted; those on right were not transplanted.

papers folded in inverted V shape and held in place with stones, earth, or other material.

The quickest crop to mature is the radish. Lettuce, turnips, peas, beets, and beans usually require 6 to 9 weeks to mature; cabbage, potatoes, early peas, onion sets, and salad greens, 10 to 12 weeks; corn from 11 to 13 weeks, and potatoes from 15 to 16 weeks.

SUCCESSIONS AND ROTATIONS.

Since a number of vegetables reach maturity early in the season, it is possible to utilize the space they occupied for successive plantings of the same vegetables or for rotation plantings of different plants. The earliest of all the vegetables to mature is the radish. The gardener generally can count on being able to utilize anew the space occupied by the first planting of these vegetables in from 5 to 7 weeks, depending on the rapidity with which they are consumed. In intensive gardening, however, it is not necessary to wait until all the radishes of the first planting have been removed before other plantings can be made. Enough of the roots can be removed at intervals to make places for setting lettuce, cabbage, cauliflower, Brussels sprouts, or other plants, and the two crops—radishes and the interplanted crop—can continue growing side by side until the former is used. In a similar way onion sets may be set out in rows that are to be occupied later by tomato plants, room being made for the latter by the removal of a few onions when the proper planting time for tomatoes arrives. Various combinations of this sort can be worked out between quick-maturing crops and the plants grown in frames or seed beds for later planting in the open.

The gardener should not plant all of his radish, lettuce, or spinach seed at once, but should make several successive plantings at intervals of about two weeks. In this way the season for these vegetables will be lengthened greatly. Successive planting is possible also with beets, peas, beans, sweet corn, and a number of other vegetables. The best of the successive crops of the quick-maturing vegetables must be crowded into the early part of the season, since most such plants do not thrive well when planted in hot weather. This is especially true of radishes and lettuce. In the case of lettuce this disadvantage can be overcome to a certain extent by artificial shading.

In all sections but the extreme north it usually is possible to grow fall crops of certain vegetables, notably carrots, beans, radishes, Irish potatoes, and turnips. In the southern part of the country an even larger number of vegetables may be grown in the fall. The seeds for these late crops are planted from July to September, depending on whether the garden is in the northern or southern States.

In planting rotations of crops, whether the rotations be during the same or in succeeding seasons, certain general principles should be kept in mind. In type and character of growth the succeeding plant should differ as widely as possible from the plant which it follows. This is both for the purpose of avoiding attacks by insects and diseases, and to insure that the second crop shall be properly nourished. A good plan is not to have root plants, such as beets and carrots, nor plants of the same family, such as cabbage and Brussels sprouts, or tomatoes and peppers, follow each other. It is well to divide the plants into root crops, fruiting crops, and foliage crops, and have members of the different groups alternate.

For the convenience of gardeners who wish to plan to use their soil to best advantage by means of successive plantings and rotations, the following groupings of vegetables are made:

1. Crops Occupying the Ground all Season.

Asparagus.	Salsify.	Eggplant.
Rhubarb.	Corn, late.	Peppers.
Beans, pole snap.	Cucumbers.	Onions (from seeds).
Beans, pole Lima.	Melons.	Leeks.
Beets, late.	Squash.	Okra.
Carrots, late.	Pumpkins.	Potatoes, main crop.
Parsnips.	Tomatoes.	Rutabagas.

2. Successive Crops.

Radish.	Peas.	Turnips.
Spinach.	Beans, dwarf.	Kohl-rabi.
Lettuce.	Parsley.	

3. Early Crops Which May be Followed by Others.[1]

Onion sets.	Turnips, early.	Corn, early.
Beets, early.	Carrots, early.	Cabbage, early.

4. Late Crops Which May Follow Others.[2]

Beets, late.	Cabbage, late.	Kale.
Spinach.	Brussels sprouts.	Endive.
Peas, late.	Cauliflower.	Flat turnips.
Celery.		

CULTIVATION.

The importance of cultivation has been referred to in the discussion of the preparation of the seed bed. It is, however, after the seeds have sprouted or after the plants have been set in their permanent locations that cultivation becomes of major importance. The gardener should never permit the surface of the soil to become baked or even to form an appreciable crust. Constant stirring with hand tools or a wheel cultivator should be practiced between the rows and about the plants. Such a stirring permits the air to penetrate the soil, where it facilitates chemical action and bacterial activity, destroys weeds which otherwise would utilize large amounts of plant food, and, finally, conserves the moisture supply. The rake is perhaps the gardener's most valuable tool in cultivating. This can be passed backward and forward over the ground until it is in an open, mellow condition. Where vegetables grow closely in the rows it often

---

[1] In addition to the vegetables listed in this group, all of those listed in Group II may be followed by other crops.
[2] Group II crops also may follow early crops.

will be necessary to supplement the cultivation by hand weeding. Small implements are made for this purpose, and may be purchased cheaply. It is well also in some cases to pull up weeds by hand, especially where they grow closely about the stalks of the garden plants.

STIRRING THE SOIL AFTER RAINS.

Just as the gardener should be careful in early spring not to dig the ground when the soil is too moist, so he should be careful later in the season not to cultivate too soon after rains. The stirring of very muddy soil " puddles " it into a compact, cement-like mass in which the plant food is securely locked. The garden will require attention, however, as soon as the excess moisture from a rain has soaked in or partially evaporated. Unless the ground is stirred at this time a crust will form almost inevitably. Such a crust, besides restricting the plants, prevents the access of air, and also facilitates the loss of moisture through evaporation.

IRRIGATION.

When, during prolonged dry spells, the plants give evidence of suffering because of the lack of moisture, water must, if possible, be supplied artificially. Where a supply of piped water is at hand, perhaps the most usual method of irrigation is by sprinkling with a hose. If sprinkling is practiced it should be done late in the afternoon. It is not sufficient merely to dampen the surface; a thorough wetting should be given. A more satisfactory and more economical method of irrigation, however, is to open small furrows between the rows of growing plants and to supply water in these ditches from a hose or pipe. Several hours after the water has soaked in, the dry earth should be drawn back into place.

PROTECTING PLANTS FROM DISEASES AND PESTS.

Unfortunately the gardener is not assured of success when his plants have started to grow thriftily. He must count almost inevitably upon the presence in his garden of plant diseases and pests, which, if not combated, will interfere seriously with his yields or even destroy his plants. It is hard for some gardeners to realize the importance of making early provision to combat these enemies of plant life. It can not be too strongly emphasized, however, that such provision is of equal importance with other phases of gardening and that it should under no circumstances be neglected. The wise gardener does not wait for the appearance of insects and diseases, but takes steps to combat them by spraying the plants at reasonable intervals from early spring until his crops have been harvested, or by other protective measures. He thus insures himself against the likelihood of loss.

The necessary implements and materials for protecting the home garden against insects and diseases should be assembled early in the season. These consist of a substantial hand sprayer and the necessary concentrated solutions, which, after dilution with water, are to be sprayed on the plants.

The diseases which affect garden plants may be divided into two groups, parasitic and constitutional diseases. The parasitic maladies, such as the blights, are caused by fungi or germs, and usually may be prevented or controlled by spraying with Bordeaux mixture. Little is known, however, of the so-called constitutional diseases, and little can be done to prevent their ravages. If some malady which does not yield to treatment with Bordeaux mixture manifests itself on isolated plants in the garden, it may be well to pull up these plants and burn them.

The insects which attack garden plants may be divided into two groups—those which eat or chew the fruit or foliage, and those which suck the plant juices. Eating insects may be killed usually by spraying poisonous solutions or dusting powders on the plants which they attack. Arsenate of lead is the poison in most general use for this purpose. This substance is poisonous to persons as well as to insects and must be used with care. It should not be applied to vegetables that are to be used soon. All vegetables should be washed carefully before they are eaten, regardless of whether they have been sprayed.

Most of the garden plants may be guarded against disease and at the same time protected from attack by eating insects by spraying at intervals of two weeks with a combination of Bordeaux mixture and arsenate of lead.

Other methods of protecting plants from the larger eating insects are to pick the pests by hand or knock them with a stick into a pan containing water on which a thin film of kerosene is floating. Insects collected by hand should be destroyed promptly. Young plants may be protected by setting over them wooden frames covered with mosquito netting, wire mesh, or cheesecloth. Cutworms may be kept from plants by setting tin or paper collars into the ground around the stalks.

Sucking insects, such as plant lice, can not be killed by poisoning the surface of the leaves and fruit, since they feed by puncturing the plants and extracting the internal juices. Poisons which will kill by contact or substances which envelop and smother the pests are, therefore, employed against the sucking insects. The principal remedies of this sort are nicotine solutions, fish-oil and other soap solutions, and kerosene emulsion.

The following table lists the insects most likely to appear in the vegetable garden and furnishes information in regard to the plants attacked and the treatment recommended:

Principal insects and remedies.[1]

Insect.	Plants attacked.	Treatment.
Eating type:		
Tomato worms	Tomato	Hand pick or spray with arsenate of lead.
Cabbage worm	Cabbage group	Hand pick or apply arsenate of lead.
Cucumber beetles	Cucumber	Cover with frames. Apply tobacco dust or spray with Bordeaux mixture or arsenate of lead.
Cutworms	Tomato, cabbage, onion	Apply poison bait; place tin or paper collars around plants; hand pick; apply Paris green or arsenate of lead.
Potato beetle	Potato, eggplant, and tomato	Hand pick and apply arsenate of lead.
Sucking type:		
Squash bug	Squash, pumpkin, melons, etc.	Hand pick; spray with kerosene emulsion or nicotine sulphate.
Aphis (plant lice)	Cabbage group and other plants.	Spray with kerosene emulsion, a solution of hard soap, or nicotine sulphate.

Gardeners desiring additional information in regard to insects affecting the vegetable garden should apply direct to the Bureau of Entomology, United States Department of Agriculture, but it should be understood that there is no publication covering the entire subject. Specimens of insects with some account of food plants and ravages should accompany correspondence.

The gardener should remember that many plant diseases and insects exist in the garden from year to year. At the end of the growing season, therefore, the garden should be carefully cleaned of rubbish, the

FIG. 11.—Head lettuce produces very tender, almost white leaves in the center of the heads, but is somewhat harder to grow than the loose-leaf sorts.

stems of plants, leaves, etc. It is necessary to burn this débris promptly, as any disease spores or insects which may be present are then surely destroyed.

[1] Methods of protecting gardens against grasshoppers are given in Farmers' Bulletin 691, "Grasshoppers and Their Control on Sugar Beets and Truck Crops."

Fig. 12.—Loose-leaf or open-headed lettuce is excellent for growing in the home garden, since its cultural requirements are not so exacting as those of head lettuce.

CULTURAL SUGGESTIONS FOR THE COMMONER VEGETABLES.

RADISH.

Radishes are so hardy that they may be grown through the winter in cold frames in the latitude of Washington and farther South in the open ground. In the North they require hotbeds, but can be sown in the open ground as soon as the soil is moderately warm. They should be planted in drills 12 to 18 inches apart and thinned slightly as soon as the plants are up. On a quick, rich soil some of the earlier varieties can be matured in from three to four weeks after planting. If the plants are allowed to remain long in the open ground, the roots lose their crispness and delicate flavor, and in order to secure a constant supply successive plantings should be made every two weeks. One ounce of radish seed is sufficient to plant 100 feet of row. A large percentage of the seed germinates, and if the sowing is done carefully later thinning may be unnecessary. The first radishes to appear may be pulled as soon as they are of sufficient size, and this will leave enough room for those that are a little later. The plant is not suited to hot weather, but should be planted in the early spring and late autumn.

LETTUCE.

Lettuce does not withstand heat well and thrives best, therefore, in the early spring or late autumn. In order to have the leaves crisp and tender it is necessary to force the growth of the plant. The usual method of growing lettuce for home use is to sow the seeds broadcast in the bed and to remove the leaves as rapidly as they become large enough for use. It is better, however, to sow the seeds in rows 14 to 16 inches apart, and when the plants come up to thin them to the desired distance. With the heading type this should be about 12 inches apart. This will result in the formation of rather compact heads and the entire plant may then be cut for use. For an early crop in the North, the plants should be started in a hotbed or cold frame and transplanted as soon as hard freezes are over. In many sections of the South the seeds are sown during the autumn and the plant allowed to remain in the ground over winter. Frequent shallow cultivation should be given the crop and, if crisp, tender lettuce is desired during the summer months, some form of partial shading may be necessary.

For head lettuce (fig. 11), Big Boston, Hanson, and California Cream Butter are good varieties. For loose-leaf lettuce (fig. 12), Grand Rapids or Black-seeded Simpson is recommended.

PEAS.

Garden peas are not injured easily by light frosts and may be planted as soon as the soil can be put in order in the spring. By selecting a number of varieties it is possible to have a continuous supply of peas throughout a large portion of the growing season. In order to accomplish this plantings should be made every 10 days or 2 weeks until warm weather comes. The first plantings should be of small-growing, quick-maturing varieties, such as Alaska, First and Best, and Gradus. These kinds do not require supports. They

FIG. 13.—Tall-growing garden peas supported by brush stuck into the ground.

should be followed by the large wrinkled type of peas, such as Champion of England, Telephone, and Prize Taker. These may be supported on brush (fig. 13), on strings attached to stakes driven in the ground, or on wire netting.

Peas should be planted about 2 to 3 inches deep in rows 3 to 4 feet apart. Some gardeners, however, follow the practice of planting in double rows 6 inches apart, with the ordinary space of 3 to 4 feet between these pairs of rows. With varieties requiring support this is a good practice, as the supports can be placed in the narrow space between the rows.

ONIONS.

The onion will thrive under a wide range of climate and soil conditions, but a rich sandy loam containing plenty of humus is best suited to it. (Fig. 14.) As the crop requires shallow cultivation and it may be necessary to resort to hand work in order to keep it free from weeds, it is very desirable that the land should be in such condition that it is easily worked. As a general rule it is well to have the crop follow some other that has been kept under the hoe and free from weeds the previous season.

In the North seed is sown as early in the spring as the soil

FIG. 14.—Onions are easily grown on good soil and require little attention besides weeding.

can be brought to the proper condition. In the South onion sets are frequently put out in the autumn and carried through the winter with the protection of a little hay or straw. There are three methods of propagating onions: The first by sowing the seed in rows where the crop is to grow; second, by sowing the seed in specially prepared beds and transplanting the seedlings to the open ground; and, third, by planting sets which have been kept through the winter. The first method is used by large commercial growers on account of the amount of labor involved in the others.

On small areas, however, it may be preferable to plant sets. Under normal conditions these usually may be obtained at planting time for about 25 or 30 cents a quart. This should be enough for the average family. Onions planted from sets will ripen earlier than those from seed sown in the fields.

When the transplanting method is used, the seed is sown in greenhouses, hotbeds, cold frames, or specially prepared beds at the rate of $3\frac{1}{2}$ to 4 pounds for each acre to be planted. One-half ounce should furnish plants sufficient for the home garden. The seedlings are transplanted when they are somewhat smaller than a lead pencil and rather stocky. The root end of the seedling is pushed into the soil with one finger, and the soil is then firmed about the plant.

The seed is sown thickly in drills about 12 to 14 inches apart. After the plants become established they are thinned to 2 or 3 inches apart. The maturity of the bulbs may be hastened by preventing the continued growth of the tops. This is sometimes accomplished by rolling an empty barrel over the rows and breaking down the tops. After these are practically dead the onion bulbs may be pulled up by hand from the soil and spread in a dry, well-ventilated place to cure. Thereafter they may be stored in crates or bags for winter use. In the North the crop ripens and is harvested during the latter part of the summer and early autumn. In the Southern States, where the crop is grown during the winter, the harvesting and marketing period takes place during the spring months.

There are several kinds of onions that may remain in the soil over winter. The multiplier, or potato onion, for example, can be planted from sets in the autumn and will produce excellent green early onions. A large onion of this type contains a number of distinct hearts, and, if planted, will produce a number of small onions. On the other hand, a small onion contains but one heart and will produce a large onion. A few of the large ones may be planted each year to produce sets for the following year's planting.

The shallot is a variety of small onion that is frequently planted in early spring for its small bulbs, or "cloves," which are used in the same manner as onions. The leaves are utilized for flavoring. Another onion-like plant is the chive, the small, round, hollow leaves of which are used for flavoring soups. These leaves may be cut freely, as they are soon replaced by others.

THE PRINCIPAL ROOT CROPS.

Beets (fig. 15) can be planted comparatively early in the season. It is not necessary to wait until the ground has become warm, if the danger of frost is past. The seed should be sown in drills 14 to 18 inches apart and covered to a depth of about 1 inch. As soon as the plants are well up they should be thinned to stand 3 to 4 inches apart. From 2 to 3 plantings should be made in order to have a continuous supply of young, tender beets.

Parsnips, salsify, carrots, and turnips are all handled much like beets. Of the five, carrots can perhaps be left closer in the row than the others, about 2 or 3 inches apart. This plant, too, is less exacting in so far as fertility is concerned. Salsify, on the other hand, demands very fertile and finely cultivated soil.

POTATOES.[1]

The potato plant thrives best in sandy or gravelly loam soils. It may be grown with a fair degree of success on any type of soil except loose sand and a heavy, sticky clay, provided the land is well drained and contains the necessary plant food.

Successful potato production is dependent to a large extent on the thoroughness with which the land is prepared before planting the crop. Where a horse can be used, the land should be plowed from 8 to 10 inches deep, provided the surface soil is of a sufficient depth to permit it. It is never advisable to turn up more than 1 inch of raw subsoil at any one plowing; so if previous plowings have not been over 6 inches, the maximum depth at which it should be plowed is 7 inches.

Where hand labor is employed the same rule should govern as to depth. In spading, especially on grass or waste land, turn the earth bottom side up. Whether the land is plowed or spaded, it should be thoroughly pulverized immediately afterwards. Where horse labor can be used, the land after plowing should be thoroughly disked first, then spring-toothed, and finally finished with a smoothing harrow. Where land must be prepared by hand, it is good practice to pulverize the soil as much as possible when spading it up, after which it can be put in a fine condition of mellowness with a steel garden rake. The importance of thoroughly fining the soil can not be overemphasized.

FIG. 15.—Both the roots and foliage of young beets may be eaten, cooked together or separately.

VARIETIES ADAPTED TO DIFFERENT LOCALITIES.

Early varieties.—In the Northeastern United States and along the South Atlantic seaboard, the Irish Cobbler, Early Petoskey, or Early

---

[1] Circular 87 of the Bureau of Entomology deals with the Colorado potato beetle, and Farmers' Bulletin 557 deals with the Potato tuber moth.

Standard, all of which are practically identical, may be expected to produce larger crops and be more generally satisfactory for an early crop than the others mentioned. Quick Lunch and New Queen would be regarded as second choices for this section.

In the South Central and Southwestern States, the Triumph may be expected to give results equal to or even better than the Irish Cobbler.

In the Middle West, the Early Ohio should do well, while the Early Harvest and Early Rose may be regarded as second choices.

Late varieties.—In the New England States, Long Island, and northern New York, the Green Mountain, Gold Coin, Delaware, and other late varieties of that class do best.

In northern Michigan, Wisconsin, and Minnesota, the late varieties named above do about as well as the Rural New Yorker No. 2, and are superior to it in table quality.

In western New York, southern Michigan and Wisconsin, and Iowa, the Rural New Yorker No. 2, Sir Walter Raleigh, and Carman No. 3 are the best adapted varieties, and divide honors with the Green Mountain in the northern portions of these States.

Throughout Maryland, Virginia, the Carolinas, Tennessee, and Georgia, the variety known as McCormick is quite generally grown as a late variety. In a favorable season the Green Mountain can also be grown.

WHEN TO PLANT POTATOES.

The date of planting necessarily must be governed by climatic conditions. In attempting to produce as early a crop as possible some risk must always be incurred of the plants being injured by late spring frosts. As a general proposition it is best to plant potatoes as soon as there is little likelihood of killing frosts after the plants are up and the ground is in condition to work.

The following dates of planting for various cities should be regarded only as the approximate time at which early potatoes might safely be planted:

March 15 to 25: Washington, Baltimore, Philadelphia, Cincinnati, Louisville, St. Louis.

March 25 to April 5: New York, Indianapolis, Detroit, Chicago.

April 5 to 15: Boston, Albany, Rochester, etc.

In the northern cities late varieties should be planted from three to four weeks later.

PLANTING PRACTICES.

The usual method of preparing potatoes for planting is to cut them into rather large pieces, containing several eyes. When seed potatoes are unusually expensive, however, it may be well to cut cone-shaped segments of meat around each eye and to use the remaining portion of the tubers for food. Under this plan it is not necessary to prepare the seed all at one time. From day to day the cones for seeding can be cut from the potatoes as they are being prepared for the table. The cuttings then should be spread out on a piece of paper in a moderately cool room (about 50° F.) and allowed to remain there until they have cured; that is, until the cut surface has become dry. A day or two should suffice for this, and potatoes then should be put in a shallow box or tray and placed where it is still cooler. Any storage condition that will insure them against frost on the one hand and undue shriveling on the other should prove satisfactory.

These seeds can be started indoors, provided it is possible to secure suitable soil and boxes. In such cases it may be desirable to plant the eye cuttings at once, and allow them to start into growth indoors with the idea of transplanting them into the open ground when danger of frost is past and the ground is dry enough to be cultivated.

The smaller the size of the set, or seed piece, used the more thorough must be the preparation of the soil. The more finely the soil is pulverized and the more uniform the moisture conditions which can be preserved in the soil, the better is the chance for the small seed piece to establish itself. A small set in rough, lumpy, or dried-out soil has little chance to live.

Generally speaking, the smaller the size of the set the closer it should be planted in the row if maximum yields are to be secured. Such sets may be expected to give the best yields if not spaced more than 10 to 12 inches apart in the row. Plant the small eye cuttings from 1½ to 3 inches deep, depending upon the character of the soil—the lighter the soil the greater the depth of planting. Larger sets may be planted 4 inches deep.

SPACING.

If an early variety is planted, and the work is to be done by hand, the rows may be spaced as close as 26 inches, whereas if cultivation is to be done with a horse, 30 to 34 inches usually is allowed. In order to give the gardener some idea of the number of sets required to plant a plot of ground 50 by 100 feet at different spacings, the following table is submitted:

To plant a plat 50 by 100 feet.

Space between rows.	Space in row between plants.	Sets required.	Space between rows.	Space in row between plants.	Sets required.
Inches.	Inches.		Inches.	Inches.	
26	10	2,769	30	10	2,400
26	12	2,487	30	12	2,000
28	10	2,678	32	12	1,874
28	12	2,231	34	12	1,765

If a late variety is planted, the spacing should be greater, say, 34 to 36 inches between the rows and 12 to 14 inches between the plants in the row. The closeness of planting should be determined, first, by the variety, and, second, by the amount of available plant food and moisture in the soil or that can be applied to it.

CORN.

Corn (fig. 16) to be at its best should be eaten within a few hours after it is picked, for its sugar content disappears very rapidly after it is removed from the garden. For this reason and because of its very general popularity it is an excellent vegetable to grow in the home garden. It should be planted on rich land and cultivated in the same manner as field corn. Beginning as soon as the soil is warm, successive plantings may be made every two or three weeks until late summer. Another method of prolonging the supply is to plant early, medium, and late varieties. The seed should be planted about

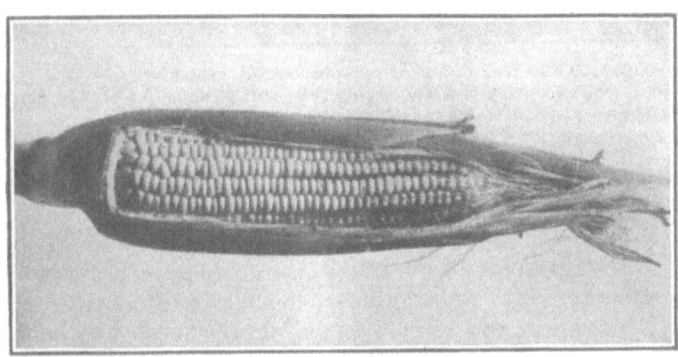

Fig. 16.—Green corn is one of the vegetables which loses much of its flavor if kept long after it is cut before being eaten. It should, therefore, be grown in the home garden if space permits.

2 inches deep, in drills 3 feet apart, and thinned to a single stalk every 10 to 14 inches.

The following varieties are recommended: For early corn, Golden Bantam and Adams Early, and for medium and late varieties, Black Mexican or Crosby's Early, Country Gentleman, and Stowell's Evergreen. The last-named variety has the largest ears and is the most productive.

Corn should be planted on rich land. The cultivation should be frequent and thorough and all weeds should be kept down and suckers removed from around the base of the plant.

TOMATOES.

Tomato plants should be started in the house or in a hotbed and should be transplanted once or twice in order that strong and vigorous plants may be secured by the time all danger from frost is past.

FIG. 17.—Tomato vines tied to stakes produce cleaner, healthier fruit than those permitted to trail on the ground, and giving the garden a more attractive appearance. The stakes need not be so large as those here pictured.

Pot-grown plants are especially desirable, as they may be brought to the blooming period by the time it is warm enough to plant them with safety in the garden. If the plants are not to be trained (fig. 17), but are to be allowed to lie on the ground, they should be set about 4 feet apart each way. If trimmed and tied to stakes they may be planted in rows 3 feet apart and 18 inches apart in the row. The home gardener will find the latter method preferable.

In common with all plants grown in a house, hotbed, or cold frame, tomatoes require to be hardened off before they are planted in the garden. By this process the plants are gradually acclimated to the effects of the sun and wind, so that they will stand transplanting to the open ground. Hardening off usually is accomplished by ventilating freely and by reducing the amount of water applied to the plant bed. The bed, however, should not become so dry that the plants will wilt or become seriously checked in their growth. After a few days it will be possible to leave the plants uncovered during the entire day and on mild nights.

EGGPLANTS AND PEPPERS.

Eggplants (fig. 18) and peppers are started and handled in the same way as the tomato. The soil best adapted for their production is a fine, rich sandy loam, well drained. The plants should be set in rows 3 feet apart and 2 feet apart in the row. Free cultivation is desirable, and the plants should be kept growing rapidly. A dozen good healthy plants each of eggplant and pepper should supply enough fruits for the average sized family throughout the season. Both of these vegetables are heat-loving and should not be set in the open until the ground has become warm.

BEANS.

Beans are more susceptible to cold than peas and should not be planted until danger of frost is past and the ground begins to warm up. They are, however, among the most desirable vegetables that the home gardener can raise. There are many different kinds and varieties of beans, but for garden purposes they may be divided into two classes—string and Lima. Both classes are grown in practically all parts of the United States where the frost-free period is greater than three months and adapt themselves to a wide diversity of soils and climate. They grow rapidly and, therefore, leave the area in which they have been planted free for another crop. To secure a continuous supply, it is desirable to make plantings at

FIG. 18.—When grown under good soil and cultural conditions the eggplant is a prolific yielder. All the fruits shown in this illustration are on a single plant.

Fig. 19.—Pole lima beans are prolific bearers, as the illustration shows. Like other beans, they thrive on almost any soil. Vegetables that may be trained on poles or fences help to economize space in the small garden.

intervals of 10 days or 2 weeks from the time that the ground is reasonably warm until hot weather sets in.

Both string and Lima beans are subdivided into pole and bush types. Pole Lima beans (fig. 19) should be planted with from 8 to

10 seeds in the hill, and after the plants become established should be thinned to 3 or 4. The hills should be 4 or 5 feet apart. Bush Lima beans are planted 5 or 6 inches apart in rows 30 to 36 inches apart. Bush beans of the string type may be planted somewhat closer—the plants standing 3 or 4 inches apart in rows from 20 to 24 inches apart if hand cultivation only is to be employed.

Beans of any kind should not be planted any deeper than is necessary to secure good germination. This should never be over 2 inches and on heavy soil it should not be more than $1\frac{1}{4}$ to $1\frac{1}{2}$ inches.

Beans are useful in the home garden, since they thrive on practically any type of soil. The pole varieties are especially convenient, since they can be planted along the edges of the yard and permitted to climb on the fences. Some of the pole beans, both snap and Lima, will continue to bear until frost. If the pole beans are planted in the hills in the garden proper, it will be necessary to sink a pole at each hill or to provide some other form of support. Extra long poles may be used and the tops of three or four from different hills fastened together tent fashion.

FIG. 20.—Hubbard squash vines occupy considerable space but may be grown in the larger home gardens.

If it is desired to keep the garden free from poles, substantial posts may be set at each end of the row and a wire or strong cord stretched between their tops. Cords may then be extended from small stakes in each hill to the wire.

CUCUMBERS, SQUASHES, AND MELONS.

Cucumbers, squashes[1] (fig. 20), and melons all belong to the melon family and demand much the same treatment. All are heat-loving and should not be planted in the open until the ground has become warm. It is easily possible, however, to give the plants an early start in the house and so gain several weeks in earliness of maturity. One way is to plant seven or eight seeds in berry boxes filled with soil. Each box of growing plants should have its bottom removed at planting time and should then be sunk in the garden to constitute a hill of plants.

Instead of growing the plants in boxes of ordinary soil they may be grown on sods in a suitable receptacle. Cut sods 6 inches square

---

[1] An insect that attacks squashes and other crops of this class is described in Farmers' Bulletin 668, "The Squash-vine Borer."

from spots which the growth of grass shows to be rich. Turn these grass side down and press the seeds in among the roots and soil. Cover with about an inch and a half of good soil and keep moist and warm. At planting time the sods may be lifted and placed in hills, which first should have manure worked into them.

These plants are rank growers and occupy much space. In very small gardens it may be well, therefore, to omit them. If squashes are grown, it may be well to plant only bunch varieties. Space may be conserved by growing a few cucumber vines near the edge of the garden and training them on a fence. This is possible, too, of course, with some melons and pumpkins, but supports will be necessary for the fruits. If the plants of this group are grown in the main garden, they must be spaced from 6 to 12 feet apart each way.

CABBAGE, CAULIFLOWER, AND BRUSSELS SPROUTS.

Cabbage and the other two members of the cabbage family mentioned here require much the same treatment.[1] All three are grown in hotbeds, frames, or flats for the early crop and are set out when all danger of frost is past. Of the three, Brussels sprouts (fig. 21) is the hardiest. Cabbage is fairly hardy, but cauliflower is somewhat tender. All require rather moist soil and plenty of plant food. Fertilizer may be conserved by placing it

FIG. 21.—A single plant of Brussels sprouts. The miniature "heads" on the stalk are cut off and cooked like cabbage.

under each "hill" before the plants are set. The settings should be made 18 to 24 inches apart in rows spaced about 24 inches.

MISCELLANEOUS SALAD VEGETABLES.

Besides lettuce there are a number of vegetables for use as salads or cooked greens that may be grown easily in the home garden. Of the salad plants corn salad, garden cress, and endive are perhaps best known. The first two may be planted early. Endive, however,

---

[1] Accounts of two insects that attack cabbage are given in Farmers' Bulletin 766, "The Common Cabbage Worm," and Circular 103 of the Bureau of Entomology, "The Harlequin Cabbage Bug."

is planted in June and July. All are grown in drills about 14 inches apart and are thinned to proper distances as they grow.

Spinach and mustard are useful greens for cooking. Spinach may be grown either in the spring or in the fall. It is grown in drills, the use of the larger plants first automatically taking care of thinning.

Mustard greens may be produced on almost any good soil. The basal leaves are used for greens and are cooked like spinach. The plants require but a short time to reach the proper stage for use and frequent sowings should be made. The seeds are sowed thickly in drills as early as possible in spring or for late use in September or October. Ostrich Plume is a reliable variety.

For use both as a salad plant and for cooked greens Swiss chard (fig. 22), a beet which has been developed for foliage, should be more extensively grown. One of the good points about this vegetable is that crop after crop of leaves may be cut without injuring the plant. Chard is planted like beets in drills 12 to 14 inches apart and thinned to 4 to 6 inches.

PERMANENT VEGETABLES.

A number of vegetables, once established, will furnish a supply of their products year after year. Asparagus, rhubarb, and a number of garnishing and flavoring herbs are the best-known members of this group. Because they permanently occupy the space in which they grow, such plants should be in beds separated from the cultivated vegetables.

FIG. 22.—Swiss chard, a beet which has been bred for salad foliage instead of for root. The leaves and stalks may be cut repeatedly and used like spinach. Since the plant furnishes salad greens throughout the season it may well be grown instead of spinach, which furnishes but one crop, or after spinach.

For the asparagus bed a well drained, early location should be chosen. Prepare the bed by digging a trench 18 inches wide and 20 inches deep. Fill this one-third full with well-rotted manure and tramp it down well. Half fill the remaining space with good soil, and on this set the root clumps of asparagus, 1 foot apart. Such roots, one, two, or three years old, may be purchased from seedsmen or nurseries. Cover the roots by filling the trench to the surface of the ground with good soil. The stalks should not be cut until a year after planting, and then but lightly. Full harvests may be taken after this. From a dozen to two dozen roots should be enough for the average family.

Rhubarb is also grown from root clumps. A row of six or eight plants, 4 feet apart, should furnish stalks enough for the average family. Each hill should be well prepared with manure and good soil. Set the crowns about 4 inches underground. Stalks should not be cut until a year after planting.

Parsley seeds are sown in a drill in spring. The plants will die down in the fall and put out fresh foliage the next spring. The plant is a biennial and must be replanted at two-year intervals.

Sage is a useful perennial herb which can be grown easily in the home garden. One or two bushes will furnish an abundance of leaves. These, when full grown, should be thoroughly dried and stored in cans or jars.

ANNUAL PLANTS USED FOR SEASONING.

Chives are small onionlike plants having flat, hollow leaves. These are cut and used for flavoring soups, sauces, etc. The plants are propagated by bulbs. A patch of the plants a foot or so square should be enough for the home garden.

Okra, or gumbo, produces pods which are used to season and thicken soups. The seeds of okra should be sown in the open after the ground has become quite warm, or the plants may be started in berry boxes in the hotbed or in the house and transplanted in the garden after all danger of frost has passed. The rows should be 4 feet apart for the dwarf sorts and 5 feet apart for the tall kinds, with the plants 2 feet apart in the row.[1] If the pods are removed before they are allowed to ripen, the plants will continue to produce them until killed by frost.

Cabbage, carrots, turnips, and rutabagas, in addition to their use as early crops, may be planted early in summer and the products which mature in autumn may then be held for winter use.

---

[1] Detailed information on this plant is contained in Farmers' Bulletin 232, "Okra: Its Culture and Uses."

VEGETABLES FOR WINTER USE.

For a late crop of cabbage it is customary to plant the seeds in a bed in the open ground in May or June and transplant them to the garden in July. For cabbage of this character the soil should be heavier and more retentive of moisture than for early cabbage, which requires a rich, warm soil in order to reach maturity quickly. For the late variety it is not desirable to have too rich a soil, as the heads are liable to burst. Cabbages should be set in rows 30 to 36 inches apart, the plants standing 14 to 18 inches apart in the row.

To store cabbage for winter the heads should be buried in pits or placed in cellars. One method is to dig a trench about 18 inches deep and 3 feet wide and set the cabbage upright with the heads close together and the roots embedded in the soil. When cold weather comes the heads are covered lightly with straw and 3 or 4 inches of earth put in. Slight freezing does not injure cabbage, but it should not be subjected to repeated freezing and thawing.

Parsnips will occupy the ground from early spring until fall. The seeds should be sown as early as convenient in the spring in rows 18 inches to 3 feet apart. The plants should later be thinned to stand 3 inches apart in the row. A rich soil with frequent cultivation is necessary for success with this crop. The roots are dug late in the fall and stored in cellars or pits, much as cabbage is, or else are allowed to remain where they are grown and are dug as required for use. All roots not dug during the winter, however, should be removed from the garden, as they will produce seed the second season and become of a weedy nature. When the parsnip has been allowed to run wild in this way the root is considered to be poisonous.

Carrots may be sown early, used during the late summer, and the surplus stored. If desired, a later crop may be sown after the removal of an early vegetable, especially for winter use. Carrots are grown in practically the same way as parsnips, but are not thinned so much and are allowed to grow almost as thickly as planted. They are dug in the autumn and stored in the same manner as parsnips or turnips.

Turnips require a rich soil and may be grown either as an early or late crop. For a late crop it is customary to sow the seeds broadcast on land from which some early crop has been removed. In the North this is generally done during July and August, but the usual time is later in the South. The seed also may be sown in drills 12 to 18 inches apart as for the early crop. After the plants appear they are thinned to about 3 inches.

The rutabaga is similar to the turnip and is grown in much the same way. It requires more space, however, and a longer period for its growth. It is used to a considerable extent for stock feed and has the advantage of being quite hardy.

FRUITS IN THE SMALL GARDEN.

BERRIES.

If there is sufficient space in the home garden, it may be desirable to have it supply fruits as well as vegetables. The small fruits, such as strawberries, raspberries, blackberries, currants, and gooseberries, may be produced with little trouble. A few dozen strawberry plants, and even fewer of the other plants mentioned, should be sufficient for a start. The plantings can be increased from year to year by resetting the young plants which spring up from runners and roots. All the small fruit plants mentioned may be set out in spring. Since most of these plants will occupy the same space year after year, they should be segregated from the part of the garden devoted to annual vegetables.

Grapes may, in many instances, be grown in the home garden more easily than the small bush fruits, since they may be planted near fences and permitted to run upon them. Grape plants also may be set out in spring before the sap rises. Fairly large holes should be dug, and these filled with rich soil mixed with wood ashes.

TREE FRUITS.

Tree fruits probably can not be grown in most small home gardens because of the relatively large areas of soil their roots occupy. The use of dwarf trees, however, makes possible the growing of a few fruit trees in the larger yards and garden inclosures. Though strawberries, cucumbers, and a few other vegetables may be grown near the trees while the latter are small, most vegetables must be grown in the open, where they will receive abundant sunlight. If fruit trees are grown in connection with gardening operations, therefore, they should, where possible, be well removed from the main garden plot.

Apple, peach, cherry, pear, plum, apricot, and quince trees may be purchased on dwarfing stocks. All may be set out in the spring before growth starts. The trees should be set in holes several feet square in which rich soil has been placed. They should be set an inch or so lower than in the nursery.

○

U. S. DEPARTMENT OF AGRICULTURE
FARMERS' BULLETIN No. 1673

The FARM GARDEN

FARM GARDENS, maintained on about four-fifths of the farms in the United States as a source of wholesome family food supply, are annually saving millions of dollars for the farmers of the country. A well-cared-for garden will yield a greater return per acre than any similar area on the farm devoted to regular farm crops.

A good garden adds very materially to the well-being of the farm family by supplying foods that might not otherwise be provided. Fresh vegetables direct from the garden are superior in quality to those generally sold on the market, and in addition are readily available when wanted for use.

Certain crops may be grown in southern gardens throughout the winter; in fact, there are thousands of southern farm gardens that produce at least one or two fresh vegetables every day in the year. The northern gardening season may be greatly extended by the use of hotbeds and coldframes, also by planting the more hardy late-summer and fall crops.

This bulletin supersedes Farmers' Bulletins 934, Home Gardening in the South, and 937, The Farm Garden in the North.

INDEX OF VEGETABLES

	Page		Page
Artichoke, Jerusalem	43	Kohlrabi	59
Asparagus	28	Leek	60
Beans	52	Lettuce	39
Beet	41	Martynia	66
Broccoli, heading	55	Muskmelon	50
Broccoli, sprouting	55	Mustard	34
Brussels sprouts	55	Okra	66
Cabbage	56	Onion	61
Cabbage, Chinese	57	Parsley	40
Cardoon	31	Parsley, turnip-rooted	48
Carrot	42	Parsnip	44
Cauliflower	58	Peas	54
Celeriac	43	Peppers	63
Celery	36	Physalis	66
Chard	32	Poke	30
Chervil	43	Potato	44
Chicory, witloof	38	Pumpkin	50
Chives	59	Radish	45
Collards	59	Rhubarb	30
Corn salad	38	Rutabaga	47
Corn, sweet	66	Salsify	46
Cress, upland	40	Shallot	62
Cress, water	41	Sorrel	36
Cucumber	49	Spinach	34
Dandelion	83	Spinach, New Zealand	35
Dasheen	43	Squash	51
Eggplant	63	Sweetpotato	46
Endive	38	Tomato	64
Fennel, Florence	65	Turnip	47
Garlic	60	Turnip greens	36
Horseradish	29	Watermelon	51
Kale	33		

THE FARM GARDEN

By J. H. BEATTIE, *Associate Horticulturist*, and W. R. BEATTIE, *Senior Horticulturist, Division of Horticultural Crops and Diseases, Bureau of Plant Industry*

CONTENTS

	Page		Page
General information	1	General information—Continued.	25
Value of the farm garden	1	Irrigation	25
Soil and location	1	Paper mulch	26
Protecting the garden	2	Insects and diseases	27
Fertilizers	3	Canning and storing vegetables at home	
Lime	5	Culture of specific garden crops	27
Soil preparation	6	Perennial vegetables	27
Plan and arrangement	6	Greens	31
Seed supply	8	Salad crops	36
Starting early plants	6	Root and tuber-root crops	41
Southern-grown plants	12	Vine crops (cucurbits)	48
Transplanting	12	Legumes	52
Time of planting	14	Cabbage group	54
Planting the garden	18	Onion group	59
Succession of crops	23	Fleshy-fruited warm-season crops	63
The late summer and fall garden	23	Miscellaneous vegetables	65
Cultivation	24		

GENERAL INFORMATION

VALUE OF THE FARM GARDEN

FARM GARDENS are maintained on approximately 79 per cent of all farms in the United States, the average value of the products per garden being estimated at $68, or a total of about $350,000,000. A half-acre garden, if properly cared for, will supply vegetables having a market value of at least $100 to $150, sufficient for a family of five or six. The main arguments in favor of a good garden on the farm, however, are that the vegetables are available when needed, are fresh, and have high quality and flavor. These characteristics are not present to the same degree in vegetables bought on the markets, especially those shipped long distances or kept in storage and subjected to handling and exposure.

During busy periods on the farm it is not always possible to go to market for fresh vegetables, and the farm garden becomes a convenient time-saving source of supply. Recent discoveries as to the vitamin content of fresh vegetables, especially the leafy kinds, emphasize the value of the garden in safeguarding the family's health. Crops that require considerable space, such as sweet corn, potatoes, sweetpotatoes, winter squashes, and melons, generally may be grown to best advantage outside the garden and in connection with the cultivation of field crops, leaving the smaller crops to the garden proper.

SOIL AND LOCATION

Good soil is the first essential for a successful garden. The type of soil is not so important as that it be well drained, well supplied with organic matter, retentive of moisture, easy to work, and reasonably free from weeds. Sandy loam soils usually can be worked earlier in the spring than the stiff clay loams, but crops on the clay loams frequently withstand dry weather better than those on the lighter soils. By means of drainage, irrigation, manuring, and the right type of cultivation any reasonably good soil can be made suitable for the intensive production of vegetables.

The slope of the land has considerable influence upon the time when the garden can be planted. A gentle slope toward the south or southeast is favorable for early crops. A location that is protected on the north by a hill, a group of close-growing trees, buildings, a stone wall, or a tight board fence is desirable in sections where winds are likely to cause damage to crops.

Hedges make good windbreaks, but owing to their heavy shade and draft on soil moisture and plant food they may prove undesirable in some locations. Arborvitae and California and Amur River privet are most commonly used for hedges around gardens, and if kept closely pruned they are in general fairly satisfactory. In place of a hedge, strips of burlap fastened to the garden fence or to lines of stakes around and through the garden give a fair protection against soil blowing and wind damage. Frequently irrigation is employed to prevent soil blowing and consequent injury to crops. Tightly constructed board fences make good windbreaks for gardens.

Good drainage is essential, and, if possible, the garden should be located on well-drained land. The drainage may often be improved by the addition of tile drains, open ditches, or the loosening of the soil by subsoiling. The garden should be free from depressions in which water might stand after a heavy rain. Waste water from surrounding land should not be allowed to drain upon the garden, and the fall below the garden should be such that there will be no danger of flood water backing up on it. The garden should not be located on creek or river-bottom land subject to overflow during the growing season.

The location of the garden for convenience both in caring for the crops and in gathering the vegetables is of great importance. It should be as near the dwelling as circumstances permit.

Sunlight is a vital factor in the production of vegetables, and for this reason the garden should be situated where it will receive the direct rays of the sun. Certain crops may stand more shading than others, but no amount of fertilizer, water, or care will replace sunshine. Trees not only shade the garden but draw heavily upon the moisture and fertility of the soil. Even where trees are so located that they do not shade the garden, their presence is a menace, for their roots may penetrate far into the garden and rob the crops of moisture and plant food.

PROTECTING THE GARDEN

Under most conditions the garden should be surrounded by a fence sufficiently high and close-woven to keep out poultry, dogs, rabbits, and other animals. In certain sections wild deer frequently destroy gardens, in which case it may be necessary to surround the garden with a fence 8 to 12 feet high. In the Great Plains area jack rabbits are a menace to gardens, but they may be kept out by the use of a rabbit-tight fence. Where the common cottontail rabbit is troublesome, gardens may be protected by either a woven wire or a closely spaced picket fence.

Poultry, especially chickens, are the most common source of injury to farm gardens. Two methods of protection are open to the garden owner—fencing the garden or confining the poultry to a definite inclosure, whichever may be the more desirable or practical. In any event, if crops are to be grown, poultry must be kept out of the garden.

Rodents of various kinds are sources of trouble to garden crops in certain sections of the country. In the East, moles and two or three species of mice cause much injury. They can be controlled by trapping, poisoning, and the use of poisons or repellents placed in their runs. Temporary relief from these rodents can generally be obtained by injecting small quantities of carbon disulphide into their runs. The exhaust gas from an automobile has the same effect. Moth balls dropped into the runs may be effective in driving off moles, but can hardly be depended on as a certain protection. In the West where ground squirrels and prairie dogs are prevalent, poisoning is the usual and most effective remedy.[1]

FERTILIZERS

Stable or barn-lot manure is the best garden fertilizer for use on most soils, except where the land is already oversupplied with organic matter, which is rarely the case. An initial application of 20 large wagonloads of partly rotted manure on a half-acre garden is not excessive. Following this, 8 to 10 tons of manure should be applied each year, unless there is evidence that the soil is becoming too rich in organic matter for certain crops like tomatoes and beans. After this stage is reached, the manure should be applied only to that portion of the garden on which crops that require heavy fertilizing are to be planted. The time of applying the manure will vary, but as a rule it should be spread just before plowing. Inasmuch as the garden is usually planted very shortly after plowing, it is desirable that the manure should be well rotted and rather fine. Coarse or strawy manure not only may interfere with the cultivation of the crops, but does not give as good results as does thoroughly rotted manure. Some farmers follow the practice of first plowing the garden, then spreading several loads of well-composted manure over the surface and working it into the soil with a disk harrow.

The addition of 50 to 80 pounds of superphosphate to each ton of manure, either in the stable or during the composting period, will aid in the decomposition of the manure and also greatly increase its value as a fertilizer. The usual method of composting manure is to place the required quantity in a low, flat pile and turn it once every week or 10 days until it has been turned three or four times. After the third or fourth turning the manure can be allowed to remain in a flat pile until wanted for spreading on the garden. If the manure is dry, water should be added to prevent burning.

---

[1] Full information on the poisoning of rodents can be procured from the Bureau of Biological Survey, U. S. Department of Agriculture.

Where large quantities of manure are being hauled from a feed lot to the fields, it is often possible to save a few loads of the finer material or scrapings for use on the garden.

Sheep and goat manures are extensively used in parts of the West and Southwest. On farms where large flocks of poultry are kept there is often a considerable accumulation of poultry manure, which may be used at a rate not exceeding 100 pounds for each 1,000 square feet. It should be borne in mind that sheep, goat, and poultry manures contain a high percentage of nitrogen and therefore should be used sparingly; otherwise injury to crops may occur. This is particularly true when commercial pulverized sheep manure is applied directly around growing plants, and great care must be taken to spread the manure thinly and mix it with the soil rather than to place it in direct contact with the plants. Where poultry, sheep, or goat manure is being used in making hills for cucumbers, melons, or squashes, it should be mixed with the soil to a depth of at least 6 inches over an area 18 to 24 inches in diameter.

SPECIAL FERTILIZERS AND COMPOST

Every farm garden should be provided with a compost pile from which a supply of fine, rich soil for growing plants may be available at all times. The ideal method of making a compost pile is to stack sods or turf with an equal quantity of manure, let the pile rot, then mix and screen for use. It usually requires about a year for material of this kind to rot, and it may be necessary to add a little water from time to time to give it the right degree of moisture for proper decay. Spading or turning the compost heap occasionally will hasten the process of decay, but, as a rule, merely piling the materials together in a heap will give fair results. The manure from the hotbed, sods or rich soil that may be available, and the poultry-house floor cleanings all may go into the compost pile to form soil for use on the garden or for growing early plants. The refuse from garden crops should not go into the compost because of the danger of spreading plant diseases.

Sterilizing the soil used for starting early plants by baking it slowly in the oven for an hour or two not only will greatly reduce the danger of plant losses from soil-borne diseases but will also destroy many of the weed seeds that are present in the soil.

Commercial fertilizers may be used to advantage in many farm gardens, the composition and rate of application depending on the locality, soil, and crops to be grown. For general use, a fertilizer containing 5 per cent nitrogen, 10 per cent phosphoric acid, and 5 or 6 per cent potash will give good results. Leafy crops, such as spinach, cabbage, kale, and lettuce, often require a higher percentage of nitrogen and may be stimulated by side dressings of nitrate of soda or some other form of readily available nitrogen. As a rule the root crops, including beets, carrots, turnips, and parsnips, need a higher percentage of potash. A fertilizer for potatoes may contain as much as 8 or 10 per cent of potash in addition to nitrogen and phosphoric acid.

The quantity of fertilizer to use will depend upon the condition of the soil, its natural fertility, and the crops being grown. Tomatoes and beans, for example, do not normally require a great amount of fertilizer, especially nitrogen; whereas onions, celery, lettuce, the root crops, and potatoes will respond to relatively large applications. In some cases 300 pounds of commercial fertilizer may be sufficient on a half-acre garden;[2] in other cases 1,000 or 1,200 pounds can be used to advantage. All depends upon the condition of the soil and its previous treatment, especially with regard to the manure and fertilizers used upon it during the preceding two or three years.

Commercial fertilizers as a rule should be applied either a few days before planting or at the time the crops are planted. The usual practice is to plow the land and give it its first harrowing, then spread the fertilizer from a pail or with a fertilizer distributor, harrowing the soil two or three times to get it in proper condition and at the same time mixing the fertilizer with it. For crops like potatoes and sweetpotatoes it is customary to scatter the fertilizer in the rows, taking care to mix it thoroughly with the soil before the seed is dropped, or, in the case of sweetpotatoes, before the ridges are thrown up.

The roots of most garden crops spread to considerable distances. The application of fertilizer to the entire area, therefore, will provide a uniform source of food for the plants to feed on. Care must be taken not to place fertilizer too near seedlings or young plants, as burning of the roots is likely to occur. Like caution must be exercised in using nitrate of soda or sulphate of ammonia as a side dressing for growing crops. On a half-acre garden 75 to 100 pounds of any of these concentrated sources of nitrogen is sufficient for one application, and where only a part of the garden is treated the quantity should be regulated accordingly. The fertilizer should be sown alongside the rows and cultivated into the topsoil.

LIME

Lime improves the texture of certain heavy soils, but its excessive use may prove injurious to most garden crops. As a general rule, asparagus, celery, beets, spinach, and sometimes carrots are benefited by the moderate use of lime, especially on soils that are naturally deficient in lime. Most of the garden vegetables do best on soils that are slightly acid, and all vegetables are injured by the application of lime in excess of their requirement. For this reason lime should be applied only where it is definitely shown by actual test to be necessary, and in no case should it be applied in large quantities. As a matter of fact most garden soils in a state of high fertility do not require the addition of lime. With good drainage, plenty of manure in the soil, and the moderate use of commercial fertilizers, the growth requirements of nearly all vegetables may be fully met.

Where lime is applied, it should be spread after plowing and be well mixed with the topsoil by harrowing. It should not be applied at the same time as, or mixed with, commercial fertilizers or manure, as the chemical changes that take place result in the loss of nitrogen and thus destroy the effectiveness of the fertilizers. As a rule, lime

---

[2] There are 43,560 square feet in an acre, or an area each of the four sides of which measures approximately 208½ feet. A piece of land 208 feet in length and 105 feet in width will contain practically one-half acre. A piece of land 220 feet in length and 100 feet in width will also contain practically one-half acre.

should not be applied in the fall, as it leaches from the soil during the winter. Any of the various forms of lime, such as hydrated lime and air-slaked lime, may be used. In some cases the unburned but finely ground limerock is used, but its action is slower than that of the burned lime. Finely ground oyster shells and marl are frequently used as substitutes for lime. Owing to its influence on the development of potato scab, lime should not be used on land that is being planted to potatoes.

SOIL PREPARATION

The time and method of preparing the garden for planting depend on the type of soil and location. Heavy clay soils in the northern sections are frequently benefited by fall plowing and exposure to freezing and thawing during the winter. Gardens in the dry-land areas should be plowed and leveled in the fall, so that the soil will absorb and retain all moisture that falls during the winter. The sandy soils of the South as a rule should not be plowed until near the time of planting. Wherever there is a heavy growth of crabgrass or a green cover crop the land should be plowed well in advance of planting and the soil disked several times to aid in the decay and incorporation of this material. Soils on which gardens are ordinarily planted should not be plowed or worked while wet. Sandy soils generally bear plowing a trifle sooner than heavy clay soils. The usual test is to squeeze together a handful of soil. If it adheres in a ball and does not readily crumble when slight pressure is exerted by the thumb and finger, it is too wet for plowing or working.

Fall-plowed land may be prepared as a rule by disking and harrowing. Spring-plowed land should be harrowed immediately after plowing, and if the soil is inclined to be lumpy a plank drag or a roller should be used for pulverizing it. Seeds grow more readily on a fine well-prepared soil than on a coarse or lumpy one, and thorough preparation greatly reduces the work of planting and caring for the crops. Spading is sometimes advisable in preparing small areas, such as beds for extra early crops of lettuce, onions, beets, and carrots, but the main portion of the garden should be plowed and harrowed. As a rule the tools ordinarily used on the farm will be suitable for preparing the garden for planting. In laying out the garden provision should be made for a gate or opening through which to haul manure or to bring in teams or a tractor as well as the tools for preparing and cultivating the garden.

PLAN AND ARRANGEMENT

It would be difficult to give a plan or specific arrangement for a garden that would suit all demands. Such a plan must be devised by each individual grower. Suggestive arrangements, however, are here presented, with the idea that they can readily be changed to suit local conditions.

The first consideration in planning the arrangement of a garden is the kind of cultivation that is to be employed. When the work is to be done mainly by means of horse tools the site and the arrangement should be such as to give the longest possible rows, and straight lines should be followed. (Fig. 1.) The garden should be free from

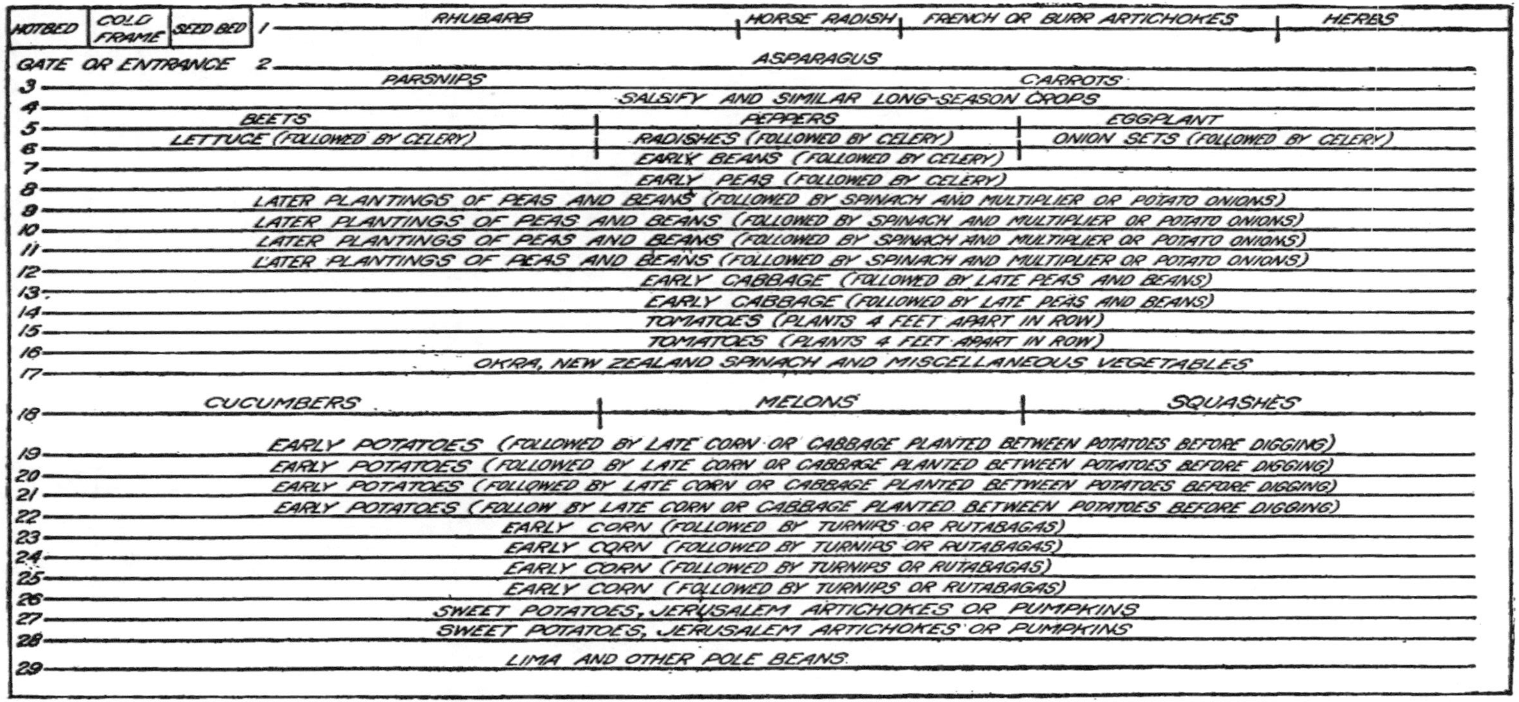

HOTBED	COLD FRAME	SEED BED

1.
2. GATE OR ENTRANCE
— HERBS
— FRENCH OR BURR ARTICHOKES
— HORSE-RADISH
— RHUBARB
3. PARSNIPS
4. BEETS
5. LETTUCE (FOLLOWED BY CELERY)
— CARROTS
— ASPARAGUS
— EGGPLANT
— PEPPERS
— ONION SETS (FOLLOWED BY CELERY)
— SALSIFY AND SIMILAR LONG-SEASON CROPS
— RADISHES (FOLLOWED BY CELERY)
6. EARLY BEANS (FOLLOWED BY CELERY)
7. EARLY PEAS (FOLLOWED BY CELERY)
8. LATER PLANTINGS OF PEAS AND BEANS (FOLLOWED BY SPINACH AND MULTIPLIER OR POTATO ONIONS)
9. LATER PLANTINGS OF PEAS AND BEANS (FOLLOWED BY SPINACH AND MULTIPLIER OR POTATO ONIONS)
10. LATER PLANTINGS OF PEAS AND BEANS (FOLLOWED BY SPINACH AND MULTIPLIER OR POTATO ONIONS)
11. LATER PLANTINGS OF PEAS AND BEANS (FOLLOWED BY SPINACH AND MULTIPLIER OR POTATO ONIONS)
12. LATER PLANTINGS OF PEAS AND BEANS (FOLLOWED BY SPINACH AND MULTIPLIER OR POTATO ONIONS)
13. EARLY CABBAGE (FOLLOWED BY LATE PEAS AND BEANS)
14. EARLY CABBAGE (FOLLOWED BY LATE PEAS AND BEANS)
15. TOMATOES (PLANTS 4 FEET APART IN ROW)
16. TOMATOES (PLANTS 4 FEET APART IN ROW)
17. OKRA, NEW ZEALAND SPINACH AND MISCELLANEOUS VEGETABLES
— SQUASHES
— MELONS
18. CUCUMBERS
19. EARLY POTATOES (FOLLOWED BY LATE CORN OR CABBAGE PLANTED BETWEEN POTATOES BEFORE DIGGING)
20. EARLY POTATOES (FOLLOWED BY LATE CORN OR CABBAGE PLANTED BETWEEN POTATOES BEFORE DIGGING)
21. EARLY POTATOES (FOLLOWED BY LATE CORN OR CABBAGE PLANTED BETWEEN POTATOES BEFORE DIGGING)
22. EARLY POTATOES (FOLLOWED BY LATE CORN OR CABBAGE PLANTED BETWEEN POTATOES BEFORE DIGGING)
23. EARLY CORN (FOLLOWED BY TURNIPS OR RUTABAGAS)
24. EARLY CORN (FOLLOWED BY TURNIPS OR RUTABAGAS)
25. EARLY CORN (FOLLOWED BY TURNIPS OR RUTABAGAS)
26. EARLY CORN (FOLLOWED BY TURNIPS OR RUTABAGAS)
27. SWEET POTATOES, JERUSALEM ARTICHOKES OR PUMPKINS
28. SWEET POTATOES, JERUSALEM ARTICHOKES OR PUMPKINS
29. LIMA AND OTHER POLE BEANS

FIGURE 1.—Plan of a half-acre garden. Length 220 feet; width, 100 feet. A half-acre garden will produce all the vegetables the average family can use throughout the growing season and a surplus for canning, storing, and drying

paths across the rows, and turning spaces should be provided at the ends. For hand cultivation the arrangement can be quite different, as the garden may be laid off in sections, with transverse walks, and the rows for most crops may be much closer. Horse cultivation is recommended whenever possible, as it very materially lessens the labor and cost of caring for the crops.

Where there is any great variation in the composition of the soil in different parts of the garden it will be advisable to take this into consideration when arranging for the location of the various crops. If a part of the land is low and moist, such crops as celery, onions, and late cucumbers should be placed there. If part of the soil is high, warm, and dry, there is the proper location for early crops and those that need quick, warm soil.

Permanent crops, such as asparagus and rhubarb, also any of the small fruits that may be planted in the garden, should be located where they will not interfere with the plowing and cultivation of the annual crops. If a hotbed, a coldframe, or a special seed bed is provided, it should be either in one corner of the garden or located outside of the garden entirely.

Tall-growing crops should be so located that they will not shade or interfere with the growth of the smaller crops. There seems to be little choice as to whether the rows run east and west or north and south, but they should conform to the general shape of the garden with convenience of cultivation in mind. In general, the smaller crops, especially those worked by hand, should be located nearest the house, with the larger crops like potatoes, sweet corn, and the vine crops in that portion of the garden most distant from the house. However, the general location of crops will depend largely on the character of the soil and convenience in cultivating.

SEED SUPPLY

Seeds for the farm garden should be ordered well in advance of planting time. Make a plan (fig. 1) of the garden, indicating the space each crop is to have, and order the seeds accordingly, allowing for replanting in case of a poor stand due to adverse weather conditions or other causes.[3] In making the plan it is a good idea to measure the garden carefully to be sure that the required space is available for each crop included. It pays to use garden seeds of high quality, especially those bred and selected for disease resistance.

Seeds saved at home from the previous year's garden should be carefully inspected so that in case they are not in good condition fresh ones may be ordered. In estimating the supply, allowance should always be made for two or more plantings of certain vegetables and for the tastes and requirements of the different members of the family. After careful checking to see that the order has been completely filled, the seeds should be stored in a dry place at a temperature 10 to 15 degrees below that of the average living room until planting time. A tin box or a large tin can makes a suitable container for storing vegetable seeds, especially as it gives protection from mice. Seeds of many of the garden vegetables will keep from four to six years if properly stored, while others lose their vitality quickly.

---

[3] The approximate quantities of seed that should be provided for planting a garden to supply vegetables for a family of five or six persons are given in the table on page 22.

STARTING EARLY PLANTS

Under southern conditions practically all vegetable plants may be started in specially prepared beds in the open with little or no covering. In the middle section and throughout the North and West, if an early garden is desired, it is essential that certain crops such as tomatoes, peppers, eggplant, cabbage, and cauliflower, and occasionally lettuce, onions, beets, cucumbers, squashes, and melons, be started indoors or in coldframes.

THE SEED BOX IN THE HOUSE

The simplest method of growing early plants is to provide a flat tray or box, such as is shown in Figure 2, which may be fitted into a south window of any room that is kept reasonably warm. Fill this

FIGURE 2.—Window box for starting early plants in the house

box with sifted soil, and in it sow the seeds of tomato, eggplant, peppers, and cabbage. When the plants are 10 to 20 days old, they can be transplanted to other boxes filled with reasonably rich sifted soil from the compost pile. Plants grown in this manner in the house, however, are inclined to be spindling, and better results may be obtained where a hotbed or a coldframe is employed.

HOTBEDS AND COLDFRAMES

In the South the hotbed will not be necessary as a rule, but a coldframe or sash-covered pit on the south side of a building will be found satisfactory for starting the early plants. In colder sections some form of heat is essential, and a manure-heated hotbed is usually the best type to provide. In the North the hotbed should be started in February or early in March, in order that the plants may be well grown in time to plant in the open ground.

The hotbed should always face the south and should be located on the south side of a building, a tight board fence, or a protecting wall, preferably near the house, where it can be given proper attention. A hotbed consists of a pit about 18 inches deep filled with fermenting horse-stable manure to furnish the heat. Material that is about half manure and half straw bedding is desirable. Place the manure in a low, flat pile, and turn it over once or twice as it begins to heat, in order to have it uniform; then place it in the hotbed pit in thin layers, shaking the manure out loosely as it is spread. Each successive layer, as it is put in, should be well trampled, and, if dry, a small quantity of water added so that the manure will pack solidly in the pit.

After the manure has been properly leveled and trampled in the bed, the frame to support the sash is placed in position. Generally the frame is made to carry four or five standard hotbed sash, or where only a small bed is required, one to three sash. The front or south side of the frame should be 8 to 12 inches lower than the back, in order to get the greatest benefit from the sunlight and so that water will drain from the glass. From 3 to 5 inches of good screened garden loam or specially prepared soil from the compost heap is then spread evenly over the manure in the frame, the sash are put on, and the bed is allowed to heat. At first the temperature of the bed will run somewhat high, but no seeds should be planted until the soil temperature falls below 80° F., which in most cases will be in about three or four days. It is not safe to judge the temperature by feeling the soil with the hand. A thermometer, its bulb buried in the soil, is the best means of telling when the bed falls to the proper temperature.

Standard hotbed sash in common use are 3 by 6 feet, containing three to five rows of glass. The sash may be purchased unpainted and unglazed or fully painted and filled with glass as desired. They should have at least two coats of paint consisting of white lead and linseed oil. In glazing the sash the glass should be bedded in putty, the panes overlapping about one-fourth inch and fastened securely in place with zinc glazing nails made for the purpose. No putty should be placed on the surface of the glass, the glass being simply bedded in putty and all surplus putty trimmed off.

In the colder parts of the country, board shutters, straw, or burlap mats, in addition to the sash, will be required as a covering during cold nights. It is also desirable to have a supply of straw or loose manure on hand to throw over the bed in extremely cold weather.

On bright days, when the hotbed heats very quickly from the sunshine on the glass, the sash should be raised slightly on the side opposite from the wind. In ventilating, care should be taken to protect the plants from a direct draft of cold air. Toward evening the sash should be closed, in order that the bed may become sufficiently warm before nightfall. Hotbeds should be watered on bright days, preferably in the morning. If it is necessary to water late in the day, the sash should be left open for a short time until the plants dry off. Plants grown in hotbeds are frequently lost by a disease known as damping off, which can be largely prevented by careful watering and proper ventilation.

Coldframes are constructed like hotbeds, except that no manure or other heating material is used. (Fig. 3.) They are covered with ordinary hotbed sash, but cotton cloth may be substituted for the sash. In the South coldframes are used for growing early plants; in the North they are used for hardening off plants that have been started in hotbeds or in the house. The same general rules for the care of a hotbed apply to a coldframe, but the latter is usually

FIGURE 3.—A sash-covered frame (coldframe) for starting early plants

ventilated more freely. Toward the close of the plant-growing period the sash or cloth covering of the frame may be left off entirely,

FIGURE 4.—Methods of starting early plants for the garden indoors by the use of (A) quart berry boxes and (B) paper bands

to adapt the plants to outdoor conditions, but the covering should be kept near by in case of a sudden drop in temperature.

SPECIAL METHODS FOR STARTING EARLY PLANTS

Early plants for the garden may be started indoors in quart berry boxes (fig. 4, A), paper drinking cups, paper bands (fig. 4, B), or in regular clay flowerpots. The containers are filled with sifted soil and placed in the hotbed, or if in the house they are placed in a shallow box. A small amount of seed is sown in each container, and after the plants are well under way they are transferred to the garden, the container usually being removed from about the roots of the plants when set in the planting hole. In the case of clay flowerpots the ball of earth containing the roots is simply jarred loose and removed from the pot. Soft paper bands or peat pots need not be removed, the roots of the plants being simply allowed to grow through the container and into the soil about them.

Market gardeners generally spot the plants in the hotbed or coldframe 4 or 5 inches apart in each direction. In moving them to the garden a knife is run to a depth of 4 or 5 inches in each direction between the plants, cutting the soil in blocks as shown in Figure 5. Each block, with the plant in its center, is removed direct to the garden. Plants moved in this manner should be watered when set, unless the soil is very moist.

FIGURE 5.—Tomato plant for the early garden, grown in hotbed or coldframe by the blocking method

SOUTHERN-GROWN PLANTS

Southern vegetable plants grown in the open and shipped to all parts of the country are now to a considerable degree taking the place of the plants formerly grown locally in hotbeds, coldframes, and special seed beds. These plants are grown very cheaply and withstand transplanting remarkably well. They may not in all cases be as good as home-grown plants, but they save the trouble of starting plants in the house or in a hotbed, and when planted they usually grow very rapidly. The disadvantages of using these plants are the occasional delay in obtaining them and the possibility of transmitting certain diseases, such as the wilt disease of the tomato, black rot of cabbage, and diseases caused by nematodes, which are common on various crops in the South. Southern-grown plants are now offered for sale by most of the northern seedsmen and often by local hardware and supply houses.

TRANSPLANTING

Plants started in the house or in hotbeds should be transplanted to give them more room about the time the first true leaves are formed. The small plants may be transplanted to flat boxes or to the coldframe to stand 2 to 5 inches apart each way. Where clay flowerpots or any of the containers mentioned are used, and a single plant is set in each container, excellent early plants may be grown, with the advantage that the roots will not be disturbed when they are set in the garden. Toward the end of the protected period the plants should be exposed more and more to outdoor conditions. Such plants usually withstand transfer to the garden with little check and few losses. Plants while undergoing the hardening process should be watered sparingly, but just before they are moved to the garden they should be given a thorough watering.

When the time comes to set the plants in the open ground, everything should be in readiness, the soil in good condition, and water available for watering the plants in case there is not enough moisture in the soil. Plants grown in the coldframe or in specially prepared seed beds should be lifted carefully with a trowel or a spade, as much soil being kept on their roots as possible. Plants do best if moved on a cloudy day or just before a rain, or late in the evening. In using water when setting out plants, first set the plant in the hole and partly fill the hole with soil; next apply the water, allowing it

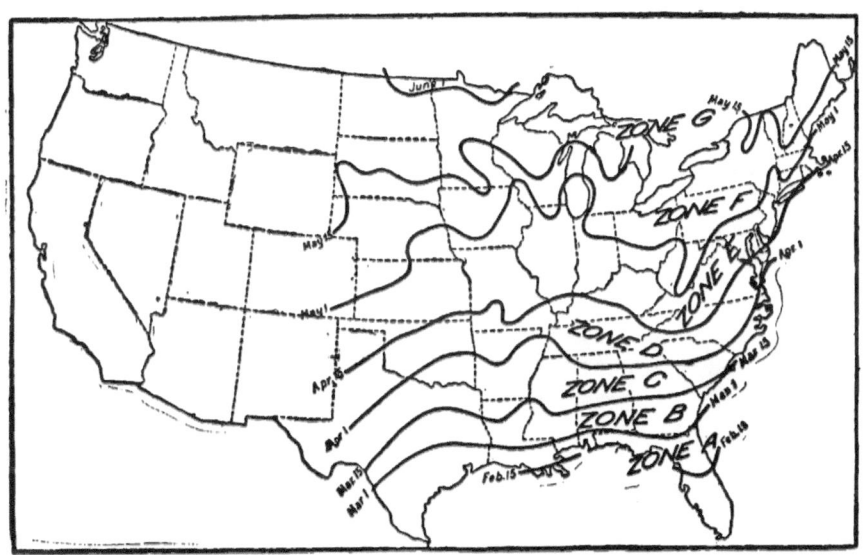

FIGURE 6.—A zone map of the United States, based on the average dates of the latest killing frost in spring east of the Rocky Mountains

to soak well into the soil. Then fill around the plant with the drier soil, and firm it about the plants. Plants set in this manner seldom wilt. When setting a small number of plants in the garden during a dry period it is often possible to protect them from the midday sun by setting a shingle or a small piece of board at a slant on the south side of each plant. If the plants are protected thus for two or three days after setting, few of them will be lost.

Cabbage and other vegetable plants that are moved direct from the seed bed should be carefully lifted by running a trowel or a spade beneath them, as much soil as possible being left on their roots. Plants handled in this manner should be set either when there is an abundance of moisture in the soil or just before a rain, with the soil firmly packed about their roots. If the soil is dry, a pint or more of water should be poured about the roots of each plant.

TIME OF PLANTING

The earliest dates for planting the various vegetables depend upon the locality, beginning during December or January in the extreme South and following the advance of the season northward until approximately June 10 in the extreme North. Garden crops may be divided into four groups: Crops that can be planted before the time of the last killing frost in the spring, those that can be planted about the time the last killing frost is expected, those that can not be planted until danger of frost is past, and those that can not be planted until the ground and the weather are warm. The zone map shown in Figure 6 is applicable to that portion of the United States east of the Rocky Mountains and is based on the dates of the last killing frost in the spring. This map and Table 1 furnish a reasonably safe guide, although conditions may vary from year to year. There is also a difference of several days within the zones themselves, owing to elevation and proximity to bodies of water.

TABLE 1.—*Earliest safe dates for planting vegetable seeds in the open in the zones of the United States illustrated in Figure 6*

Crop	Zone A	Zone B	Zone C	Zone D	Zone E	Zone F	Zone G
Asparagus		Feb. 1 to Mar. 1	Mar. 1 to 15	Mar. 15 to Apr. 15	Apr. 15 to May 1	May 1 to 15	May 15 to June 1.
Beans:							
Lima	Mar. 1 to 15	Mar. 15 to Apr. 1	Apr. 1 to 15		May 15 to June 1	May 15 to June 15	May 15 to June 15.
Snap	Feb. 15 to Mar. 1	Mar. 1 to 15	Mar. 15 to 30	May 1 to 15	May 1 to 15	May 15 to June 1	May 15 to June 15.
Beet	Feb. 1 to 15	Feb. 15 to Mar. 1	Mar. 1 to 15	Apr. 1 to May 1	Apr. 15 to May 1	May 1 to 15	
Broccoli:				Mar. 15 to Apr. 15			
Heading [1]	Jan. 1 to Feb. 1	Jan. 15 to Feb. 15	Feb. 15 to Mar. 1	Mar. 1 to 15	Mar. 15 to Apr. 15	Apr. 15 to May 1	May 1 to 15.
Sprouting [1]	do	do	do	do	do	do	Do.
Brussels sprouts	do	do	do	do	do	do	Do.
Cabbage	do	do	do	do	do	do	Do.
Cabbage, Chinese	do	do	do	do	do	do	Do.
Cardoon							
Carrot	Feb. 1 to 15	Feb. 15 to Mar. 1	Mar. 1 to 15	Mar. 15 to Apr. 1	Apr. 15 to May 1	May 1 to 15	May 1 to June 1.
Cauliflower [1]	Jan. 1 to Feb. 1	Jan. 15 to Feb. 15	Feb. 15 to Mar. 1	Mar. 1 to 15	Mar. 15 to Apr. 15	Apr. 15 to May 1	May 1 to 15.
Celeriac	do	do	do	do	do	do	Do.
Celery [1]	do	do	do	do	do	do	Do.
Chard	do	do	do	do	do	do	Do.
Chervil	do	do	do	do	do	do	Do.
Chicory, witloof							
Chives	Jan. 1 to Feb. 1	Feb. 1 to 15	Feb. 15 to Mar. 1	Mar. 1 to 15	June 1 to 15	June 15 to July 1	May 1 to 15.
Collards [1]	do	do	do	do	Mar. 15 to Apr. 15	Apr. 1 to May 1	Do.
Corn salad	Feb. 1 to 15	Feb. 15 to Mar. 1	Mar. 1 to 15	Mar. 15 to Apr. 15	Apr. 1 to May 1	May 1 to 15	May 15 to June 1.
Corn, sweet	Feb. 15 to Mar. 1	Mar. 1 to 15	Mar. 15 to Apr. 1	Apr. 1 to May 1	Apr. 15 to May 15	May 1 to June 1	May 15 to June 15.
Cress:							
Upland	Feb. 1 to 15	Feb. 15 to Mar. 1	Mar. 1 to 15	Mar. 15 to Apr. 1	Apr. 1 to May 1	May 1 to 15	May 15 to June 1.
Water	do	do	do	do	do	do	Do.
Cucumber	Mar. 1 to 15	Mar. 15 to Apr. 1	Apr. 1 to 15	Apr. 15 to May 1	May 1 to June 1	May 15 to June 15	June 1 to 15.
Dandelion	Jan. 1 to Feb. 1	Jan. 15 to Feb. 15	Feb. 1 to Mar. 15				
Dasheen	Mar. 1 to 15	Mar. 15 to Apr. 15	Apr. 15 to May 15				
Eggplant [1]	Feb. 1 to 15	Feb. 15 to Mar. 1	Mar. 1 to 15	Apr. 15 to May 1	May 1 to June 1	May 15 to June 15	June 1 to 15.
Endive				Mar. 1 to Apr. 1	Apr. 1 to May 1	May 1 to 15	May 15 to June 1.
Florence fennel	Jan. 1 to Feb. 1	Feb. 1 to 15	Feb. 15 to Mar. 1	Mar. 15 to Apr. 15	Mar. 15 to Apr. 15	Apr. 15 to May 1	May 1 to June 1.
Garlic	do	do	do	Mar. 1 to 15			Do.
Horseradish [1]	Feb. 1 to 15	Feb. 15 to Mar. 1	Mar. 1 to 15	Mar. 15 to Apr. 1	Mar. 15 to Apr. 15	Apr. 1 to May 1	May 1 to June 15.
Jerusalem artichoke	Jan. 1 to Feb. 1	Feb. 1 to 15	Feb. 15 to Mar. 1	Apr. 1 to 15	Mar. 15 to Apr. 15	May 1 to 15	May 1 to 15.
Kale	Feb. 1 to 15	Feb. 15 to Mar. 1	Mar. 1 to 15	Mar. 1 to 15	Apr. 1 to May 1	Apr. 1 to May 1	May 15 to June 1.
Kohlrabi	Jan. 1 to Feb. 1	Feb. 1 to 15	Feb. 15 to Mar. 1	Mar. 1 to 15	Mar. 15 to Apr. 15	Apr. 1 to May 1	May 1 to 15.
Leek	Feb. 1 to 15	Feb. 15 to Mar. 1	Mar. 1 to 15	Mar. 15 to Apr. 15	Apr. 1 to May 1	May 1 to 15	May 15 to June 15.
Lettuce	Mar. 1 to 15	Mar. 15 to Apr. 1	Apr. 1 to 15	Apr. 15 to May 1	June 1 to June 15	June 1 to 15	June 1 to June 15.
Martynia		do	do	do	do	do	Do.
Muskmelon	Feb. 1 to 15	Feb. 15 to Mar. 1	Mar. 1 to 15	Mar. 15 to Apr. 15	Apr. 1 to May 1	May 1 to 15	May 15 to June 1.
Mustard	Feb. 15 to Mar. 1	Mar. 1 to 15	Mar. 15 to 30	Apr. 15 to May 1	May 1 to June 1	May 15 to June 1	May 15 to June 1.
Okra							

[1] Plants.

TABLE 1.—*Earliest safe dates for planting vegetable seeds in the open in the zones of the United States illustrated in Figure 6*—Continued

Crop	Zone A	Zone B	Zone C	Zone D	Zone E	Zone F	Zone G
Onion:							
Plants	Jan. 1 to Feb. 1	Feb. 1 to 15	Feb. 15 to Mar. 1	Mar. 1 to 15	Mar. 15 to Apr. 15	Apr. 1 to May 1	May 1 to 15.
Seed	Feb. 1 to 15	Feb. 15 to Mar. 1	Mar. 1 to 15	Mar. 15 to Apr. 1	Apr. 1 to May 1	May 1 to 15	May 15 to June 1.
Sets	Jan. 1 to Feb. 1	Feb. 1 to 15	Feb. 15 to Mar. 1	Mar. 1 to 15	Mar. 15 to Apr. 15	Apr. 1 to May 1	May 1 to 15.
Parsley	Feb. 1 to 15	Feb. 15 to Mar. 1	Mar. 1 to 15	Mar. 15 to Apr. 1	Apr. 1 to May 1	May 1 to 15	May 15 to June 1.
Parsley, turnip-rooted	do	do	do	do	do	do	Do.
Parsnip	do	do	do	do	do	do	Do.
Peas	Jan. 1 to Feb. 1	Feb. 1 to 15	Feb. 15 to Mar. 1	Mar. 1 to 15	Mar. 15 to Apr. 15	Apr. 15 to May 1	May 1 to June 1.
Peppers[1]	Mar. 1 to 15	Mar. 15 to Apr. 1	Apr. 1 to 15	Apr. 15 to May 1	May 1 to June 1	June 1 to 15	June 1 to 15.
Physalis	do	do	do	do	do	do	May 1 to 15.
Poke				Mar. 1 to 15	Mar. 15 to Apr. 15	Apr. 15 to May 1	May 1 to June 1.
Potato	Jan. 1 to Feb. 1	Feb. 1 to 15	Feb. 15 to Mar. 1	do	do	June 1 to 15	
Pumpkin	Mar. 1 to 15	Mar. 15 to Apr. 1	Apr. 1 to 15	Apr. 15 to May 1	May 1 to June 1	Apr. 15 to May 15	May 1 to 15.
Radish	Jan. 1 to Feb. 1	Feb. 1 to 15	Feb. 15 to Mar. 1	Mar. 15 to Apr. 15	Mar. 15 to Apr. 15	Apr. 15 to May 15	May 15 to June 1.
Rhubarb[1]					Apr. 15 to May 1	May 1 to 15	May 1 to 15.
Salsify	Feb. 1 to 15	Feb. 15 to Mar. 1	Mar. 1 to 15	Mar. 15 to Apr. 15	Apr. 15 to May 1	May 15 to June 1	May 15 to June 1.
Shallots	Jan. 1 to Feb. 1	Feb. 1 to 15	Feb. 15 to Mar. 1	Mar. 1 to 15	Apr. 15 to May 1	Apr. 15 to May 1	Do.
Sorrel	Feb. 1 to 15	Feb. 15 to Mar. 1	Mar. 1 to 15	Mar. 1 to Apr. 1	Apr. 15 to May 15	May 1 to 15.	
Spinach	Mar. 1 to 15	Mar. 15 to Apr. 1	Apr. 1 to 15	May 1 to 15	Mar. 15 to June 1	May 15 to June 15	June 1 to 15.
Spinach, New Zealand	do	do	do	Apr. 15 to May 1	May 1 to June 1	June 1 to 15	
Squash	do	do	do	do	do	do	
Sweetpotato[1]	do	do	do	do	do	do	June 15 to 30.
Tomato[1]	Jan. 1 to Feb. 1	Feb. 1 to 15	Feb. 15 to Mar. 1	Mar. 1 to 15	Mar. 15 to Apr. 15	Apr. 15 to May 1	May 1 to 15.
Turnip greens	do	do	do	do	do	do	Do.
Turnips and rutabagas	do	do	do	do	do	do	
Watermelon	Mar. 1 to 15	Mar. 15 to Apr. 1	Apr. 1 to 15	Apr. 15 to May 1	May 1 to June 1	June 1 to 15	

[1] Plants.

By referring to Figure 7 it will be noted that the dates when the last killing frost may be expected in the western part of the country are extremely variable. For example, at certain points in Colorado this date is as late as June 12 or 16; at points in Wyoming to the northward it is as early as May 4; in California there is a variation from January 25 to June 22; and in Arizona, from February 15 to

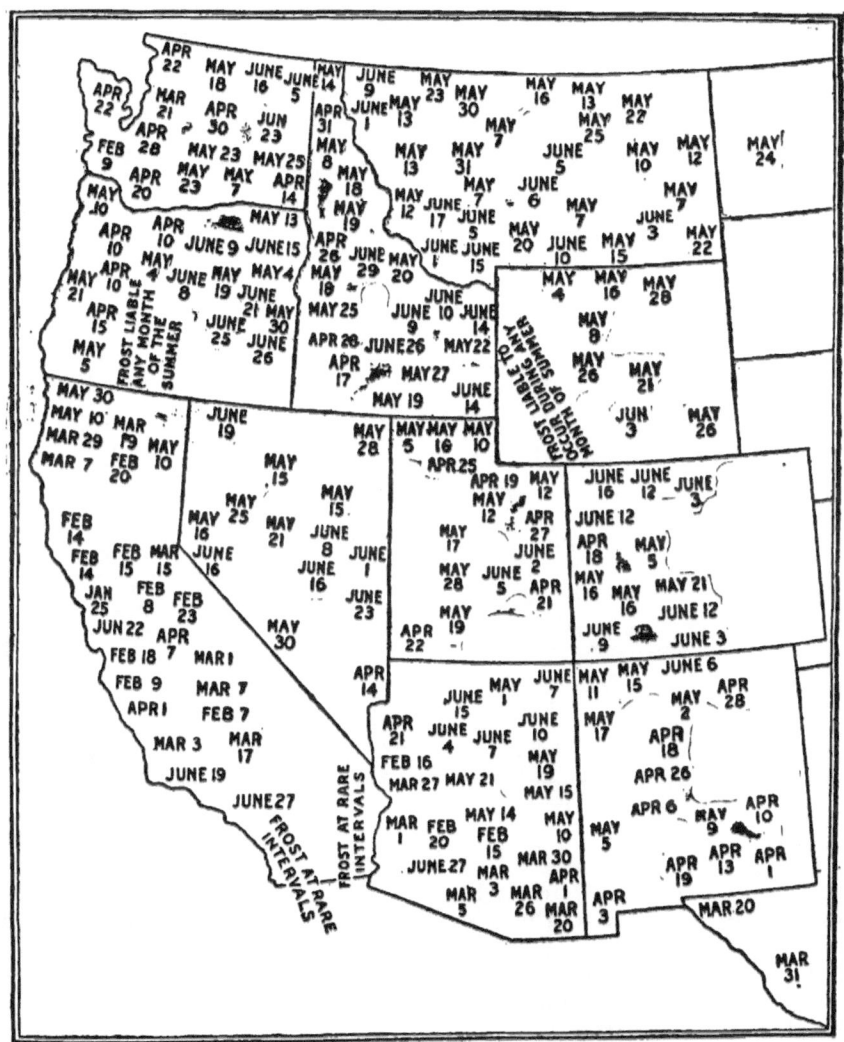

FIGURE 7.—Outline map showing the average date of the last killing frost in spring in the western portion of the United States

June 27. Primarily these variations are owing to differences in the elevations of the stations where the observations were made rather than to the location of the stations in different zones.

Of equal importance are the latest dates on which various crops may be planted and yet mature before the earliest killing frost in the autumn. The zone map shown in Figure 8 gives the approximate dates of the earliest autumn frosts in the central and eastern part of the United States, while the outline map shown in Figure 9 gives this information for the Rocky Mountain and Pacific coast regions. It will be noted that in the latter area there is one section where frost rarely ever occurs and two sections where frost is liable to occur during any month of the year. By referring to Table 2 the approximate latest date for planting any given crop may be determined.

Most farmers know by experience and by the blossoming of certain native trees when it is reasonably safe to plant the various garden crops. Exceptional seasonal variations, however, are likely to occur, and it is always desirable to have a reserve supply of plants for replanting in case the first are lost by frost. Potatoes are injured even by moderate frost. On the other hand, they require a considerable period between the time of planting and their appearance above

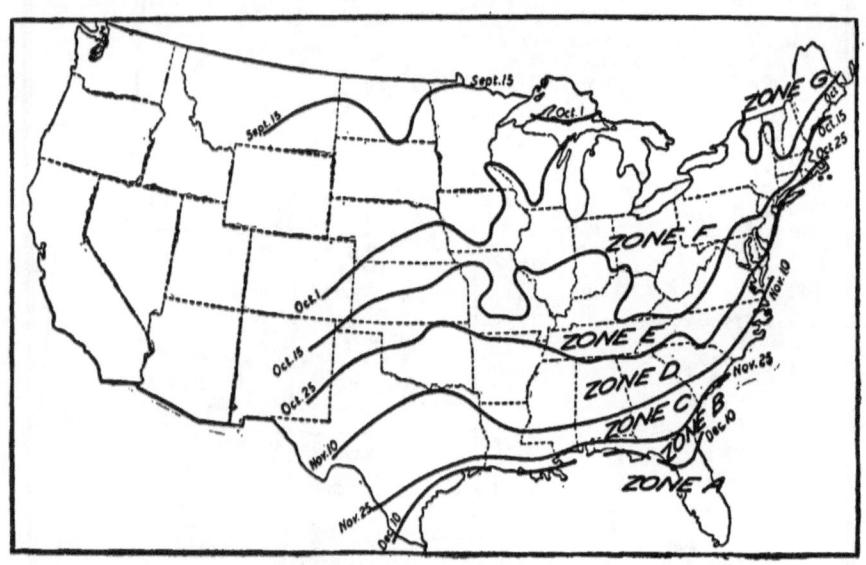

FIGURE 8.—Zone map of the central and eastern part of the United States based on average date of first killing frost in autumn. By referring to Table 2 the latest safe date for planting any crop in any one of the various zones may be determined

ground, and so may be planted well in advance of the date on which the last killing frost of the season may be expected. Potatoes that are just above ground can often be saved from frost by covering the plants with soil. Peas, onions, cabbage, kale, spinach, turnips, and beets will stand considerable frost. It frequently pays to take a reasonable chance of putting them in fairly early. If they are not killed, it means early vegetables; if they are, nothing is lost but the seed and the labor of replanting. Summer squashes, cucumbers, and melons frequently may be planted in advance of their normal season, the hills being protected from wind and frost by paper or glass covers. In addition these covers protect the plants from insects.

PLANTING THE GARDEN

Methods of planting garden crops vary with the locality and the type of soil. In some sections of the South, especially along the

South Atlantic coast and in the Gulf States, it may be necessary to plant on beds or ridges in order to obtain good drainage. Level planting is recommended on the lighter sandy soils and on the majority of the sandy loam and clay loam soils of the North and North-

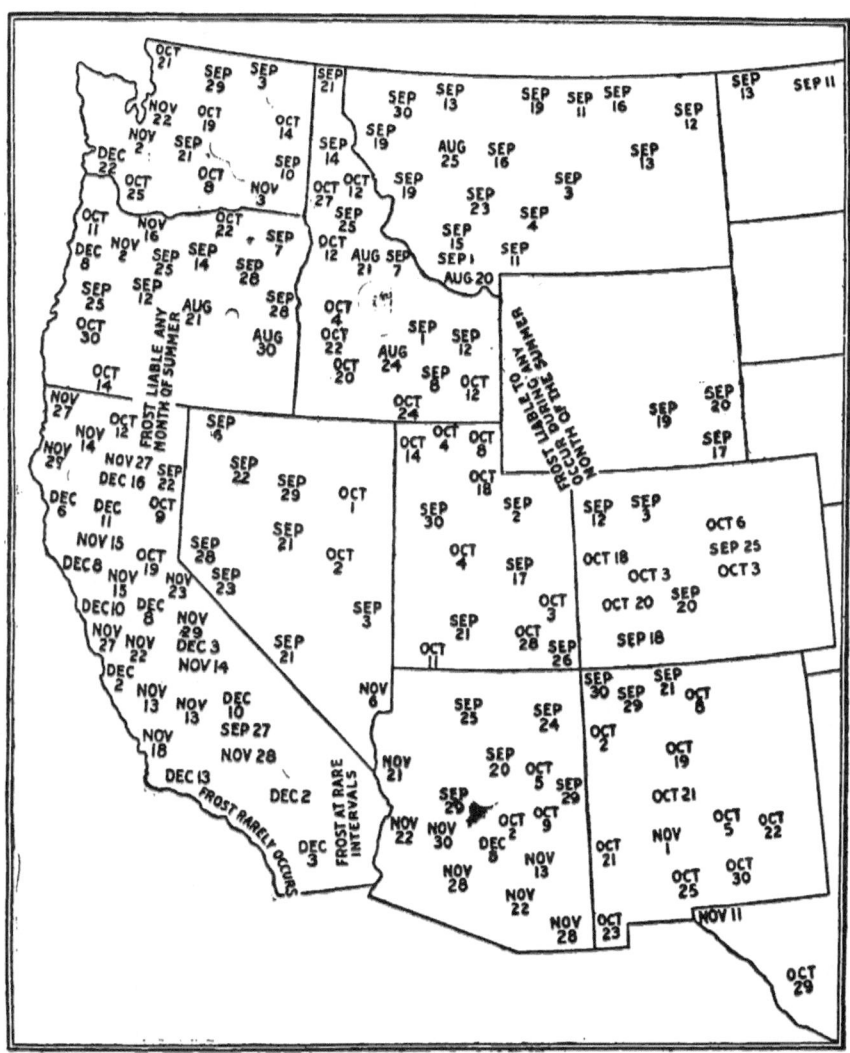

FIGURE 9.—Outline map showing average date of first killing frost in the autumn in the western portion of the United States

east. In the irrigated sections of the West the seeds are usually planted on the side of the furrows a little above the irrigation water level. In all cases the method of planting should conform to the approved customs of the region and the type of soil upon which the garden is located.

TABLE 2.—*Latest safe dates for planting vegetable seeds and plants in the open in the zones of the United States illustrated in Figure 8*

Crop	Zone A	Zone B	Zone C	Zone D	Zone E	Zone F	Zone G
Asparagus		Nov. 1 to Dec. 1	Nov. 1 to Dec. 1	Nov. 1 to Dec. 1	Nov. 1 to Dec. 1	Oct. 15 to Nov. 15	Oct. 1 to Nov. 1
Beans:							
Lima	Oct. 1	Oct. 15	Sept. 1				
Snap	do.	do.	do.	Aug. 15	Aug. 1	Aug. 15	Aug. 15
Beet	Nov. 1	Oct. 1	do.	do.	do.	July 15	July 1
Broccoli:							
Heading[1]	do.	do.	do.	do.	Aug. 1	July 15	Do.
Sprouting[1]	do.	do.	do.	do.	do.	do.	Do.
Brussels sprouts	do.	do.	do.	do.	July 15	Aug. 1	Do.
Cabbage[1]	do.	do.	Oct. 1	Sept. 1	Aug. 1	July 15	Do.
Cabbage, Chinese	do.	do.	Sept. 1	Aug. 15	do.	do.	Do.
Cardoon	do.	do.	do.	do.	do.	do.	Do.
Carrot	do.	do.	do.	do.	do.	do.	Do.
Cauliflower[1]							
Celeriac			Oct. 1	Sept. 1	Aug. 1	July 1	June 15
Celery[1]	Nov. 1	Oct. 1	do.	do.	July 15	do.	Do.
Chard	do.	do.	do.	do.	do.	do.	Do.
Chervil	do.	do.	do.	do.	do.	do.	
Chicory, witloof	Dec. 1	Nov. 1	do.	Aug. 15			
Chives				July 1	June 15	June 1	May 15
Collards[1]	Nov. 1	Oct. 1	Sept. 1	Aug. 15	July 15	July 1	June 1
Corn salad	Dec. 1	Nov. 15	Nov. 1	Oct. 1	Sept. 15	Aug. 15	July 15
Corn, sweet	Oct. 1	Sept. 1	Aug. 15	Aug. 1	July 15	July 1	June 15
Cress:							
Upland	Dec. 1	Nov. 15	Nov. 1	Oct. 15	Oct. 1	Sept. 1	
Water	do.	do.	do.	do.	do.	do.	
Cucumber			Aug. 15	Aug. 1	July 15	July 1	June 1
Dandelion	Dec. 1	Nov. 1	Oct. 15	Oct. 1	Sept. 15	Sept. 1	
Dasheen[1]							
Eggplant[1]				July 1	June 15	June 1	Aug. 1
Endive	Sept. 1		July 15	Oct. 15	Oct. 1	Sept. 1	July 1
Florence fennel	Nov. 1	Nov. 1	Nov. 1	Sept. 1	Aug. 1	July 1	
Garlic[2]			Oct. 1				
Horseradish[1]							
Jerusalem artichoke							
Kale	Nov. 1	Nov. 1	Nov. 1	Oct. 1	Sept. 15	July 1	Do.
Kohlrabi	do.	Oct. 1	Sept. 1	Aug. 15	July 15		June 15
Leek	do.	do.	do.	July 15	June 15	June 1	May 15
Lettuce	Dec. 1	Nov. 1	Oct. 15	Sept. 1	July 1	July 15	July 1
Martynia	Nov. 15	do.	Oct. 15	Oct. 1	Aug. 1	Aug. 15	July 15
Muskmelon[2]					Sept. 1		
Mustard	Dec. 1	Nov. 15	Nov. 1	Oct. 15	Oct. 1	Sept. 1	Aug. 15
Okra	Oct. 1	Sept. 15	July 15	July 1	June 15		

Onion:					
Plants	Dec. 15	Dec. 1	do	do	June 1	May 15.
Seed	Dec. 15	Nov. 1	Oct. 15	June 15	June 1	Do.
Sets	Dec. 15	Dec. 1	July 15	Aug. 1	July 15	July 1.
Parsley	Dec. 1	Nov. 1	Nov. 1	July 1	June 15	Do.
Parsley, turnip-rooted	do	Nov. 15	do	Se t. 1		
Parsnip	do	Nov. 1	June 15	June 1		
Peas	Nov. 1	Oct. 1	Sept. 1	Aug. 15	Aug. 15	Aug. 15.
Peppers[1]	Sept. 15	Sept. 1	July 15	June 15	June 1	
Physalis	Sept. 1	do	Aug. 15	July 1	do	
Poke[2]						
Potato	Sept. 15	Sept. 1	Aug. 15	July 15	July 1	June 15.
Pumpkin	do	do	do	do	do	Do.
Radish	Dec. 1	Nov. 1	Oct. 15	Sept. 15	Sept. 1	Aug. 15.
Rhubarb[1]						Nov. 1.
Rutabagas	Nov. 15	Nov. 1		Nov. 1	Nov. 1	June 1.
Salsify	Dec. 1			July 1	July 1	
Shallots	do	do	June 15			
Sorrel	do	do	Oct. 15	Oct. 1	Aug. 15	July 15.
Spinach	Nov. 1	Oct. 1	do	do	do	Aug. 1.
Spinach, New Zealand			Aug. 1	July 15	June 15	
Squash:						
Summer	Oct. 1	Sept. 1	Aug. 15	Aug. 1	July 1	June 15.
Winter			July 15	July 1	June 15	Do.
Sweetpotato[1,2]						
Tomato[1]	Oct. 1	Sept. 1	Aug. 15	July 1	June 15	July 15.
Turnip greens	Nov. 15	Nov. 1	Oct. 15	Sept. 1	Aug. 1	July 1.
Turnips	do	do	do	Sept. 1	July 15	
Watermelon[2]						

[1] Plants. [2] Spring planting only.

Table 3 gives in general the proper depth of planting for the various vegetable seeds as well as the quantity of seeds or number of plants required for 100 feet of row and the distance apart that plants should be spaced. Special planting suggestions will be found under the discussion of cultural hints for the various garden crops.

TABLE 3.—*Quantity of seeds and number of plants required for 100 feet of row, depths of planting, and distances apart for rows and plants*

Crop	Required for 100 feet of row		Depth for planting seed	Distance apart		
				Rows		Plants in the row
	Seed	Plants		Horse cultivation	Hand cultivation	
			Inches	*Feet*		
Asparagus	1 ounce	75	1 -1½	4 -5	1½ to 2 feet	18 inches.
Beans:						
Lima, bush	1 pint		1 -1½	2½-3	2 feet	3 to 4 inches.
Lima, pole	do		1 -1½	3 -4	3 feet	3 to 4 feet.
Snap, bush	do		1 -1½	2½-3	2 feet	3 to 4 inches.
Snap, pole	½ pint		1 -1½	3 -4	do	3 feet.
Beet	2 ounces		1	2 -2½	14 to 16 inches	2 to 3 inches.
Broccoli:						
Heading	1 packet	50- 75	½	2½-3	2 to 2½ feet	14 to 24 inches.
Sprouting	do	50- 75	½	2½-3	do	Do.
Brussels sprouts	do	50- 75	½	2½-3	do	Do.
Cabbage	do	50- 75	½	2½-3	do	Do.
Cabbage, Chinese	do		½	2 -2½	18 to 24 inches	8 to 12 inches.
Cardoon	do	35	½	3	3 feet	3 feet.
Carrot	do		½	2 -2½	14 to 16 inches	2 to 3 inches.
Cauliflower	do	50- 75	½	2½-3	2 to 2½ feet	14 to 24 inches.
Celeriac	do	200-250	⅛	2½-3	18 to 24 inches	4 to 6 inches.
Celery	do	200-250	⅛	2½-3	do	Do.
Chard	2 ounces		1	2 -2½	do	6 inches.
Chervil	1 packet		½	2 -2½	14 to 16 inches	2 to 3 inches.
Chicory, witloof	do		½	2 -2½	18 to 24 inches	6 to 8 inches.
Chives	do		½	2½-3	14 to 16 inches	In clusters.
Collards	do		½	3 -3½	18 to 24 inches	18 to 24 inches.
Corn salad	do		½	2½-3	14 to 16 inches	1 foot.
Corn, sweet	¼ pint		2	3 -3½	2 to 3 feet	Drills, 14 to 16 inches; hills, 2½ to 3 feet.
Cress:						
Upland	1 packet		⅛- ¼	2 -2½	14 to 16 inches	2 to 3 inches.
Water	do		⅛- ¼	2 -2½	18 to 24 inches	4 to 6 inches.
Cucumber	do		1	6 -7	6 to 7 feet	Drills, 3 feet; hills, 6 feet.
Dandelion	do		½	2½-3	14 to 16 inches	8 to 12 inches.
Dasheen	½ peck	50	2 -3	3½-4	3½ to 4 feet	2 feet.
Eggplant	1 packet	50	½	3	2 to 2½ feet	3 feet.
Endive	do		½	2½-3	18 to 24 inches	12 inches.
Florence fennel	do		½	2½-3	do	4 to 6 inches.
Garlic	1 pound		1 -2	2½-3	14 to 16 inches	2 to 3 inches.
Horseradish	Cuttings	50- 75	2	3 -4	2 to 2½ feet	18 to 24 inches.
Jerusalem artichoke	1 to 2 quarts	25- 35	2 -3	3 -4	2 to 3 feet	2 to 3 feet.
Kale	1 packet		½	2½-3	18 to 24 inches	12 to 15 inches.
Kohlrabi	do		½	2½-3	14 to 16 inches	5 to 6 inches.
Leek	do		½-1	2½-3	do	2 to 3 inches.
Lettuce	do	100	½	2½-3	do	15 inches.
Martynia	do		1	3 -4	2½ to 3 feet	2 feet.
Muskmelon	do		1	6 -7	6 to 7 feet	Hills, 6 feet.
Mustard	do		½	2½-3	14 to 16 inches	12 inches.
Okra	2 ounces		1 -1½	3 -3½	3 to 3½ feet	2 feet.
Onion:						
Plants		400	1 -2	2 -2½	14 to 16 inches	2 to 3 inches.
Seed	1 packet		½-1	2 -2½	do	Do.
Sets	1 quart		1 -2	2 -2½	do	Do.
Parsley	1 packet		⅛	2 -2½	do	4 to 6 inches.
Parsley, turnip-rooted.	do		⅛- ¼	2 -2½	do	2 to 3 inches.
Parsnip	do		½	2 -2½	18 to 24 inches	Do.
Peas	1 pint		2 -3	2 -4	1½ to 3 feet	1 inch.
Peppers	1 packet	50- 70	½	3 -4	2 to 3 feet	18 to 24 inches.
Physalis	do		½	2 -2½	1½ to 2 feet	12 to 18 inches.
Poke	do	25- 40	½-1	3 -3½	3 to 3½ feet	3 feet.
Potato	5 to 6 pounds		4	2½-3	2 to 2½ feet	10 to 18 inches.
Pumpkin	1 ounce		1 -2	5 -8	5 to 8 feet	3 to 4 feet.

TABLE 3.—*Quantity of seeds and number of plants required for 100 feet of row, depths of planting, and distances apart for rows and plants*—Continued

Crop	Required for 100 feet of row		Depth for planting seed	Distance apart		
				Rows		
	Seed	Plants		Horse cultivation	Hand cultivation	Plants in the row
			Inches	*Feet*		
Radish	1 ounce		½	2 -2½	14 to 16 inches	1 inch.
Rhubarb		25- 35		3 -4	3 to 4 feet	3 to 4 feet.
Salsify	1 ounce		½	2 -2½	18 to 24 inches	2 to 3 inches.
Shallots	1 pound (cloves).		1 -2	2 -2½	14 to 16 inches	Do.
Sorrel	1 packet		½	2 -2½	18 to 24 inches	5 to 8 inches.
Spinach	1 ounce		½	2 -2½	14 to 16 inches	3 to 4 inches.
Spinach, New Zealand.	do		1 -1½	3 -3½	3 feet	18 inches.
Squash:						
Bush	½ ounce		1 -2	4 -5	4 to 5 feet	Drills, 15 to 18 inches; hills, 4 feet.
Vine	1 ounce		1 -2	8 -12	8 to 12 feet	Drills, 2 to 3 feet; hills, 4 feet.
Sweetpotato	5 pounds	[1] 75	2 -3	3 -3½	3 to 3½ feet	12 to 14 inches.
Tomato	1 packet	35- 50	½	3 -4	2 to 3 feet	1½ to 3 feet.
Turnip greens	do		¼- ½	2 -2½	14 to 16 inches	2 to 3 inches.
Turnips and rutabagas.	½ ounce		¼- ½	2 -2½	do	Do.
Watermelon	1 ounce		1 -2	8 -10	8 to 10 feet	Drills, 2 to 3 feet; hills, 8 feet.

[1] Slips.

SUCCESSION OF CROPS

All garden space should be kept fully occupied throughout the growing season. In the South this means the greater part of the year; in fact, throughout the South Atlantic and Gulf coast regions it is possible to have certain vegetables growing in the garden every month of the year.

In arranging the garden all early maturing crops may properly be grouped so that after their removal the ground will be available as a unit for planting later crops. As soon as one crop is removed another should take its place. It is not desirable, however, to follow a crop with another of its kind, but with some unrelated crop. For example, early peas or beans can very properly be followed by late cabbage, celery, carrots, or beets; early corn or potatoes can be followed by fall turnips or spinach. It is not always necessary to wait until the early crop is entirely removed, but a later crop may be planted between the rows of the early crop; for example, sweet corn may be planted between the rows of early potatoes. Late cabbage is frequently planted between potato rows. Crops that are attacked by the same diseases should not follow each other.

In the extreme North, where the season is relatively short, there is very little opportunity for succession cropping; therefore plenty of land should be provided to accommodate the desired range of crops.

THE LATE SUMMER AND FALL GARDEN

Farmers the country over would be justified in paying more attention to their late summer and fall gardens. Second and third plantings of crops adapted to growing late in the season not only provide a supply of fresh vegetables for the latter part of the season but give better products for canning and storing. This is particularly true of beans, beets, carrots, and celery. Late-grown beans are especially suitable for canning, while the root crops and celery when matured late in the season are crisp and tender and of better quality for having escaped the summer's heat. In parts of the South the autumn garden is really of as great importance as the early one.

CULTIVATION

Frequent shallow cultivation should be given most garden crops, mainly to keep the garden free from weeds and the surface soil loose and mellow. Weeds draw heavily on the moisture supply and the plant food of the soil; therefore the best time to destroy weeds is just after they start. If the crops are cultivated once a week, especially during the early part of the season, weeds will be controlled, and the crops will get the benefit of the moisture and soil fertility. Under no circumstances should the land be cultivated when wet, but in sections having natural rainfall the garden should be gone over with the cultivator as soon as it is dry enough after a rain to break the crust and thus prevent the baking of the surface soil. If the work is done properly and at regular intervals there will be little difficulty in controlling weeds and keeping the garden crops growing.

FIGURE 10.—A 5-shovel cultivator with attachments, adapted for garden cultivation

A 1-horse, 5-shovel cultivator with various attachments, of the type shown in Figure 10, is suited for garden cultivation. In all cases the cultivator should be fitted with a lever or some device to regulate its width. Cultivators that stir the soil deeply should not, under most circumstances, be used in the garden, except where some crops, such as potatoes, require the soil to be worked into a ridge about the plants. A sweep should not be used, except possibly in the middles between the rows. The larger crops in the garden should be cultivated with horse-drawn tools and with a minimum of hand labor. The smaller crops, such as carrots, beets, and lettuce, if planted in rows too close for horse cultivation, may be worked with a hand cultivator of the type shown in Figure 11. This implement is fitted with a variety of attachments, enabling the gardener to do many kinds of work.

Hand tools needed in the garden are mainly a hoe, a steel rake, a spade or a spading fork, a planting trowel, a watering can, and a garden line for laying off the rows. It is not necessary to have a large investment in tools. Generally the implements used for other purposes on the farm are adaptable for work in the garden.

IRRIGATION

Throughout that portion of the country where rains occur during the growing season it should not be necessary to irrigate in order to produce the ordinary garden crops. In arid regions where irrigation must be depended upon for the production of crops, the system best adapted for use in that particular locality should be employed in the garden. Wherever irrigation is practiced the water should not be applied until needed, and then the soil should be thoroughly soaked. After irrigation the land should be cultivated as soon as the surface becomes sufficiently dry, and no more water should be applied until the plants begin to show the need of additional moisture. Constant or excessive watering is very detrimental in every case. Apply the water at any time of the day that is most convenient and when the plants require it.

Overhead or sprinkler irrigation is now used extensively in commercial market gardens, especially in sections where the natural rainfall is insufficient at certain periods of the growing season. This system is also suited for use in the home garden if there is an adequate supply of water under pressure. Manufacturers of overhead or sprinkler equipment provide temporary lines of sprinkler pipe which are connected by unions and may be put together or taken apart very quickly. A hose connects the pipe with the water system. These pipes may be supported on stakes, on blocks of wood, or on crates or boxes placed in a row through the garden.[4]

FIGURE 11.—A small hand cultivator, a desirable addition to the garden equipment

PAPER MULCH

Gardening under paper, or the use of paper as a mulch, has been advocated as a means of eliminating cultivation, controlling weeds, increasing yields, conserving moisture, and raising the temperature of the soil. Under many conditions the use of paper mulch has proved to be advantageous and largely increased yields have been obtained. In some instances the advantages have not justified the expense and labor involved in applying the paper. For the home gardener, however, the chief interest in mulch paper lies in the fact that it reduces the necessity for cultivation during hot weather. The use of paper will control weeds, although a certain amount of hand weeding may be needed around individual plants or between

---

[4] For further information on overhead irrigation, see Farmers' Bulletin 1529, Spray Irrigation in the Eastern States.

the strips of paper. Paper mulch has hastened the maturity and increased the yields of certain garden crops, particularly those requiring a long season, such as sweetpotatoes, peppers, eggplant, and tomatoes, especially in the more northern States.

Paper mulch as used in home gardens has given most general satisfaction when laid in strips held with a continuous ridge of soil over the depressed edges. Following the laying of the paper over the moist garden soil, the transplants such as tomatoes, cauliflower, and peppers are set at the desired intervals through openings made in the paper with a sharp stick or dibble. Crops such as potatoes, corn, beans, and melons may be seeded through similar openings. The use of mulch paper with small-seeded drill crops requires special methods which vary with the conditions.

While the heavier (type B) mulch papers have proved most suitable for garden use, the lighter (type A) papers have sometimes proved serviceable, particularly on light soils or in regions of reduced rainfall. The cost of the heavier paper required for a plot 50 by 50 feet when used in the manner above described is about $7 and that of the lighter paper about $3.50.

INSECTS AND DISEASES

The insects and diseases that infest garden crops are so numerous that it would be impracticable even to mention them all in a bulletin of this character. There are certain control measures, however, that will often accomplish a great amount of good. In the autumn after the crops have been harvested, or as fast as any crop is disposed of, all refuse that remains should be gathered and burned. Some of the garden insects and disease-producing organisms winter in the remains of garden crops and in the trash and weeds around the garden. By burning such material many of these insects and disease organisms are destroyed.

There are two main classes of insects to be dealt with. The chewing or biting insects may for the most part be controlled by the use of stomach poisons, such as lead arsenate or Paris green, or by hand collection or other special methods. The sucking insects, especially the plant lice, must be controlled by contact poisons, such as nicotine or pyrethrum.

For the diseases of vegetables, numerous methods of control are available. Sometimes a single method is effective, but more often several measures must be combined to secure the best results. An illustration of the former is the use of varieties resistant to disease. An example of the latter is the combination of rotation of crops, seed treatment, and spraying for the control of anthracnose of cucurbits.

Among the most important disease-control measures are crop rotation, soil treatment, the use of disease-free seed and plants, seed treatment with fungicides, the use of disease-resistant varieties, spraying and dusting with fungicides, and the eradication of wild host plants on which certain diseases overwinter.[5]

---

[5] For details of these control methods see Farmers' Bulletin 1371, Diseases and Insects of Garden Vegetables, and Yearbook Separate 929, Diseases and Pests of Fruits and Vegetables.

CANNING AND STORING VEGETABLES AT HOME

In sections of the country where a constant supply of fresh vegetables can not be obtained from the garden throughout the year, it is important that the season for their use be extended by means of canning and storage. Nonacid vegetables, such as asparagus, beans, corn, peas, beets, and spinach, should be canned under steam pressure rather than by the hot-water process. Tomatoes, being an acid vegetable, may be safely canned by the boiling-water process. Pressure cookers are now standard equipment in many homes and may be used for the canning of vegetables. It is important, however, that the pressure cooker be equipped with thermometer, pressure gauge, and safety valve for proper control. There are also on the market satisfactory hand machines for sealing tin cans, making it possible to apply factory methods in the canning of vegetables in the home.[6]

The home storage of vegetables is, perhaps, of greater importance than canning because of its adaptation to all that portion of the country where freezing temperatures prevail during the winter months. There are at least 10 important vegetables that can be stored for winter use, the success attending their storage depending largely on the way the work is handled. Certain vegetables, like cabbage, turnips, beets, carrots, and celery, may be stored in pits in the open ground; potatoes, sweetpotatoes, and onions are stored to best advantage in cellars or specially designed storage houses. Temperature, moisture control, and ventilation are the main points involved in the successful home storage of vegetables.[7]

The root crops, including beets, carrots, winter radishes, and turnips, also such crops as collards, kale, and spinach, may remain where they are grown throughout the late fall and early winter in nearly all parts of the South. These crops, however, will start a new growth as soon as the weather begins to get warm in the late winter and will produce seed stalks, after which they are unfit for the table. In sections of the South where temperature conditions make it impossible to store vegetables for off-season use, canning and drying should be substituted.

CULTURE OF SPECIFIC GARDEN CROPS

PERENNIAL VEGETABLES

Perennial vegetables, especially asparagus, horseradish, and rhubarb, are among the most valuable garden products. They occupy comparatively little space and when once planted continue to yield for a number of years. It is usually best to locate these perennials along one side of the garden where they do not interfere with work on the annual plants. Unfortunately, these three important perennials are not adapted to culture in all sections and can not be grown in parts of the lower South. Because of their desirability, the perennials should be included in every garden where space and adaptability permit their culture.

---

[6] Farmers' Bulletin 1471, Canning Fruits and Vegetables at Home, gives information on proper methods of canning.
[7] Farmers' Bulletin 879, Home Storage of Vegetables, gives information relative to storage structures and methods of caring for vegetables in storage.

ASPARAGUS

Asparagus is wholesome and in many sections is among the earliest of the spring vegetables. An area about 20 feet square, or a row 50 to 75 feet long, will supply plenty of asparagus for a family of five or six persons, provided the soil is well enriched and the plants are given good attention.

Asparagus does best in locations having winters sufficiently cold to freeze the ground to a depth of at least a few inches, but it is not adapted to all portions of the lower South. In many southern locations the plants make a weak growth, producing small shoots. Elevation has some effect, but in general the latitude of south-central Georgia is about the southern limit of profitable culture.

The crop can be grown on almost any well-drained, fertile soil, and there is little possibility of having the land too rich, especially through the use of manure. As an asparagus planting will last for many years, it should be located where it will interfere as little as possible with other gardening operations.

Since asparagus roots go deep for their supply of moisture and plant food, the land should be loosened far down either by subsoil plowing or deep spading before planting. It is a good plan to throw the topsoil aside and spade manure, leaf mold, rotted leaves, or peat into the subsoil to a depth of 14 to 16 inches. From 5 to 10 pounds of a complete fertilizer should also be mixed into each 75-foot row or 20-foot bed.

FIGURE 12.—Asparagus crowns or plants being set in a trench

When ready for planting, the bottom of the trench should be about 6 inches below the natural level of the soil. (Fig. 12.) After the crowns are set and covered to a depth of an inch or two, the soil should be gradually worked into the trench around the plants during the first season. When set in beds, asparagus plants should be at least 1½ feet apart each way; when set in rows, they should be about 18 inches apart, with the rows from 4 to 5 feet apart.

Asparagus plants or crowns are grown from seed. The use of 1-year-old plants only is recommended. These should have a root spread of at least 15 inches, and larger ones are better. The home gardener will usually find it best to purchase his plants from some grower who has a good strain of a recognized variety. Mary Washington is a good variety that has the added merit of being rust resistant. In procuring asparagus crowns it is always well to be sure that they have not been allowed to dry out.

Clean cultivation encourages vigorous growth. Weeds and grass are usually responsible for unsatisfactory results with asparagus, and it behooves the gardener to keep his asparagus clean from the start. In the large farm garden with long rows most of the work can be done with a horse-drawn cultivator, but in the small garden, where the rows are short, or the asparagus is planted in beds, handwork must be resorted to.

White asparagus is produced by mounding the rows or hills with earth to keep light away from the young spears. Hilling is begun during the early spring and continued throughout the cutting season as needed, but in most cases, especially on light-textured soils, the initial hilling should be sufficient. On heavier soils the earth must be added more slowly. At the end of the cutting season these ridges are leveled down.

It is well to make an annual application of manure to asparagus. A liberal dressing of a high-grade complete fertilizer, 6 to 8 pounds to a 75-foot row, once each year, is also necessary. Both manure and fertilizer should be used at the end of the cutting season.

No shoots should be removed the year the plants are set in the permanent bed, and the period of cutting should be short the year after setting. During the cutting season in subsequent years all shoots should be removed. About July 1 to 10 cutting should cease and the tops should be allowed to grow. In the autumn, when dead, they can be removed and burned.

Asparagus rust and asparagus beetles are the chief enemies of asparagus. Directions for their control are given in Farmers' Bulletin 1371, Diseases and Insects of Garden Vegetables.[8]

HORSERADISH

Horseradish is adapted for growing in the north-temperate regions of the United States, but it is not suited for planting in the South except possibly in the high altitudes. Grated horseradish is a very desirable condiment, always best when fresh. A few plants in an out-of-the-way place in the garden, such as a corner, will supply enough for the family.

Any good soil, except possibly the lightest sands and heaviest clays, will grow horseradish, but it does best on a deep, rich, moist loam that is well supplied with organic matter. A shallow soil should be avoided, as it produces rough, prongy roots. Manure should be mixed with the soil a few months before the plants or cuttings are set. Some fertilizer may be used at the time of planting and more during each subsequent season. A top-dressing of manure each spring is advisable, but a good, deep soil in an old garden will usually grow good horseradish without heavy manuring or fertilization.

Horseradish seldom forms seed; it is propagated either by using crowns or by root cuttings. In propagating by crowns, a portion of an old plant consisting of a piece of root and crown buds is merely lifted and placed in the new location. Root cuttings are pieces of older roots 6 to 8 inches long and of the thickness of a lead pencil. These may be saved when preparing the larger roots for grating, or they may be purchased from seedsmen. A trench 4 or 5 inches deep is opened with a hoe and the root cuttings placed at an angle with their tops near the surface of the ground. Each cutting will sprout in several places, and after they are well established the soil should be carefully removed by hand from around the cuttings. All but one good cluster of leaves near the top of each cutting should be removed. The soil should then be replaced. These plants usually

---

[8] Additional information on asparagus culture is given in Farmers' Bulletins 1242, Permanent Fruit and Vegetable Gardens, and 1646, Asparagus Culture.

make good roots the first year. As a rule the plants in the home garden are allowed to grow from year to year, and portions of the roots are removed as needed. Pieces of roots and crowns remaining in the soil are usually sufficient to reestablish the plants.

Horseradish is prepared by cleaning and grating the roots directly into white wine vinegar or distilled vinegar of $4\frac{1}{2}$ to 5 per cent acid content. Bottled and sealed immediately, it keeps for a few weeks. Dried, ground, and bottled, it keeps for some time, but this product is not as good as when the horseradish is grated fresh and mixed with vinegar. Cider vinegar should not be used, as it causes the horseradish to turn dark.

POKE

Poke, also known as scoke and garget, is grown and used to some extent as an early spring vegetable. The plant is commonly found growing wild along fences and around farmyards and in other places where rich, moist soil is to be found. Poke is a common carrier of the mosaic disease, and it should not be grown with crops susceptible to this disease.

Poke is propagated by taking portions from the crowns of the plant and setting these in a new location. The culture of poke is similar to that of asparagus. Poke must have a fertile soil; but given that, no additional fertilization is needed. Like horseradish, poke may be planted along one side of the garden where it can remain for years. New plants soon arise from the old, and a few crowns spaced 2 to 3 feet apart soon occupy as much space as the average gardener cares to give it.

The young shoots that come up first in spring are used for food. They are taken just as they come through the loose earth and while they are still white and tender. Mulching with leaves or straw will aid in keeping the shoots white and tender. They are cut in the same way as asparagus, but care should be taken to avoid taking any portion of the root, as it contains a poisonous alkaloid. Poke is cooked, seasoned, and eaten in the same way as asparagus or as greens.

RHUBARB

Rhubarb thrives best in regions having cool moist summers and winters sufficiently cold to freeze the ground to a depth of several inches. It is not adapted to most portions of the South, but in certain regions of higher elevation it does fairly well. Rhubarb, like asparagus, is a perennial, and a few hills along the garden fence will supply all that a family can use. In sections where it thrives, rhubarb should be in the garden, for it comes early in the spring and has fine dietetic qualities.

Any deep, well-drained, fertile soil is suitable for rhubarb. It should be spaded or plowed to a depth of 12 to 16 inches, and rotted manure, leaf mold, decayed hardwood leaves, sods, or some other form of organic matter should be mixed with it. The methods of soil preparation suggested for asparagus are suitable for rhubarb; but as rhubarb is planted in hills 3 to 4 feet apart, it is usually sufficient to prepare each hill separately.

Rhubarb plants may be started from seed and transplanted, but seedlings vary from the parent plant. The usual method of starting the plants is to obtain pieces of crowns from established hills and set them in prepared hills. Cultivation is confined to the control of weeds. The planting should be top-dressed with a heavy application of manure in either early spring or late fall. Fresh horse manure applied over the hills during early spring greatly hastens growth or "forces" the plant.

If plenty of manure can be obtained, rhubarb needs little if any commercial fertilizer. However, a pound of complete commercial fertilizer high in nitrogen applied around each hill every year insures an abundant supply of plant food. In the absence of manure the plants can be mulched with green grass or weeds, and commercial fertilizer may be applied more liberally, but some manure is very desirable.

Seed stalks should be removed as soon as they form, because seed bearing greatly weakens the plant. No leaf stems should be harvested before the second year and but few until the third. Moreover, the harvest season must be largely confined to early spring as the plants should be allowed to grow undisturbed during summer. The hills should be divided and reset every seven or eight years. If not, they become too thick and produce only slender stems.

Only the leaf stem of the rhubarb is used as a vegetable. The leaves contain injurious materials such as oxalic acid, and in no case should they be used for food. They make excellent covers to protect tomato, cabbage, and other plants for the first day or two after setting.

GREENS

Greens may be defined as the leaves and stems of young plants, such as spinach, which in their green state are boiled for food. The classification of greens in this bulletin is an arrangement of convenience, for plants such as collards are really greens also. The plants treated here as greens are hardy vegetables most of which are adapted to fall sowing and winter culture over the entire South and the more temperate portions of the North. Their culture may be extended over a wider area of the North by growing them with some protection, such as mulching or frames. Greens are especially valuable vegetables in that they are high in salts and vitamins.

CARDOON

Cardoon is a large thistlelike plant (fig. 13) which is grown for its fleshy leaf stems. In the North the seeds are sown in early spring in a hotbed or coldframe and the plants transplanted later to the open ground. In the South the seed may be sown in the rows where the plants are to be grown. The plants should be placed about 3 feet apart each way in rich soil with plenty of moisture, but they do not thrive on poorly drained land. Toward autumn the leaves are drawn together and blanched by wrapping with paper, by slipping a draintile over each plant, or by other methods of excluding light. If intended for winter use, the leaves are not blanched in the garden, but the plants are lifted with considerable earth adhering to the roots and stored in a cellar or pit to blanch.

FIGURE 13.—Cardoon, a large thistlelike plant which is bleached for use

The leafstalks are boiled and served as a green or used in the making of soups and stews. Cardoon is usually somewhat bitter, and it has only a limited field of usefulness as a home garden crop.

CHARD

Chard, or Swiss chard, is a type of beet that has been developed for its tops instead of its roots. The leaves are cooked and used as greens in very much the same way as spinach. The thickened leaf stems are sometimes cooked and used in much the same way as asparagus. One of the advantages of this vegetable is that crop after crop of the outer leaves may be harvested without injuring the plant. Only one planting is necessary, and a row 30 to 40 feet long will supply a family for the entire summer. Figure 14 shows the habit of growth of Swiss chard. Its culture is practically the same as that of beets, but the plants grow larger and should be thinned to at least 6 inches apart in the row. In common with beets, chard demands a rich mellow soil; and as it is sensitive to soil acidity, it is usually wise to use a little lime on the land before planting it. The seed clusters each contain several seeds, and fairly wide spacing will facilitate thinning.

FIGURE 14.—Swiss chard, excellent hot-weather greens

DANDELION

The dandelion is hardy and adapted to much the same conditions as kale and mustard. It will grow on almost any garden soil. In the North the seeds are usually sown during early spring in rows about 18 inches apart and covered to a depth of about half an inch. The plants should be thinned to 8 to 12 inches apart in the rows and cultivated throughout the summer. (Fig. 15.) In the colder parts of the country it may be desirable to mulch slightly during the winter, using leaves, straw, or strawy manure. Early the following spring the plants will be ready for use as greens. In the South, the seed may be sown during the autumn, and the plants will be ready for use in the spring. Dandelion is greatly improved if blanched by being covered with paper or by having two boards set in the form of a letter A over the row. The blanching not only makes the leaves more tender but destroys part of the bitter taste.

FIGURE 15.—Dandelion, which under favorable conditions gives a heavy yield of greens

KALE

Kale, or borecole, is hardy like spinach and lives over winter in latitudes as far north as northern Maryland and southern Pennsylvania and in other locations where similar winter conditions prevail. It is also resistant to heat and may be grown in summer, but its real merit is as cool-weather greens.

Kale is a member of the cabbage family, and the best garden varieties are low-growing, spreading plants with thick, more or less crinkled leaves. (Fig. 16.) Scotch Curled and Siberian are two of the best-known garden varieties.

In the home garden in the North kale may be seeded almost any time from early

FIGURE 16.—Kale, hardy and popular greens

spring until a few weeks before hard frost. In northern regions where it lives over winter the last sowing should be about six weeks before frost in order that the plants may become well established. In the South it may be seeded almost any time, but it has little to commend it during midsummer and is seldom sown to mature during this season. No other plant is so well adapted to fall sowing throughout a wide area both North and South or in regions characterized by winters of moderate severity. It may well follow green beans, potatoes, peas, or some other vegetable that has occupied the ground during the early season.

Almost any garden soil will grow good kale. When it follows in the same season another crop that has been fertilized, kale should need little if any additional plant food. It may be broadcast like turnips, particularly when seeded during the autumn; but for spring sowings, made at a time when weeds are troublesome, row seeding is advised. The seed should be covered lightly, usually by being raked in with a garden rake. Cultivation is limited to that necessary for the control of weeds.

Kale may be harvested either by cutting the entire plant or by taking the larger leaves while young. Old kale is liable to be tough and stringy. The culture of kale is easy, and the gardener is advised to pay more attention to this excellent green.

MUSTARD

Almost any good soil will produce a crop of mustard. The basal leaves are used for greens; and as the plants require but a short time to reach the proper stage for use, frequent sowings should be made. Sow the seeds thickly in drills as early as possible in the spring, or for late use sow in September or October. The forms of Chinese or Japanese mustard, the leaves of which are often curled and frilled, are generally used. Mustard greens are cooked like spinach.

SPINACH

Spinach is by far the most popular of the greens. It is a reasonably hardy cool-weather plant that withstands winter conditions throughout most portions of the South. In colder portions of the Southern States it may need some protection during the winter, for, like cabbage and other hardy crops, it is sometimes severely injured or even killed by low temperatures. In most portions of the North spinach is primarily an early spring and late fall crop, but in certain locations where summer temperatures are mild it may be grown continuously from early spring until late fall. It should be emphasized that the summer and winter culture of spinach is possible only where moderate temperatures prevail.

Spinach will grow on almost any type of well-drained, fertile soil where sufficient moisture is available. If possible a rich friable loam with an abundance of organic matter should be used. The home gardener will find spinach adapted to his land whether it be a heavy clay or a peat so long as it is well-drained and rich. Spinach is very sensitive to acid soil; if any doubt exists regarding the need of the soil for lime, it may be wise to apply a few pounds to the portion of the garden devoted to spinach, irrespective of the treatment given the remainder of the area.

The general application of both manure and fertilizer to the garden has been advised in an earlier portion of this bulletin. Spinach will profitably use additional supplies of both. A pound of rotted manure to each square foot and 3 to 4 pounds of commercial fertilizer to each 100 square feet of land is suggested as suitable rates of application for spinach in the home garden. Both manure and fertilizer should be applied broadcast and raked in before the spinach is sown.

In the North spinach may be sown as early in the spring as it is possible to prepare the ground. Two or three successive plantings at intervals of one week should be made until the approach of hot weather or about June 1, but these later plantings can not be expected to yield as heavily as the earlier ones. Plantings may again be started during the late summer and continue until about six weeks before frost. In sections having cool summers, plantings may be made in succession throughout the growing season or until a few weeks before frost. In the South the time of planting depends upon locality and season. In general it extends from early fall to late spring, but it is useless to attempt spinach culture in midsummer. The zone maps and tables give the approximate dates for sowing spinach in various parts of the country.

Bloomsdale Savoy, Prickly Seeded, and Victoria are desirable varieties. The first-named should not be used for the later sowings in the spring, because it shoots to seed readily in hot weather. Virginia Savoy is a most valuable variety for fall planting because of its superior hardiness and resistance to " blight," which may occur in the autumn, but it is not suitable for spring planting. Great care should be taken to obtain seed that is fresh and of good quality. For horse cultivation the rows should be not less than 24 inches apart, and when land is plentiful they may be 30 inches apart. For garden tractor, wheel hoe, or handwork the rows should be 12 to 18 inches apart. Spinach may be drilled by hand in furrows about 1 inch deep made with a hoe or other device and covered with fine earth not more than one-half inch deep, or it may be drilled with a seed drill, which distributes the seed more evenly than is ordinarily possible by hand. The use of the drill is advised. The plants should be thinned to 3 or 4 inches apart before they crowd in the row.

NEW ZEALAND SPINACH

New Zealand spinach is not related to common spinach. It is a large plant with thickish leaves and stems and grows with a branching, spreading habit to a height of 2 or more feet. It thrives in hot weather and is grown as a substitute at seasons when the ordinary spinach can not withstand the heat. New Zealand spinach thrives on soils suitable for common spinach. Because of the larger size of these plants they must be given more room. The rows should be at least 3 feet apart, with the plants about 2 feet apart in the rows. The seeds may be sown 1 to 1½ inches deep as soon as danger of frost is past. As some difficulty may be experienced in getting the seeds to germinate promptly, they should be soaked for one or two hours in water at 120° F. before planting. Successive harvests of the tips may be made from a single planting, since new leaves and branches are readily produced. Care must be taken not to remove too large a portion of the plant at one time lest later harvests suffer. New Zealand spinach is cooked the same way as common spinach.

SORREL

Sorrel is not well known to the majority of gardeners, yet it is highly prized by many, especially for cooking with spinach to give it added flavor. It is a perennial plant that is usually started from seeds. It requires a rich, mellow, well-drained soil. Rows may be of any convenient width, and the plants should be thinned to about 8 inches apart in the rows. If the leaves alone are gathered and the plants are cultivated to prevent the growth of weeds, a planting should last three or four years. Broad-Leaved French is a well-known variety.

TURNIP GREENS

Varieties of turnips usually grown for the roots are also planted especially for the greens. Strains of turnips especially suitable for greens are now available under different names. In some cases turnips are seeded thickly and thinned for use as greens, the rest being left to develop as a root crop. Turnip greens are especially adapted to winter and early spring culture in the South. The cultural methods employed are the same as those described under Turnip and Rutabaga (p. 47).

The Seven-Top turnip is also sown and allowed to grow until young succulent seed stalks are formed, these being cut and used as greens. These sprouts are sometimes erroneously called " brockley " or broccoli.

SALAD CROPS

The group known as salad crops includes vegetables that are usually eaten raw with salt, vinegar, pepper, or salad oils, or with mayonnaise or other dressings. This classification is entirely one of convenience, as other vegetables not included in this group are also used in the same way. Some members of this class are sometimes cooked and used as greens.

Lettuce and celery far outweigh all the other plants of this group in popularity. Practically every garden includes a bed or a few rows of lettuce, and it would be more generally grown if gardeners fully appreciated its possibilities.

CELERY

Like most other vegetables, celery can be grown in home gardens in practically all parts of the country at some time during the year. It is a cool-weather crop and adapted to winter culture in the lower South. In the upper South and in the North it may be grown either as an early spring or as a late fall crop. Farther north in certain favored locations it can be grown throughout the summer.

Rich, moist, but well-drained, deeply prepared, mellow soil is essential for celery. Soil varying from sand to clay loam and to peat may be used as long as these requirements are met. Unless the ground is very fertile, plenty of well-rotted barnyard manure, supplemented by liberal applications of commercial fertilizer, is necessary. For a 100-foot row of celery, four or five wheelbarrow loads of manure and 5 pounds of a high-grade complete fertilizer thoroughly mixed with the soil is none too much. The celery row should be prepared a week or two before the plants are set.

The most common mistake with celery is failure to allow enough time for growing the plants. It requires about 10 weeks to grow good celery plants such as those shown in Figure 17. For the early crop in the North, which is set outdoors as soon as frosts are over, or about April 15 in the latitude of Indianapolis, Ind., the seeds must be sown in the hotbed or greenhouse about February 1. For the late crop in the same latitude, which is set about July 1, the plants must be started about April 15. The zone tables and maps indicate the planting dates for the various regions. Celery seed is small and germinates slowly. A good method is to place the seeds in a muslin bag and to soak them overnight, after which they are mixed with dry sand and distributed in shallow trenches in the seed flats or seed bed and covered with leaf mold or similar material to a depth of not more than one-eighth inch. The bed should be kept from drying out by covering with burlap sacks which are kept moist, or by similar means. Celery plants are very delicate and must be kept free from weeds. They are made more stocky by transplanting once before they are set in the garden, but this practice retards their growth. When they are to be transplanted before setting in the garden, the rows in the seed box or seed bed may be only a few inches apart; but if they are to remain in the box until transplanted to the garden, the plants should be about 2 inches apart each way. In beds, the rows should be 10 to 12 inches apart, with the seedlings 1 to 1½ inches apart in the row.

FIGURE 17.—Two celery plants: Left, transplanted once before time for setting in the field; right, not transplanted from original seed bed

Celery may be set in single or double rows about 4 feet apart or in a bed. In single rows the plants are spaced about 6 inches apart; in double rows the spacing is the same, but two rows are placed side by side about 1 foot apart. In bed culture the plants may be set 1 foot apart each way. Row culture is usually best, especially when the celery is to be banked with earth. Set celery on a cool or cloudy day, if possible; and if the soil is at all dry, set the plants in place, cover the roots lightly, water, and then place more soil around them. If the plants are large, it is best to pinch off the outer leaves 3 or 4 inches from the base before setting. In bright weather it is also well to shade the plants for a day or two after setting. Small branches bearing green leaves, stuck in the ground, protect the plants from intense sun without excluding air. As soon as the plants attain some size the leaves should be drawn together and the soil gradually worked around the plants to keep them upright. Care must be taken to avoid getting soil into the hearts of the plants. Early celery is blanched with boards, paper, draintiles, or other devices for excluding the light. In addition to these means, late celery may be blanched also by banking with earth or by storing in the dark. Banking celery with soil in warm weather causes it to decay.

Late celery may be kept for early winter use by banking with earth and covering the tops with leaves or straw to keep them from freezing, or it may be dug and stored in a cellar or a coldframe, with the roots well embedded in moist soil. While in storage it must be kept as cool as possible without freezing.[9]

WITLOOF CHICORY

Witloof chicory, sometimes called French endive, is grown for both roots and tops. It is a hardy plant that is not especially sensitive to heat or cold, but it does need a deep, rich, loamy soil without too much organic matter. The tops are harvested while young and boiled and eaten like spinach. It is necessary when boiling chicory to change the water once or twice to remove the bitterness. The roots are lifted in autumn and placed in a box or bed of moist soil in a warm cellar for forcing. They must be covered with a foot or two of manure, or a few inches of sand. Under this covering the leaves form in a solid head which is known on the market as witloof. These blanched leaves may be used as a raw salad or cooked and eaten like spinach or chard.

The culture of chicory is simple. The seeds are sown during spring or early summer in drills about 18 inches apart and the plants thinned to 6 or 8 inches apart in the rows. If sown too early the plants shoot to seed and are worthless for forcing. The kind known as witloof is most generally used.

CORN SALAD

Corn salad is also known as lamb's-lettuce and fetticus. The seed is sown during the early spring in drills and the plants cultivated the same as for lettuce or mustard. For an extra-early crop the seed may be planted during the autumn and the plants covered lightly during the winter. In the Southern States the covering is not necessary, and the plants are ready for use during February and March. The leaves are frequently used in their natural green state, but they may be blanched by covering the rows with anything that will exclude the light. Corn salad is used as a salad in place of lettuce, or mixed with lettuce or water cress. Its flavor is very mild, and it is improved by mixing with some other salad plant. It is also boiled with mustard for greens.

ENDIVE

Endive closely resembles lettuce in its requirements and habits of growth, except that it is not so sensitive to heat. It may be substituted for lettuce when the culture of lettuce is impracticable. In the South it is mainly a winter crop. In the North it is grown during the spring, summer, and autumn and is also forced during the winter. Endive is often known on the markets as escarolle. Broad-Leaved Batavian is a good sort.

The time of seeding is given in Tables 1 and 2 and depends upon the location. Sow the seeds thinly; and when the plants are established, thin to the same distance as for lettuce, or about 1 foot apart in the rows. When the plants are large and well-formed, draw the leaves together and tie so the heart will blanch. For winter use the

---

[9] For additional information on celery, see Farmers' Bulletin 1269, Celery Growing.

plants should be lifted with a ball of earth, placed in a cellar or coldframe where they will not freeze, and tied and blanched as needed.

Endive is used in the same way as lettuce. Its agreeable flavor makes it a most excellent addition to the list of vegetables. Figure 18 shows the appearance and character of endive.

LETTUCE

Lettuce should be found in every home garden. It is a cool-weather crop, being as sensitive to heat as any vegetable grown. In the South lettuce culture is confined to late fall, winter, and spring. In colder portions of the South lettuce may not live through the winter, especially during seasons of low temperature. In the North lettuce culture is practically limited to the spring and autumn, as both winter and summer are too severe for it. In some favored locations, such as areas of high altitude or in far-northern latitudes, lettuce grows to perfection during the summer. In general, zones

FIGURE 18.—Broad-Leaved Batavian and Moss-Curled varieties of endive. The former is often called escarolle

A, B, and C shown in Figure 6 are adapted to fall, winter, and spring culture, and zones D, E, F, and G to spring and autumn culture. Frequent complaints from gardeners regarding poor results obtained with lettuce have been traced almost invariably to failure to realize its limitations, resulting in planting at the wrong season.

Any rich soil is adapted to lettuce. The plant is sensitive to lack of lime, and if the soil is strongly acid a few pounds of lime should be applied. A commercial fertilizer with a heavy proportion of phosphorus will also help. Rotted manure may well be applied to lettuce ground, but the use of fresh strawy manure should be avoided.

Spring lettuce should be started indoors or in a hotbed and transplanted to the garden when the plants have four or five leaves. Gardeners need not wait for the cessation of light frosts, as lettuce is not usually harmed by a temperature as low as 25° F. if the plants have been properly hardened. About six weeks should be allowed for growing the plants. Gardeners in northern Virginia, who set their plants in the open about April 15, must sow the seeds indoors about March 1. When plants can not be grown indoors or purchased, seeding should be done as early as the ground can be worked. For the fall crop the seed may be sown directly in the row and thinned, as there is no gain in transplanting.

For horse cultivation lettuce plants should be set 12 to 15 inches apart in rows 24 to 30 inches apart, and for hand culture about 12 to 15 inches apart each way. When the seed is sown directly in the row the plants should be thinned to the distances just mentioned. Where gardeners grow leaf lettuce, or desire merely the leaves and not well-developed heads, the spacing in the rows may be much closer. In any case it is usually best to cut the entire plant instead of removing the leaves.

There are many excellent varieties of lettuce, all of which do well in the garden when conditions are right. Of the loose-leaf kinds, Early Curled Simpson and Prize Head are among the best. Grown by the transplanting method described, individual plants of either of these may attain a weight of as much as $2\frac{1}{2}$ pounds. Of the heading sorts, May King, Unrivaled, Big Boston, New York, Iceberg, and Hanson are all excellent. Both New York and Iceberg need more time than May King, Unrivaled, and Big Boston. In regions where warm weather comes early, it is seldom worth while to sow head lettuce seed in the open ground in the spring with the expectation that firm heads will be obtained.

PARSLEY

Parsley is hardy to cold but sensitive to heat. It will thrive under much the same temperature conditions as kale, lettuce, or spinach. If given a little protection it may be carried over winter throughout most of the North, but it can not withstand extreme heat.

Parsley will thrive on any good soil, but as the plant is delicate during its early stages of growth, the land should be mellow, not subject to baking, and free from clods and stones. In common with most vegetables, parsley needs plenty of soil fertility.

The seeds of parsley are small, and they germinate slowly. Soaking in water overnight will hasten germination. In northern locations it is a good plan to sow the seeds indoors and transplant the plants to the garden, thereby obtaining the crop ahead of hot weather. In the South it is usually possible to sow the seeds directly in drills. For the fall crop in the North, row seeding is also practiced. After seeding it is well to lay a board over the row for a few days until the first seedlings begin to appear. After its removal the plants should be watered from day to day to insure germination of as many seeds as possible. Parsley rows should be 14 to 16 inches apart, with the plants 4 to 5 inches apart in the rows.

The leaves of parsley are used for garnishing and for flavoring soups and vegetables. A few feet of row will supply the family, and a few plants transplanted to the coldframe in the autumn will give a supply during early spring.

UPLAND CRESS

Upland cress, sometimes erroneously called peppergrass, is a hardy plant. It may be sown in all the milder portions of the country during autumn. In the colder sections it is sown during early spring as soon as the ground can be worked. The seeds are small and must not be covered deeply. After the plants are well established, thin to 4 to 6 inches apart in the rows. It is a short-season crop that should be planted in quick succession to insure a steady supply. The leaves and young shoots are used as a green salad or cooked like greens.

WATER CRESS

Water cress is one of the few vegetable crops that can be grown in wet surroundings. In the more moderate portions of the North it grows practically the year round and winter is its best season in the South. It is best and most easily produced in water from springs in limestone regions; the limestone regions of Virginia, Maryland, Kentucky, and the Ozarks give almost ideal conditions. A supply for the family may be grown in a small spring-fed brook or a series of shallow pools where the water is about 1 foot deep. Care must be taken, though, to have a clean supply of water, otherwise the cress is unfit for use.

Water cress is started from seed and from pieces of plant. It is best to prepare the bed, using plenty of rotted manure, and turn the water on after the seeds or cuttings are in place. Early spring is the best time to plant water cress. Often seeds or cuttings may be placed in the rich, moist soil found at the edges of springs or brooks. No special care is required. The plant grows profusely in the wild state. A bed will yield a good crop the first season. Cress is used in salads for its pleasant pungency.

ROOT AND TUBER-ROOT CROPS

Potatoes in the North and sweetpotatoes in the South are found in almost every garden. Other members of this group, especially beets, carrots, and turnips, are of almost the same importance. The vegetables in this classification may be used throughout the growing season and also be kept for winter. Without the supply of root crops from the home garden many families would have a restricted diet. They represent a very large proportion of the total value of home-garden crops.

BEET

The beet is well adapted to all parts of the country. It is not especially sensitive to heat, and it is also resistant to cold; however, it will not withstand severe freezing, and in the lower South, where beets are usually grown the year round, they are sometimes killed by winter freezes. Farther north the winters are too severe, but spring, summer, and autumn culture is practiced. Owing to its wide adaptability and fine qualities, including the presence of vitamins B and C, the beet ranks near the top among home-garden vegetables.

The approximate time for sowing beets in the different parts of the country is shown in Table 1. As a rule, beets may be sown in the North as early as the ground can be worked in the spring; in the South they may be planted at almost any time, but midsummer heat and drought may interfere with germination. By covering the seeds with sandy soil, leaf mold, or some other material that will not bake, and by keeping the soil damp until the plants are up, much of this trouble can be avoided. Successive sowings should be made at intervals of about three weeks in order to have a continuous supply of young, tender beets throughout the season. Beets are sensitive to the reaction of the soil, and it is usually wise to apply lime if the soil is known to be strongly acid. Good quality depends upon quick development, and the land must be fertile, well drained, and in good physical condition. Well-rotted manure, supplemented by commercial fertilizer having a high proportion of both phosphorus and potash is recommended, both the manure and fertilizer to be applied broadcast before the seed is planted.

In gardens where cultivation is done by hand the rows may be about 16 inches apart; for horse cultivation they must be wider. Beet seed as purchased consists of small fruits each containing several seeds. These must be spaced thinly to avoid crowding. On most soils the seed should be covered to a depth of about an inch. After the plants are well established they should be thinned to stand 2 to 3 inches apart in the rows.

Early Wonder and Crosby Egyptian are standard varieties of beets suitable for early home-garden culture. Detroit Dark Red is an excellent variety for fall culture for winter use.[10]

CARROT

Since about 1920 the carrot has made a remarkable rise in the esteem of gardeners. It was formerly grown mainly for storage for winter use, but the American housewife has learned to appreciate the worth of young, tender carrots, and they are now planted in succession and grown in much the same way as beets, thereby insuring a continuous supply of tender, succulent roots. From a dietetic standpoint carrots are particularly desirable, especially for children, as they are rich sources of vitamins A, B, and C. Moreover, they contain a yellow coloring matter known as carotin, which is also beneficial.

The carrot is hardy and is fairly resistant to heat. In the South carrots are largely grown during fall, winter, and spring, and gardeners in that part of the country can have a practically continuous supply. In the North the carrot can be grown and used throughout the summer and the surplus stored for winter. The carrot will grow on almost any type of soil as long as it is moist, fertile, loose, and free from clods and stones, but sandy loams and peats are best.

On account of their hardiness carrots may be seeded as early in the spring as the ground can be worked. Succession plantings at intervals of three weeks will insure a continuous supply of tender carrots. The application of coarse manure immediately before the carrot crop is planted is not advisable, as it makes the roots prongy and rough. Commercial fertilizer should be used. Planting distances are given in Table 3. Carrot seed should be covered about one-half inch on most soils; on heavy lands the depth should be less, usually about one-fourth inch. With care in seeding, little thinning is necessary, as carrots will stand some crowding, especially on loose soils. They should be no thicker than 15 to 20 plants per foot of row.

Chantenay, Nantes, and Danvers Half Long are standard sorts. Carrots should be stored before hard frosts occur, as the roots are injured by cold.

---

[10] Information on the storage of this and other root crops may be obtained from Farmers' Bulletin 879, Home Storage of Vegetables.

CELERIAC

Celeriac, sometimes called turnip-rooted celery, has been developed for the root instead of the top. Its culture is the same as that of celery, and the enlarged roots can be used at any time after they attain sufficient size. Celeriac may be stored for winter use, but only the late summer crop should be used for storage. In regions having mild winters the roots may be left in the ground and covered with a mulch of several inches of straw or leaves, or they may be lifted and packed in moist sand and stored in a cool cellar.

CHERVIL

Two distinct types of chervil are cultivated, the so-called salad chervil and the turnip-rooted chervil. The first is used for garnishing and for other purposes instead of parsley; by many it is considered superior to parsley. Its culture is practically the same as for parsley. The seeds must be bedded in damp sand for a few weeks before sowing, otherwise their germination is very slow.

Turnip-rooted chervil thrives in practically all parts of the country where fertile soil and sufficient moisture are to be had. In the South the seeds are usually sown during the fall but may not germinate until spring. In the North the seeds are sown during the autumn to germinate in the spring, or the plants are started indoors during late winter and transplanted to the open ground later on. Burying the seeds for a few weeks in damp sand materially hastens germination. Spacing and culture are about the same as for beets and carrots. Tables 1 and 2 give the approximate planting dates and the usual spacing of the crop.

DASHEEN

The dasheen is closely related to the ordinary elephant ear. It is a long-season crop adapted for culture only in the lower South, where there is normally a very warm frostless season of at least seven months. It needs a rich loamy soil, an abundance of moisture with good drainage, and a fairly moist atmosphere. In portions of the South where it is adapted the dasheen is coming into prominence as a home and truck garden crop. Small tubers, those from 2 to 5 ounces in weight, are used for planting in much the same way as potatoes. Planting may be done two or three weeks before frosts are over, and the season may be lengthened by starting the plants indoors and setting them out after frost is past. The dasheen is a large-growing plant, similar in appearance to the well-known elephant ear, and the plants should be set in 3½ to 4 foot rows about 2 feet apart in the row. Dasheens may be dug and dried on the ground in much the same way as sweetpotatoes, and stored at 50° F. with ventilation. They are cooked and used in much the same way as potatoes.

JERUSALEM ARTICHOKE

The Jerusalem artichoke is of interest to gardeners as a substitute for potatoes, but its tendency to become a weed should cause some caution in starting it. It is a near relative to the sunflower and can be grown practically throughout the United States. It is started from pieces of the tubers in the same way as potatoes. A quart of the tubers will set about 30 hills. The tubers are not injured by freezing and may remain in the ground over winter. Approximate planting dates are given in Table 1.

PARSNIP

The parsnip is adapted to culture over a wide portion of the United States. While it must have warm soil and weather at planting time, it does not thrive in midsummer in the South, as the temperatures seem to be too high for it. Approximate dates for planting are given in Table 1. While both soil and weather conditions must be taken into account in selecting a planting date, some consideration must also be given to the length of the growing season. In many parts of the South parsnips are grown and used during early summer, but it would not pay to plant them at a season when they would come to maturity during midsummer. Moreover, it is difficult to obtain good germination during the summer, which limits their culture during the autumn. In the North it does not pay to plant parsnips too early or to give them too long a growing season, as they are liable to become oversize, tough, and fibrous.

Any deep fertile soil will grow parsnips, but those of a light, friable nature with no tendency to bake are best. Old garden land, spaded or plowed to a depth of about a foot and well enriched with fine well-rotted manure and commercial fertilizer, is almost ideal. Stony or lumpy soils are objectionable, as they are inclined to cause rough, prongy roots. Nor is coarse manure in direct contact with the roots advisable, for the same reason.

Spacing and seeding rates are given in Table 3. Parsnip seed must be fresh, that is, not over a year old, and it is well to sow rather thickly and thin to about 3 inches apart. Parsnips germinate slowly, but it is possible to help germination by covering the seed with leaf mold, sand, a mixture of sifted coal ashes and soil, peat, or some similar material that will not bake. Rolling the soil over the row or trampling it firmly after seeding usually hastens and improves germination. Boards are sometimes laid over the rows until the plants begin to come up. Hollow Crown and Guernsey are suitable varieties. The cultivation of parsnips is the same as that for similar crops.

Parsnips may be dug and stored in a cellar or pit or left in the ground until used. Roots placed in cold storage gain in quality faster than those left in the ground, and freezing in the ground in winter improves the quality. There is no basis for the belief that parsnips that remain in the ground over winter and start growth in the spring are poisonous. The reported cases of poisoning from eating so-called wild parsnips have all been traced to water hemlock (Cicuta), which belongs to the same family. The plant resembles the parsnip somewhat, and anyone should be very careful in gathering wild plants of this description.

POTATO

Any good, well-drained garden soil is suitable for potato production. The crop needs much fertilizer and well-rotted manure. High-grade complete fertilizer may be advantageously applied to most soils for potatoes. Rates of application may be about the same as for other heavy-feeding vegetables, such as onions and cabbage. Preparation of soil for potatoes should be the same as for general garden crops.

In preparing seed potatoes it is desirable to cut them into blocky rather than wedge-shaped pieces. If good seed is scarce and high priced, it may be permissible to cut to single-eye pieces, provided the seed bed is especially well prepared and the conditions for germination are satisfactory. It should be remembered that the smaller the size of the seed piece the more necessary it becomes to have the growing conditions as favorable as possible.

Early potatoes should be planted as soon in the spring as the land can be worked, irrespective of locality. Late potatoes, extensively grown in the North, should be planted late in May or during June. The rows should be not less than 2 feet nor more than 3 feet apart and the hills 10 to 15 inches apart in the row. Lay off the rows with a 1-horse plow or lister, and drop the seed in the bottom of the furrow. Cover the seed to a depth of about 4 inches, using a hoe or a 1-horse plow. One to three weeks will be required for the potatoes to come up, depending entirely upon the temperature of the soil. The ground may freeze slightly after the planting has been done, but so long as the frost does not reach the seed potatoes no harm will result, and growth will begin as soon as the soil becomes sufficiently warm. Yields of potatoes may be materially increased by the use of certified seed that is relatively free from virus and other diseases. Certified seed is now sold by seedsmen and dealers almost everywhere, and its cost is only slightly above that of seed that has been grown without inspection or certification.

As soon as the potatoes appear above ground and the rows can be followed, the surface soil should be well stirred by means of one of the harrow-toothed cultivators. Good cultivation should be maintained throughout the growing season, with occasional hand hoeing, if necessary, to keep the ground free from weeds. After the vines begin to die, the soil may be well worked up around the plants in order to hold them erect and protect the tubers from the sun.

After the potatoes are dug they should not be allowed to lie exposed to the sun or to any light while in storage, as they soon become green and unfit for table use. Early potatoes especially should not be stored in a damp place during the heat of summer and will keep best if covered with straw in a cool, shady shed until autumn weather sets in, after which they can be placed in a dry cellar or buried in the open ground. The ideal temperature for keeping potatoes is between 40° and 45° F., but they will not withstand any freezing.[11]

RADISH

Radishes are hardy but they can not withstand heat. In the South they do well during the autumn, winter, and spring, but do not thrive in summer. In the North they may be grown in the spring and autumn, and in sections having mild winters they may

---

[11] For additional information on potatoes, consult the following Farmers' Bulletins: No. 1205, Potato Production in the South; No. 1064, Production of Late or Main-Crop Potatoes; No. 1190, How to Grow an Acre of Potatoes; No. 1371, Diseases and Insects of Garden Vegetables; No. 879, Home Storage of Vegetables; No. 847, Potato Storage and Storage Houses.

be grown in coldframes at this season. In high altitudes and in northern locations having cool summers, they will thrive from early spring to late autumn.

Radishes are not sensitive to the type of soil, so long as it is rich, moist, and friable. Fertility from decayed manure and commercial fertilizer is essential. Some additional fertility applied when the seeds are sown is advisable, as conditions must be favorable for quick growth. Radishes that grow slowly have a pungent flavor and are undesirable.

Radishes mature the quickest of our garden crops. They remain in prime condition only a few days, and the gardener should plan to make small plantings every two weeks. A few yards of row will supply all the radishes a family will consume during the time they are at their best. Tables 1, 2, and 3 give approximate planting dates, rates of seeding, and spacing. Care in spacing the seeds saves labor in thinning.

There are two types of radishes, the mild, small, quick-maturing sorts, such as Scarlet Globe, French Breakfast, and Cincinnati Market, all of which reach edible size in from 20 to 40 days; and the more pungent, large, so-called winter radishes, such as Long Black Spanish and Rose China, which require 75 days or more for growth. These latter are planted so as to reach a desirable size in the autumn and are gathered and stored like other root crops. Winter radishes deserve the attention of more gardeners.

SALSIFY

Salsify, or vegetable oyster, has a wide adaptation and may be grown in practically all parts of the country. It is very similar to parsnips in its requirements but needs a slightly longer growing season. For this reason it can not be grown as far north as parsnips. Salsify, however, is somewhat more hardy and can be sown earlier in the spring.

Soil for salsify should be thoroughly pulverized to a depth of at least a foot. If heavy, the garden soil should be lightened by adding sifted coal ashes, sand, or some other material. Like parsnips, salsify must have plenty of plant food, but fresh, rough manure should be avoided, as this causes rough, prongy roots.

Sandwich Island is the best-known variety. An ounce of seed will sow a 100-foot row, and a 50-foot row will meet the requirements of most families. As salsify seed retains its vitality only one year, fresh seed should always be used. Approximate dates for sowing are given in Table 1. Width of rows, depth of planting, and the stand in the rows are given in Table 3.

Cultivation is the same as for other root crops. Salsify may be left in the ground over winter or lifted and stored like parsnips or other root crops. This fine vegetable should be grown more generally.

SWEETPOTATO

The sweetpotato is of tropical origin and succeeds best in the South. It is grown in home gardens as far north as southern New York and Michigan. Even farther north, in sections having especially mild climates, such as the Pacific Northwest, sweetpotato culture is possible. In general, sweetpotatoes may be grown in any locality where there is a frost-free period of about 150 days with relatively high temperature. The plant succeeds with a minimum supply of moisture, differing in this respect from many other home-garden vegetables.

A well-drained, moderately deep sandy soil of medium fertility is best for sweetpotatoes. Very deep, open soils encourage the formation of long stringy roots and should be avoided. To improve drainage the plants usually are set on top of wide ridges. For best results the soil should be moderately fertilized throughout, but most areas that have been used for home gardening probably will produce a good crop of sweetpotatoes without additional fertilization. A little well-rotted manure and some commercial fertilizer may be advantageously applied to poor soils. If applied under the rows, both manure and fertilizer should be well mixed with the soil.

Toward the northern part of the area over which sweetpotatoes are grown it is necessary to start the plants in a hotbed, because the season is too short to produce a crop after the weather warms enough to start plants out of doors. The roots too small for marketing are used for seed, bedded close together in the hotbed, and covered with about 2 inches of sand or fine soil such as leaf mold. The seed should be bedded about five or six weeks before it is safe to set the plants in the open ground. Toward the last the hotbed should be ventilated freely to harden off the plants.

The ridges for planting sweetpotatoes should be 3 to 5 feet apart and the plants about 14 inches apart in the row. Cultivate sufficiently to keep the surface soil loose and free from weeds. As soon as the vines cover the ground no cultivation is necessary.

Sweetpotatoes are dug as soon as the vines are nipped by frost. They should be dug on a bright, drying day, when the soil is not too wet. On a small scale they may be dug with a spading fork, great care being taken not to bruise or injure the roots. The roots should lie exposed for two or three hours to dry thoroughly, after which they may be placed in a warm, well-ventilated room to cure for several days. The proper temperature for curing is 80° to 90° F. for about 10 days, and then store them at 50° to 55° afterwards. A small crop may be cured around the kitchen stove and later stored in a dry room where there is no danger of their becoming too cold. Sweetpotatoes should be handled as little as possible, especially after they are cured.[12]

TURNIP AND RUTABAGA

Turnips and rutabagas are similar and are treated together. They are among the most commonly grown and widely adapted root crops in the United States. Being essentially cool-weather vegetables, they are grown in the South chiefly during the fall, winter, and spring, while in the North their culture is confined largely to the spring and autumn. Rutabaga does best in the more northerly locations, and gardeners south of the latitude of Indianapolis, Ind., or northern Virginia are advised to grow turnips instead.

---

[12] For additional information on sweetpotatoes, the following Farmers' Bulletins may be consulted: No. 999, Sweet-Potato Growing; No. 1059, Sweet-Potato Diseases; No. 1442, Storage of Sweet Potatoes; and No. 879, Home Storage of Vegetables.

Turnips reach a good size in from 60 to 80 days, but rutabagas need about a month longer. Being susceptible to heat and hardy, these crops for fall use should be planted as late as possible, allowing time for maturity before hard frost. In the South, turnips are very popular during the winter and spring, but in the North fall seeding following early potatoes, peas, or spinach is usually practiced.

Both turnips and rutabagas need a fertile soil. However, land that has been in some heavily fertilized crop, such as early potatoes, usually gives a good crop without additional fertilization. The soil need not be prepared deeply, but the surface should be fine and smooth. For spring culture, row planting similar to that described for beets should be practiced. The importance of planting turnips as early as possible for the spring crop is emphasized. When seeding in rows, cover the seeds lightly; and when broadcasting, rake the seeds in with a garden rake. A half ounce of seed will sow a 100-foot row or broadcast 100 square feet. Turnips may be thinned as they grow, and the tops used for greens.

The common varieties of turnip and rutabaga differ mainly in color and shape of root. Although there are both white-fleshed and yellow-fleshed varieties of each, most turnips are white-fleshed, while most rutabaga varieties are yellow-fleshed. Both may have white, green, or purplish red crowns. Purple-Top Strap Leaf and Purple-Top White Milan are well-known white-fleshed turnips. Golden Ball and Petrowski are good yellow-fleshed sorts. American Purple-Top is a yellow-fleshed rutabaga, and White Russian or Sweet Russian is a white-fleshed rutabaga.

TURNIP-ROOTED PARSLEY

The root is the edible portion of turnip-rooted parsley. It has a superficial resemblance to the parsnip, and the flesh is whitish and dry, with much the same flavor as celeriac. It is boiled and used like celeriac or other root crops.

Turnip-rooted parsley requires the same climate, soil, and culture as parsley. It is hardy and able to withstand much cold, but is difficult to start in dry, hot weather. The seeds are small and usually germinate slowly. It is well to soak them in water overnight before sowing and to mix them with dry sand to obtain better distribution in the rows. The plants should be thinned to about 3 inches apart in the rows. Planting dates and spacing are given in Tables 1 and 3. This vegetable may remain in the ground until after hard frosts. It may be lifted and stored like other root crops.

VINE CROPS (CUCURBITS)

The vine crops, including cucumbers, muskmelons, pumpkins, squashes, watermelons, and citrons, are grouped together because of the similarity of their culture. In importance to the home gardener they do not compare with some other groups, especially the root crops and the greens, but there is a place in most gardens for at least bush squashes and a few hills of cucumbers. In large gardens a few hills of muskmelons and watermelons are often desirable.

CUCUMBER

The cucumber is distinctly a warm-weather crop. It may be grown during the warmer months over a wide portion of the country, but it is not adapted to winter growing in any but a few of the most southerly locations. Moreover, the extreme heat of midsummer in some locations is too severe, and cucumber culture in these regions is limited to spring and autumn. Tables 1 and 2 give the approximate dates when cucumbers may be planted in the various sections.

The cucumber demands an exceedingly fertile, mellow soil. In addition to the manuring and fertilization suggested in an earlier portion of this bulletin, some well-rotted manure and commercial fertilizer is advisable under the rows or hills, but the gardener should be sure that the manure contains no remains of any vine crops, as these might carry injurious diseases. Three or four wheelbarrow loads of manure and 5 pounds of commercial fertilizer to a 50-foot drill or each 10 hills is enough. The manure and fertilizer should be well mixed with the top 8 to 10 inches of soil.

Cucumbers are sensitive to cold, and they should not be planted until the ground has warmed up. For an early crop the seed may be started in berry boxes, plant bands, pots, or on sods in a hotbed, and moved to the garden after danger of late frost is past. During early growth and in cool periods cucumbers and other tender plants may be covered with plant protectors made of panes of glass with a top of cheesecloth, parchment paper, or muslin. A few hills will supply the family with pickling and slicing stock, and the few precautions necessary to insure success are well repaid.

Cucumbers make a rank growth and must have plenty of room. When planted in drills, the rows should be 6 or 7 feet apart, with the plants thinned to 2 to 3 feet apart in the rows. With the hill method of planting, the hills should be at least 6 feet apart each way, with the plants thinned to two to each hill. It is always wise to plant 8 or 10 seeds in each hill, thinning to the desired stand. Cucumber seeds should be covered to a depth of about 1 inch; and if the soil is inclined to bake they should be covered with loose earth, such as a mixture of soil and sifted coal ashes, sand, or other material that will not harden and keep the plants from coming through.

When grown primarily for pickling, one of the special small-sized pickling varieties, such as Chicago Pickling or Snow's Pickling, should be used; if for slicing, such varieties as White Spine and Early Fortune should be employed. It is usually desirable to plant a few hills of each type, but the slicing type can be planted and used for both purposes.

Cucumbers require almost constant vigilance to prevent destructive attacks by cucumber beetles. These insects not only eat the foliage but also spread cucumber wilt and other serious diseases. During the early stages of growth the plants may be protected by small frames such as a wooden barrel hoop tacked to three pegs and covered with cheesecloth or mosquito netting, the edges of the netting being covered with earth to keep it from blowing off and to prevent insects from gaining entrance. The covering may be removed while cultivating, but it must be immediately replaced, as no insects should be allowed to touch the plants. When the vines begin to run, the covering must be removed. Thorough dusting with an arsenical dust every few days helps to control cucumber beetles. For the melon aphis, another serious enemy, a nicotine dust should be used, or a combined application may be made for both.[13]

The removal of the fruits before any hard seeds form materially lengthens the life of the plants and the size of the crop.

MUSKMELON

The muskmelon needs an abundance of room, and its culture in gardens where space is scarce is seldom justified. In the larger home gardens or in the home truck patch where conditions are suitable, the muskmelon is a desirable addition to the list of crops. The climatic and soil requirements of the muskmelon are about the same as for the cucumber. It seems to develop more perfectly when grown on light-textured soils, whereas the cucumber does well on moderately heavy land. The plants are vigorous growers, and the spacing should be somewhat wider than for cucumbers. Table 3 gives the width of rows and spacing.

Muskmelons are frequently started indoors in pots, berry boxes, plant bands, or in pieces of sod and transferred to the garden later. In sections where the growing season is short or earliness desired, this practice is important. Special precautions should be taken to protect muskmelons from attacks by insects. This can be accomplished as suggested for cucumbers.

Hearts of Gold, Emerald Gem, Pollock 10–25, and Tiptop are standard varieties of the common muskmelon. Several special types of melons such as the Casaba, Honeydew, and Persian are being grown to some extent in various parts of the United States. In general, these are not well adapted to home-garden culture except in certain portions of the South and West, where they are produced under irrigation.[14]

PUMPKIN

Pumpkins are sensitive to both cold and heat. In the North they can not be planted until settled weather has arrived; in the South they do not thrive during midsummer. Approximate planting dates for different sections are given in Table 1.

Most varieties of pumpkins require an abundance of room. The gardener, therefore, is seldom justified in devoting any portion of a limited garden area to pumpkins, because many other vegetables would give greater returns from the same area. However, in large gardens where there is plenty of room and where they can be planted after some early crop like potatoes, it is often possible to grow pumpkins to advantage. If planted in hills, they should be at least 10 feet apart each way, but when started among corn, potato, or other plants they are usually spaced 8 to 10 feet apart in every third or fourth row.

The pumpkin is one of the few vegetables that thrives under partial shade and for this reason may be grown among sweet corn or other

---

[13] For additional information on cucumber culture and cucumber enemies, see Farmers' Bulletins 1563, Cucumber Growing, and 1371, Diseases and Insects of Garden Vegetables.
[14] For additional information on muskmelon culture, see Farmers' Bulletin 1468, Muskmelons.

tall-growing plants. Small Sugar and Connecticut Field are well-known orange-yellow skinned varieties. The Kentucky Cheese has a grayish orange color with salmon-colored flesh. All are good-quality, productive varieties.

Pumpkins should be gathered and stored before they are injured by hard frosts. They keep best in a well-ventilated place where the temperature is a little above 50° F.

SQUASH

Squashes are among the most commonly grown garden plants. They may be grown in practically all parts of the United States where fertile soil with sufficient moisture is found. Soils rich in organic matter are needed. The use of well-rotted manure thoroughly mixed with the soil is recommended. Although sensitive to frost, they are more hardy than melons and cucumbers. In the warmer portions of the South squashes may be grown during the winter.

There are two classes of squash varieties, summer and winter. The former includes the Bush Scallop, known in some localities as the Cymling, and the Summer Crookneck. The winter class includes the hard-shelled, later-maturing storage varieties such as Hubbard, Delicious, and Boston Marrow. The so-called vegetable marrows are also classed as summer squashes. Italian Vegetable Marrow, or Cocozelle, is the best-known sort. All the summer squashes and the marrows must be used while young and tender, easily penetrated by the thumb nail. The winter squashes have hard rinds and are well adapted for storage.

The summer varieties, such as Crookneck and Bush Scallop, are of the bush type and may be planted early. If in drills, the rows should be about 5 feet apart with the plants spaced 18 inches in the rows. If in hills, these should be about 4 by 4 feet with two plants in each hill. Such varieties as Boston Marrow and Hubbard should be in drills 10 to 12 feet apart or in hills 8 by 8 to 12 by 12 feet apart.

Summer varieties should be gathered before the seeds ripen or the rinds harden, but the winter sorts will not keep unless well matured. They should be taken in before hard frosts occur and stored in a dry, moderately warm place, such as on shelves in a basement with a furnace. Under favorable conditions such varieties as Hubbard may be kept until midwinter.[15]

WATERMELON

Like muskmelons and pumpkins, watermelons require an abundance of room, and only the larger gardeners can afford to devote space to them. Moreover, watermelons are rather sensitive to the soil on which they are grown, a sand or sandy loam being practically essential. Being warm-weather plants, it is useless to plant the seeds too early or to attempt their culture in sections where the season is too short and the temperature too low. The approximate time for planting watermelons in the different zones is given in Table 1. Watermelon hills should be at least 10 feet apart; consequently a few hills take up a large amount of space. The old plan of making the hills by mixing a half wheelbarrow load of rotted manure with

---

[15] For additional information on squashes and pumpkins, ask for the mimeographed circular on these subjects prepared by the Division of Horticultural Crops and Diseases, Bureau of Plant Industry, U. S. Department of Agriculture.

the soil in each hill is a good one, provided the manure is free from the remains of cucurbit plants that might carry disease. A half pound of commercial fertilizer also should be thoroughly mixed with the soil in the hill. It is a good plan to place several seeds in a ring about 1 foot in diameter in each hill. Later the plants should be thinned, two to each hill.

Kleckley Sweet, Florida Favorite, Stone Mountain, and Tom Watson are suitable varieties for the home garden.

The preserving type of watermelon, called citron, is not edible when raw. Its culture is the same as that for the watermelon.

LEGUMES

Beans and peas are among our oldest and most important garden plants. They contain large quantities of fats and proteins, and only a limited space is required for growing the family supply. Both beans and peas, especially in the fresh green state, as one can have them from the home garden, are among the richest sources of vitamins A, B, and C. Recent investigations have revealed that they also contain other beneficial vitamins. The popularity of both beans and peas is also due in part to their wide climatic and soil adaptation.

BEANS

From the home gardener's point of view green beans, both snap and Lima, are of more importance than dry beans. Green snap beans are among the most important vegetables grown in the garden. In the North snap beans can not be planted until the ground is thoroughly warm, but succession plantings may be made every two weeks from that time until a few weeks before frost. In the South and Southwest green beans may be grown over a wide portion of the fall, winter, and spring seasons, but they are not well adapted to midsummer. In the extreme South beans are grown throughout the winter. The approximate dates for planting beans in the different zones are given in Table 1, and the spacing and quantity of seed needed are shown in Table 3.

Green beans are not especially sensitive to the character of the soil upon which they are grown, as long as it is well drained, reasonably fertile, and of such physical nature that it does not interfere with germination and emergence of the plants. Soil that has received a general application of manure and fertilizer should need no additional fertilization. When beans follow early crops that have been fertilized the residue of this fertilizer is usually sufficient for the beans.

As it develops the bean plant pushes the two halves of the seed, or cotyledons, through the surface, and heavy-textured soils that bake are liable to interfere seriously with or prevent normal development. On heavy lands it is well to cover the seeds with sand, a mixture of sifted coal ashes and sand, peat, leaf mold, or some other material that will not bake. By keeping the surface of the ground moist but not too wet for a few days after planting the plants may be brought up without difficulty. It is very important that bean seed be covered not more than 1 inch in heavy soils and 1½ inches on sandy soils. Beans are sensitive to cold and should never be planted until the soil has warmed up and the weather is settled. The dates given for planting beans and other tender crops must often be changed to suit the season. When beans are planted in hills they may be covered with plant protectors, thereby making it possible to plant somewhat earlier than otherwise.

Burpee Stringless Green Pod and Hodson Kidney Wax are good bush varieties for use as snap or green beans. Kentucky Wonder is a good pole sort for the same use. Any of these may be dried and kept for winter. If intended primarily for use dry, White Navy and Dwarf Horticultural are excellent sorts.

Two types of Lima or so-called butter beans are grown in home gardens. In the North the large Lima (*Phaseolus lunatus macrocarpus*) is most generally grown. In the South the Sieva or Carolina type is mainly grown. Certain more northerly sections of the United States, including northern New England and the northern portions of the States along the Canadian border, are not adapted to the culture of Lima beans. Lima beans should have a growing season of about four months with relatively high temperature and can not be planted with safety until somewhat later than snap beans. Weather and soil conditions must be suitable before it is safe to put the seeds in the ground. The small butter beans will mature in a shorter period than the large-seeded Lima beans. By starting the seed indoors in berry baskets or other containers and moving them to the open ground when the weather is settled, a little may be gained in earliness. The use of plant protectors over the seeds will also aid in obtaining earliness. In the South planting dates depend upon location. In the lower South, however, midsummer plantings are seldom practicable, and in the northerly portions planting is restricted to spring and early summer.

Lima beans may be grown on almost any fertile, well-drained, mellow soil, but it is especially desirable that the soil be light-textured and not subject to baking, as the plants can not force their way through a hard crust. Covering with some material that will not bake, as suggested for other beans, is a wise precaution when using heavy soils. Lima beans need a soil somewhat richer than is necessary for kidney beans, but the excessive use of manure or fertilizer containing a high percentage of nitrogen should be avoided. Beans do well when supplied with a fertilizer containing a relatively high proportion of phosphoric acid.

Both the Sieva and the large Lima are to be had in pole and bush forms. Bush beans may be drilled in rows like green beans; pole Lima beans require more room than the bush forms. Precautions must be taken to avoid covering Lima bean seed too deep. From 1 inch to $1\frac{1}{2}$ inches is about the right depth.

In the South Henderson Bush Lima and the Small White Lima (a pole bean) are commonly used; in the North Henderson Bush Lima, Burpee Bush Lima, Siebert Pole Lima, King of the Garden, and Emerald Isle (pole beans) are largely used.

Pole beans of the kidney and Lima types require some form of support, as they normally make vines several feet long. The well-known bean pole consisting of a small sapling about 2 inches in diameter at the base and 6 or 7 feet long is very satisfactory. Sawed stakes are objectionable on account of the corners and their smoothness, which makes it difficult for the beans to climb. Beans usually need some help in getting started up the poles. They twine in a counterclockwise direction. Where poles are difficult to obtain beans may be trained to a trellis made of a top and bottom wire stretched between posts and connected every foot or two by stout twine. Some gardeners plant pole beans along the fence or beside hills of corn, which serve as supports.

The only special precaution to observe in cultivating beans is to avoid cultivating or handling the vines while wet, as this is liable to spread disease. The advent of the Mexican bean beetle in the East has brought the home gardener in these sections face to face with a difficult problem. Spraying or dusting with magnesium arsenate is recommended.[16]

PEAS

Peas have many of the merits possessed by beans. They are high in food value and rich sources of vitamins A, B, and C. They require more space than beans, and with limited garden areas only an early planting may be practicable. Fresh-picked peas are so superior in quality to those that have been off the plants for some time that every gardener who has the space and can grow them should include peas in his list of vegetables.

Peas are distinctly a cool-weather crop. In the lower South they are grown at all seasons except during the summer; farther north the seasons for peas are spring and autumn. In the northern tier of States and at high altitudes they may be grown from spring until autumn, although in many places summer heat is too severe and the season is practically limited to spring. Table 1 gives the approximate date for planting peas in the different zones. A good general rule to follow in portions of the South where freezing does not occur is to plant at any time except in the warmer months. In the North the best general rule is to plant as early as the ground can be worked, and a few succession plantings may be made at 10-day intervals. The later plantings rarely yield as well as the earlier ones. Plantings may be resumed as the cool weather of autumn approaches, but the yield is seldom as satisfactory as that from the spring crop. Planting distances and depth of covering for peas are given in Table 3.

Alaska and Long Pod Alaska are small-growing early sorts of smooth peas. Gradus, Thomas Laxton, and Telephone are wrinkled kinds that should be used for later harvests. Telephone and other varieties having a heavy vine growth require more space and some form of support, such as brush stuck in the ground, wire fencing stretched between end posts and supported every few feet by stakes, a trellis, or some other inexpensive device. To enjoy the utmost quality in garden peas, gather them while sweet and tender, and cook and serve within the hour.

CABBAGE GROUP

The cabbage or cole group includes heading broccoli, sprouting broccoli, Brussels sprouts, cabbage, Chinese cabbage, cauliflower,

---

[16] For information on insects and diseases of beans see Farmers' Bulletin 1371, Diseases and Insects of Garden Vegetables. For information on the Mexican bean beetle and its control, see Farmers' Bulletin 1407, The Mexican Bean Beetle in the East and Its Control.

collards, and kohlrabi. These plants are noteworthy because of their adaptation to culture in most portions of the country where fertile soil and sufficient moisture are to be found and because of their hardiness to cold and richness in vitamins A, B, and C. Altogether they are among the most valuable of the home-garden crops.

HEADING BROCCOLI

Heading broccoli is similar to cauliflower in appearance—even being marketed as cauliflower—but it needs a much longer period for development. In the South and certain portions of the West, broccoli plants may be set in summer and autumn and come to edible maturity during late winter and early spring. In the colder portions of the North it will not live over winter, and the growing season is not long enough for most varieties of broccoli. Early Large White French is one of the best-known varieties. In soil and cultural requirements broccoli is similar to cauliflower.

SPROUTING BROCCOLI

Sprouting broccoli is a kind that forms a loose flower head upon a tall, fleshy, branching stalk instead of compact heads or curds as in the case with both cauliflower and heading broccoli. This is one of the newer vegetables to most American gardeners, but it has been known and appreciated by Europeans for many years.

Sprouting broccoli is adapted to winter culture in regions suitable for wintering-over cabbage. It is also very resistant to heat. Spring-set plants in the latitude of Washington, D. C., have yielded good crops of sprouts until midsummer and later, under conditions that caused cauliflower to fail. In the latitude of Norfolk, Va., the plant has yielded good crops of sprouts from December until spring. It is an exceptionally promising home-garden crop.

Sprouting broccoli is grown in the same way as cabbage. Plants grown indoors during the early spring and set in the open about April 1 begin to yield sprouts about 10 weeks later. The fall crop may be handled in the same way as late cabbage, except that the seed is sown later. The sprouts carrying flower buds are cut about 6 inches long, and other sprouts arise in the axils of the leaves so that a continuous harvest may be obtained. The habits of growth are shown in Figure 19. Italian Green Sprouting is one of the best-known varieties or strains.

BRUSSELS SPROUTS

Brussels sprouts are somewhat more hardy than cabbage and will live outdoors over winter in all the milder sections of the country. It may be grown as a winter crop in the South and as early and late cabbage in the North. The sprouts, or small heads, are formed in the axils of the leaves. (Fig. 20.) As the heads begin to crowd, the lower leaves should be broken from the stem of the plant to give them more room. The top leaves should always be left, as the plant needs them to supply nourishment. For winter use in cold climates, take up the plants that are well laden with heads and set them close together in a pit, a coldframe, or a cellar with some soil tamped around the roots. Keep the stored plants as cool as possible without freezing.

FIGURE 19.—Sprouting broccoli, a worth-while addition to the list of garden vegetables

CABBAGE

Because of its wide climatic and soil adaptability and its popularity as a food, cabbage undoubtedly ranks as one of the most important home-garden crops. In the lower South it can be grown in all seasons except during the summer, and in latitudes as far north as Washington, D. C., it is frequently set during the autumn, as its extreme hardiness enables it to live over winter at relatively low temperatures and thus become available among the first garden crops of spring. Farther north it can be grown as an early summer crop and as a late fall crop for storage. Unlike many other garden crops, cabbage can be grown throughout practically the entire United States where suitable soil and sufficient moisture are to be found.

Cabbage is not at all sensitive to the type of soil on which it is grown so long as the land is very fertile, of good texture, and moist. Cabbage is a gross feeder, and no vegetable will make a greater or more rapid response to favorable growing conditions. Quality in cabbage is closely associated with quick growth, and both rotted manure or compost and commercial fertilizer should be liberally used. In addition to the applications made at planting time, cabbage may also received a side dressing or two of nitrate of soda, sulphate of ammonia, or some other quickly available nitrogenous

FIGURE 20.—Brussels sprouts. The sprouts are borne in the axils of the leaves

fertilizer. These may be applied sparingly to the soil around the plants at intervals of three weeks, not more than 1 pound being used to each 200 square feet of space, or, in terms of single plants, a third of an ounce to each plant. For late cabbage the soil should not be so rich, and the supplemental feeding with nitrates may be omitted.

Good seed is especially important. Only a few cents' worth of seed is needed for starting enough plants for the home garden, as two or three dozen heads of early cabbage are as many as the average family can use. Early Jersey Wakefield and Charleston Wakefield are standard early sorts. Copenhagen Market and All Seasons are excellent midseason kinds, while for late cabbage Flat Dutch and Danish Ball Head are largely used.

Where cabbage yellows is a serious trouble, resistant varieties should be used. The following are a few of the wilt-resistant varieties adapted to different seasons: Wisconsin Hollander, for late storage; Wisconsin All Seasons, somewhat earlier, a kraut cabbage; Marion Market, for midseason, a round-head cabbage; Globe, for midseason, a round-head cabbage.

Cabbage plants for spring setting in the North may be grown in hotbeds or greenhouses from seeding made a month to six weeks before planting time, or may be purchased from southern growers who produce them outdoors during winter. These winter-grown, hardened plants, sometimes referred to as " frost proof," are hardier than hotbed plants and may be set outdoors in most portions of the North as soon as the ground can be worked in the spring. Northern gardeners can have cabbage from their gardens much earlier by using healthy southern-grown plants or well-hardened, well-grown hotbed, or greenhouse plants. Late cabbage, prized by northern gardeners for fall use and for storage, is grown from plants produced in open seed beds from sowings made about a month ahead of planting. Late cabbage may well follow early potatoes, peas, beets, spinach, or some other early crop. Many gardeners set cabbage plants between potato rows before the potatoes are ready to dig, thereby gaining time. The approximate date for setting cabbage plants is given in Table 1. In protected locations or if plant protectors are used, it is possible always to advance dates somewhat, especially if the plants are well hardened. Planting distances for cabbage are given in Table 3.[17]

Late cabbage is one of the most satisfactory vegetables for storage for winter. The heads may be cut and packed in a barrel or a box buried in the ground or covered with soil, or the plants may be pulled and buried in a low windrow.

CHINESE CABBAGE

Chinese cabbage, which is closely related to both cabbage and turnips, is variously known as pai tsai, petsay, pe-tsai, pok choi, wong bok, etc. The name celery cabbage is popularly applied to it, although it is unrelated to celery. Another form, which might be called the nonheading type of Chinese cabbage, has been erroneously

---

[17] Complete information on the culture, storage, and enemies of cabbage is to be found in the following Farmers' Bulletins: No. 433, Cabbage; No. 879, Home Storage of Vegetables; No. 1371, Diseases and Insects of Garden Vegetables.

called white Chinese mustard. It does not form a head, but is grown for a potherb. The nonheading types are popular and deserve greater attention.

Chinese cabbage seems to do best as an autumn crop in the northern tier of States. When well grown, it is an attractive vegetable. It is not especially successful as a spring crop, and gardeners are advised to confine their attention to its fall culture in the North and its winter culture in the South.

The plant demands a very rich, well-drained, but moist soil. The seeds may be sown and the plants transplanted to the garden, or they may be drilled in the garden rows and the plants thinned to the desired stand. For the fall crop in the North, about two and one-half months before frost is a good time to sow the seeds. The approximate dates for sowing are given in Tables 1 and 2, and the spacing of the plants and depth of covering seeds are given in Table 3.

CAULIFLOWER

Cauliflower has been called "rich man's cabbage," because it is more difficult to grow. It has an attractive appearance during growth and as prepared for the table. (Fig. 21.) Although hardy, it will not withstand as much frost as cabbage. Any considerable degree of warm weather is fatal to cauliflower, causing it to fail to head. In the South its culture is limited to fall, winter, and spring; in the North it is practically confined to spring and autumn, as the summers and winters are too severe. However, in some regions of high altitude and when conditions are otherwise favorable cauliflower culture is continuous throughout the summer. In most cases it is treated as an early and a late crop in much the same way as cabbage.

FIGURE 21.—A good head of cauliflower

Like cabbage, cauliflower requires a fertile, well-drained soil. It is grown on all types of land from sands to clays and peats. Although the physical character is unimportant, the land must be fertile. Manure and commercial fertilizer are thus essential.

The time required for growing cauliflower plants is the same as for cabbage. In the North the main cause of failure with cauliflower in the spring is in not sowing the seed and setting the plants early enough. The fall crop must be planted at such a time that it will come to the heading stage during cool weather. Tables 1 and 2 give the approximate planting dates for cauliflower in the various zones. Snowball and Dwarf Erfurt are standard varieties of cauliflower.

Care should always be taken to obtain a good strain of seed; poor cauliflower seed is especially objectionable.

The only special precaution to be observed in the culture of cauliflower is to tie the leaves together when the heads or "buttons" begin to form, in order to keep the heads white. Cauliflower does not keep long after the heads form, and a dozen or two heads are sufficient for the average gardener.[18]

COLLARDS

The culture and uses of collards are the same as for cabbage. Collards withstand the heat better than other members of the cabbage group, and they are highly esteemed in the South for both summer and winter use. Collards do not form a true head, but instead a large rosette of leaves, which may be blanched by tying together or covering.

KOHLRABI

The edible portion of kohlrabi consists of the swollen stem of the plant. The early crop in the North may be started like cabbage and transplanted to the garden. In the South kohlrabi may be grown at almost any time during the year except midsummer. The approximate dates for planting and the spacing of the plants in the rows are given in Tables 1, 2, and 3. Kohlrabi seeds may be started indoors and the plants transplanted to the garden, or the seeds may be drilled in the garden rows and the plants thinned to the desired stand. In soil and cultural requirements kohlrabi is similar to cabbage. The principal requirements are fertile soil and sufficient moisture. Kohlrabi is an excellent vegetable if harvested while young and tender.

ONION GROUP

Onions and related plants are among the oldest and most popular of the home-garden crops. It would be difficult to find a home garden without at least one of this group, which includes chive, garlic, leek, onion, and shallot. Practically all of these have an exceedingly wide soil and climatic adaptation; at least some can be grown in all parts of the country where fertile soil and sufficient moisture are found.

The members of the onion group require but little garden space to produce enough for the family needs. They may be grown over a large part of the season, and dry onions are well adapted to winter storage. Moreover, these plants are good sources of vitamins A, B, and C.

CHIVES

The chive is a small onionlike plant that is used for flavoring soups and stews. (Fig. 22.) The plants will grow in any place where onions do well. They are frequently planted as a border, but they are equally adapted to culture in rows like other vegetables. Being a perennial, chive should be planted in a place where it can be left for more than one season. The approximate planting date in different zones is given in Tables 1 and 2, and spacing information is given in Table 3.

---

[18] For additional information on the culture of cauliflower, send for a mimeographed circular prepared by the Division of Horticultural Crops and Diseases, Bureau of Plant Industry, U. S. Department of Agriculture.

Chive may be started from either seed or clumps of bulbs. When once established, it is an easy matter to lift some of the bulbs and move them to a new location. When left in the same place for several years they become too thick, and an occasional resetting is desirable.

GARLIC

Garlic is more exacting in its cultural requirements than are onions, but it may be grown with a fair degree of success in almost any home garden where good results are obtained with other vegetables. Like chive, garlic is of value chiefly for seasoning; and while desirable as an addition to the list of garden crops, it must be considered of minor importance.

The approximate planting dates and spacing are given in Tables 1, 2, and 3. Garlic is propagated by planting the small cloves or bulbs which make up the large bulbs. Each large bulb contains about 10 small ones. In preparing the stock for planting, the small bulbs are carefully separated and planted singly. Each will grow into a bulb containing about 10 small ones. (Fig. 23.)

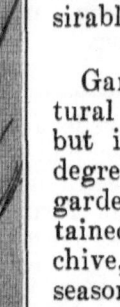

FIGURE 22.—A clump of chive

The culture of garlic is practically the same as that for onions. When mature the bulbs are pulled, dried, and braided into strings or tied in bunches, which are hung in a cool, well-ventilated place for later use. In the South, where the crop matures early, care must be taken to keep the garlic under favorable conditions, otherwise it will spoil. In the North, where the crop matures later in the season, storage is not so difficult, but care must be taken to prevent freezing.

FIGURE 23.—Garlic. Each bulb contains several small ones. These are separated for planting

LEEK

The leek is very similar to the onion in its adaptability and cultural requirements. It forms a thick fleshy structure like a large green onion instead of a bulb. (Fig. 24.) This is used in soups and stews and for almost any purpose to which the onion is adapted. Leeks are started from seeds like onions, but are usually sown in a trench, so that the plants can be more easily hilled up as growth proceeds. Tables 1, 2, and 3 give planting dates and spacing distances. Leeks are ready for use any time after they attain suitable size, but under favorable conditions they grow to 1½ inches or more in diameter, with white stalks 6 to 8 inches long. They may be lifted in the autumn and stored like celery in a coldframe or a cellar.

ONION

The onion will thrive under a wide variety of climatic and soil conditions. It does best with an abundance of moisture and a temperate climate without extremes of heat or cold during the growing season. In the South the onion will thrive during the fall, winter, and spring. Farther north winter temperatures may be too severe for certain types; yet others, such as the Potato onion, may be planted in the autumn and be ready for use in early spring. However, in the North onions are primarily a spring, summer, and fall crop. Approximate planting dates are given in Tables 1 and 2.

Any type of soil will grow onions, but it must be fertile, moist, and in the highest state of tilth. Both rotted manure and commercial fertilizer, especially one high in phosphorus and potash, should be applied to the onion plot. A pound of manure to each square foot of ground and 4 or 5 pounds of fertilizer to each 100 square feet is about right. The soil should be very fine and free from clods and foreign matter.

FIGURE 24.—Leek. This relative of the onion is used in soups and stews and in other ways

Onions may be started in the home garden by the use of sets, seedlings, or seed. Sets, or small onions, grown the previous year, are usually employed by home gardeners, but plants grown in an outdoor seed bed in the South or in a hotbed or a greenhouse are coming into more general use. The home-garden culture of onions from seed is quite satisfactory in the northern tier of States, where the summers are comparatively cool.

Several distinct types of onions may be used in the home garden. The Potato or Multiplier variety is planted in the fall or early spring for green onions. The Top or Tree onion is used in the same way. The Bermuda is a large, flat, mild-flavored type that is used extensively in home gardens for growing green onions and dry bulbs. Unfortunately, it is a poor keeper. The Valencia or Spanish variety and its modified form, the Prizetaker, is a large, mild-flavored, straw-colored, spherical onion that is a good keeper. The White Globe, American Silverskin, or White Portugal, and the Yellow Danvers, Southport Yellow Globe, and Southport Red Globe are varieties commonly used as sets and seed for the main or northern crop. All of them may be used for either green or dry onions.

Onion sets, seedlings, or seed may be planted in rows, as suggested in Table 3. The cost of sets and seedlings is about the same, but seed costs much less. In certainty of results the seedlings are best; practically none form seed stalks, and all make onions. Figure 25 shows a bunch of Prizetaker seedlings. This bunch

FIGURE 25.—A bunch of onion plants which when planted in the garden yielded over a bushel of good onions

yielded over a bushel of good onions. Seed-sown onions are uncertain unless conditions are quite favorable.

The cultivation of onions may be limited to the control of weeds. When the bulbs are well grown and the tops begin to die, the onions should be pulled and left in windrows in the garden or on wire-bottom trays placed under an open shed for a few days to dry. The tops may then be removed and the onions put in a well-ventilated place to cure.

SHALLOT

The shallot is a small onion of the Multiplier type. In its requirements it is similar to other onions; and as the bulbs have a more delicate flavor than most onions, the plant is well worth attention in the garden. Shallots seldom form seed and are propagated by means of the small cloves or divisions into which the plant splits during growth. The plant is hardy and may be left in the ground from year to year, but best results are to be had by lifting the clusters of bulbs at the end of the growing season and replanting the smaller ones at the desired time. The Jersey or False shallot is the only kind available from American seedmen. Its quality is much the same as that of the True shallot.

FLESHY-FRUITED WARM-SEASON CROPS

Eggplant, peppers, and tomatoes are closely related and are similar in their cultural requirements. Warm weather and fertile, well-drained soil are essential to obtaining good results with these crops. Tomatoes are by far the most important, and a home garden without them is rarely seen. Tomatoes are one of the best sources of vitamins A, B, and C. Moreover, the fact that the canned and dried tomatoes also contain these vitamins gives the vegetable added value.

EGGPLANT

Eggplant is extremely sensitive to the conditions under which it is grown. Distinctly a warm-weather plant, it demands a growing season of from 100 to 140 days with high average day and night temperatures. The soil, also, must be well warmed up before eggplant can safely be set outdoors.

In the South, eggplants may be grown during the spring and autumn; both midsummer and winter conditions are too severe. In the North, summer culture alone is practiced. The more northerly locations, where a short growing season and low summer temperatures prevail, are unsuitable for eggplants. Tables 1 and 2 give the approximate planting dates.

Soil for the eggplant must be extremely fertile, but it is not wise to use fresh manure or large quantities of commercial fertilizer. Garden soil that is very fertile as the result of long-continued good treatment is best for eggplant. Under such conditions a few plants will yield a large number of fruits.

Eggplant seed should be sown in the hotbed, in the greenhouse, or in warm sections outdoors about eight weeks before the plants are needed. It is important that they be kept growing without check from drying, low temperature, or other cause. They may be transplanted like tomatoes. Good plants have stems that are not hard or woody; one with a woody stem rarely develops satisfactorily. Black Beauty and Florida Highbush are good varieties.

PEPPERS

Peppers have greatly increased in popularity as a home-garden crop. Formerly looked upon as of merit mainly for seasoning, they are now used in salads, pickles, as cooked vegetables, and in many other ways.

Peppers are much like tomatoes in their requirements, but are more exacting. They may be grown over a wide portion of the

United States, in locations where fertile soil and ample moisture with a relatively long growing season of high temperature are found. Being hot-weather plants, peppers can not be planted in the North until the soil has warmed up and all danger of frost has passed. In the South planting dates vary according to the location, fall planting being practiced in some locations. Planting dates are given in Tables 1 and 2.

Plants of peppers should be started six to eight weeks before needed. The seeds and plants require a somewhat higher temperature than those of the tomato. Otherwise they are handled in exactly the same way. In the garden, peppers should be planted in rows as specified in Table 3. They need only sufficient cultivation to keep down weeds.

Varieties of peppers vary widely in their characteristics. Hot peppers, such as are used for flavoring and sauces, are represented by varieties like Small Chili and Long Red. For stuffing or for pickles, the mild-flavored Chinese Giant, Bull Nose, Sweet Mountain, and Harris Early Giant are good sorts. For slicing like tomatoes and cucumbers, Sunnybrook (fig. 26) and Red Squash are recommended.[19]

FIGURE 26.—Sunnybrook peppers, a salad variety

TOMATO

The tomato is easily entitled to a place among the half-dozen most important home garden vegetables. It grows under a wide variety of conditions, requires but small space for a large production, and its value in the diet is hard to overestimate. It is one of the richest sources of vitamins A, B, and C. Of tropical American origin, the tomato naturally requires a rather high temperature. Home gardens in the extreme South, however, may include tomatoes during the winter. Over most of the upper South and the North it is suited to spring, summer, and autumn culture. In the more northern regions the growing season is liable to be too short for obtaining heavy yields, and in much of the North it is desirable to increase earliness and the length of the growing season by starting the plants indoors. By adopting a few precautions, the home gardener may grow tomatoes in practically all locations where there is fertile soil with sufficient moisture.

---

[19] For additional information on this vegetable see the mimeographed circular obtainable from the Division of Horticultural Crops and Diseases, Bureau of Plant Industry, U. S. Department of Agriculture.

Tomatoes may be grown on any fertile, well-drained garden soil. A liberal application of manure and commercial fertilizer in preparing the soil should be sufficient for tomatoes under most conditions. In applying manure or fertilizer it is well to avoid the excessive use of such materials as poultry manure and fertilizers having a heavy proportion of nitrogen, as these might give too much vine growth and cause failure to set fruits. Heavy applications of manure and fertilizer should be broadcast, not applied in the row; but small quantities may be mixed with the soil in the row in preparing for planting.

Tomato plants should be started from five to seven weeks before they are needed. Enough plants for the home garden may be started in a window box and transplanted to small pots, paper drinking cups with the bottoms removed, so-called plant bands, which are round or square, or other boxes of soil, the seedlings being spaced 2 or 3 inches apart. Tomato seed germinates best at about 70° F., or ordinary house temperature. After transplanting, tomato plants should be grown at rather low temperatures with plenty of ventilation, as in a coldframe. This gives stocky, hardy growth. If desired tomato plants may be transplanted again to larger containers, such as 4-inch clay pots or quart cans with holes in the bottom.

Tomato plants for all but the early spring crop are usually grown in outdoor seed beds without transplanting. Thin seeding and careful weed control will give strong, stocky plants.

For early tomatoes Earliana, Bonny Best, and Break O'Day varieties are recommended. For medium and late plantings Marglobe, Globe, Greater Baltimore, and Stone are recommended. Stone is distinctly a late variety.

Tomatoes are sensitive to cold and should not be planted until danger of frost is past. By using plant protectors during cold periods the home gardener can set tomato plants somewhat earlier than would otherwise be possible. Hot, dry weather, such as occurs in midsummer in the South, is also unfavorable for planting tomatoes. Fall plantings must be made in accordance with the location. Approximate planting dates are given in Tables 1 and 2. Planting distances depend on the variety and whether the plants are to be pruned and staked or not. If pruned to one stem, trained and tied to stakes or a trellis, they may be set 18 inches apart in 3-foot rows; if not, they may be planted 3 feet apart in 4-foot rows. Pruning and staking has many advantages for the home gardener. Cultivation is easier, a greater yield may be obtained from the same area, and the fruits are always clean and easy to find.[20]

MISCELLANEOUS VEGETABLES

Florence fennel, martynia, physalis, okra, and sweet corn are grouped together because they can not be conveniently classified elsewhere.

FLORENCE FENNEL

Florence fennel is related to celery and celeriac, the enlarged, flattened leaf stalks being the portion used. For a summer crop the seeds are sown in the rows in spring, and for an autumn and winter

---

[20] For additional information on tomato culture, insects, and diseases, see Farmers' Bulletins No. 1233, Tomatoes for Canning and Manufacturing; No. 1338, Tomatoes as a Truck Crop; No. 1371, Diseases and Insects of Garden Vegetables.

crop in the South they are sown toward the end of summer. The plants should be thinned to stand about 6 inches apart. Like most vegetables, fennel needs a fertile soil and an abundance of moisture. When the leaf stalks have grown to about 2 inches in diameter the plants may be slightly mounded up and partially blanched. They should be harvested and used before they become tough and stringy. Fennel is cooked and used like celeriac and kohlrabi.

MARTYNIA

Martynia requires a good deal of heat and therefore is grown only during the warmer portion of the season. The excessive heat of southern midsummer, however, especially when accompanied by drought, is not favorable to the crop; neither is low temperature. Its growing conditions are very similar to those of cucumbers and squashes. The seeds may be started indoors and transplanted to the garden, or they may be drilled in the rows where the crop is to be grown. Planting dates and spacing are given in Tables 1, 2, and 3. The fruits, gathered while young and tender, are used for pickles.

OKRA

Okra, or gumbo, has about the same degree of hardiness as cucumbers and tomatoes and may be grown under conditions suitable for them. It will thrive on any fertile, well-drained soil. An abundance of quickly available plant food will stimulate growth and insure a good yield of tender, high-quality pods.

As okra is a warm-weather vegetable, the seeds should not be sown until the soil is warm. Planting dates are given in Table 1. The rows should be from 3 to 5 feet apart, depending on whether the variety is a dwarf or large growing. Seeds should be sown every few inches and the plants thinned to stand 18 inches to 2 feet apart in the rows. Perkins, Mammoth, Dwarf Green Prolific, White Velvet, and Lady Finger are good varieties. The pods should all be picked young and tender, and none allowed to ripen. Old pods are unfit for use and soon exhaust the plant.[21]

PHYSALIS

Physalis, also known as ground cherry and husk tomato, is closely related to the tomato and can be grown in any location where tomatoes do well. The kind ordinarily grown in gardens produces a yellow fruit about the size of a cherry. The seeds may be started indoors or sown in the rows in the garden. Planting dates and spacing are given in Tables 1, 2, and 3. The fruits are used for making preserves.

SWEET CORN

Sweet corn, like potatoes and sweetpotatoes, requires considerable space and is adapted only to large gardens. Although a warm-weather plant, it may be grown in practically all parts of the United States. It requires a fertile, well-drained, but moist soil. With these requirements met, the type of the soil does not seem to be especially important, but a clay loam is almost ideal for sweet corn.

---

[21] For additional information see Farmers' Bulletin 232, Okra: Its Culture and Uses.

In the South sweet corn is planted from early spring until autumn, but the corn earworm, drought, and heat make it difficult to obtain worth-while results in midsummer. The ears pass the edible stage very quickly, and succession plantings should be made to insure a constant supply. In the North sweet corn can not be safely planted until the ground has thoroughly warmed up. Here, too, succession plantings need to be made to insure a steady supply. Planting dates are given in Tables 1 and 2. Sweet corn is frequently planted to good advantage after early potatoes, peas, beets, lettuce, or some other early, short-season crop. In some cases, to gain time, it may be planted before the early crop is removed.

Sweet corn may be grown in either hills or drills in rows at least 3 feet apart. It is well to plant the seed rather thickly and thin to single stocks 12 to 15 inches apart, or three or four plants to each 3-foot hill. For early corn Golden Bantam, Early Minnesota, and Adams Early are suggested. Early Evergreen, Evergreen, and Country Gentleman are recommended for later planting.

Experiments have shown that in the eastern part of the country there is no advantage in removing suckers from sweet corn. Cultivation sufficient to control weeds is all that is needed.

ORGANIZATION OF THE UNITED STATES DEPARTMENT OF AGRICULTURE WHEN THIS PUBLICATION WAS LAST PRINTED

Secretary of Agriculture	ARTHUR M. HYDE.
Assistant Secretary	R. W. DUNLAP.
Director of Scientific Work	A. F. WOODS.
Director of Regulatory Work	W. G. CAMPBELL.
Director of Extension Work	C. W. WARBURTON.
Director of Personnel and Business Administration.	W. W. STOCKBERGER.
Director of Information	M. S. EISENHOWER.
Solicitor	E. L. MARSHALL.
Weather Bureau	CHARLES F. MARVIN, *Chief.*
Bureau of Animal Industry	JOHN R. MOHLER, *Chief.*
Bureau of Dairy Industry	O. E. REED, *Chief.*
Bureau of Plant Industry	WILLIAM A. TAYLOR, *Chief.*
Forest Service	R. Y. STUART, *Chief.*
Bureau of Chemistry and Soils	H. G. KNIGHT, *Chief.*
Bureau of Entomology	C. L. MARLATT, *Chief.*
Bureau of Biological Survey	PAUL G. REDINGTON, *Chief.*
Bureau of Public Roads	THOMAS H. MACDONALD, *Chief.*
Bureau of Agricultural Engineering	S. H. MCCRORY, *Chief.*
Bureau of Agricultural Economics	NILS A. OLSEN, *Chief.*
Bureau of Home Economics	LOUISE STANLEY, *Chief.*
Plant Quarantine and Control Administration	LEE A. STRONG, *Chief.*
Grain Futures Administration	J. W. T. DUVEL, *Chief.*
Food and Drug Administration	WALTER G. CAMPBELL, *Director of Regulatory Work, in Charge.*
Office of Experiment Stations	J. T. JARDINE, *Chief.*
Office of Cooperative Extension Work	C. B. SMITH, *Chief.*
Library	CLARIBEL R. BARNETT, *Librarian.*

For sale by the Superintendent of Documents, Washington, D. C. - - - - - - Price 10 cents

U. S. DEPARTMENT OF AGRICULTURE
FARMERS' BULLETIN No. 1733

PLANNING A SUBSISTENCE HOMESTEAD

MANY FAMILIES with small incomes can lower their living costs by living on a small piece of land and growing their own food, and at the same time enjoy a greater quantity and variety of fresh and canned vegetables and fruit. Gardening and poultry raising on a small piece of land is about all an employed man and his family can care for by hand. About 1 acre of good land is enough for such purposes.

But if the family wants to keep a cow and plans to buy the necessary winter feed, 2 acres of good pasture land, in addition, should be enough, and the extra work will not be excessive.

Men employed only part time or short hours who have large families and small incomes may find it economical to keep a milk cow, or milk goats, and some pigs, and raise the necessary feed in addition to having a garden and keeping poultry. This plan means the use of horse or mechanical power and should be tried only after experience and careful consideration.

Some families are so placed that their best plan involves obtaining a fairly large acreage of cheap land for general farming. In many areas this cheap land is extremely poor and has failed to yield a reasonable living under any kind of farming. For this reason extreme care must be exercised in selecting a so-called cheap farm.

Washington, D. C.　　　　　　　　　　Issued May 1934
　　　　　　　　　　　　　　　Slightly revised April 1940

PLANNING A SUBSISTENCE HOMESTEAD

By WALTER W. WILCOX, *junior agricultural economist, Division of Farm Management and Costs, Bureau of Agricultural Economics* [1]

CONTENTS

	Page		Page
Renewal of interest	1	Feed and livestock production on a subsistence homestead	12
Selecting land near cities	2	The family cow	12
Vegetable, poultry, and fruit production	3	Milk goats	14
Lay-out for a small acreage	3	Pork for family use	14
Quantity and variety of garden vegetables and small fruits	5	Feed for livestock on small acreages	16
The small poultry flock	7	Possibilities of a small wood lot	17
Production of tree fruits on small acreages	8	Limitations of small acreages as a means of self-support	17
Fertilizers	9	Production for home use on larger acreages	18
Insects, diseases, and other handicaps	9	Self-sufficing farms	18
Cash expenses for agricultural production and returns	10	Individual farms vary in productivity	18
Winter vegetable and fruit supply for a family of five	10	Farmers' bulletins of interest	19

RENEWAL OF INTEREST

GROWING FOOD for family-living purposes in connection with enough outside work to provide the family with the cash for necessary farm and family expenses is a combination that many families now want to develop. Recent hard times and still more recent Governmental policies have renewed an intensified interest in this possible combination. This kind of farming has often been called subsistence farming and a farm of this kind a subsistence homestead.

This part-time farming has certain problems of its own that are somewhat different from the usual farming problems. The family has to think of the quantity and variety of products it needs rather than of what the markets demand. Those who are inexperienced often overestimate the savings made possible by this way of living, and they often underestimate the costs in the way of the labor and cash necessary in such part-time farming.

In this kind of farming special attention is given to obtaining just the right area and kind of land; for when much of the work is done by hand, a heavy soil that is hard to work is a great disadvantage. With no power available, and with only a minimum of livestock, keeping unused land free from weeds is a burden.

---

[1] Members of the staff of the Division of Subsistence Homesteads, U.S. Department of the Interior, assisted in preparing this publication including its illustrations. W. R. Beattie, senior horticulturist, Bureau of Plant Industry, worked out the detailed plans for the garden and fruit production on the small acreages, and Medora M. Ward, assistant economist, Economics Division, Bureau of Home Economics, supplied the section regarding the winter vegetable and fruit supply for a family of five.

This combination of farming and wage work off the farm, now usually called subsistence farming, is particularly attractive to those families with several children who find it difficult to provide suitable housing and plenty of fresh fruits and vegetables from their small incomes. It is much less attractive if wages from work off the farm are not enough to meet the necessary cash expenses of the farm and the family living. Inexperienced people will find severe competition if they try to raise farm products for sale.

Many people now in town who lived on farms in their childhood inquire about subsistence or "self-sufficing" farming on 20 to 100 acres or more. Many farms that are apparently suitable for such a purpose are now for sale at relatively low prices, but many serious problems are involved in this kind of farming. Only a few of those problems are discussed here as most of them are covered in other Farmers' Bulletins, a brief list of which is given at the end of this bulletin.

This bulletin deals chiefly with the economic problems that will be met by those people who are planning to combine part-time farming and wage earning.

SELECTING LAND NEAR CITIES

Several problems are involved in selecting a small piece of land near a city in which jobs may be found. The first is the difference in the prices of land with reference to location. The price of land near a city is often based as much on residential value as on productive capacity. Two tracts of land equally valuable from the point of view of building sites may not be equally valuable for use in growing fruits and vegetables. A part-time farmer should have good, productive land. The importance of the soil cannot be overemphasized. A moderately level, fertile, well-drained piece of land that is free from stones and can be readily worked may easily be worth twice as much as another nearby tract of the same size. Sandy loam soils usually can be worked earlier in the spring than the stiff clay loams, but crops on the clay loams frequently withstand dry weather better than those on lighter soils. By draining, irrigating, manuring, and the right kind of cultivating any reasonably good soil can be made suitable for the intensive growing of vegetables.

Distance to place of employment and transportation facilities are other important considerations. Studies show that most part-time farmers do not want to drive more than 10 miles to work. Other things being equal, a location near several places where jobs might be found has many advantages over a location where a family would be rather cut off if the one industrial plant closed down.

If city water is not available at a reasonable cost, a good supply of pure well or spring water is necessary. A small tract of land that is otherwise suitable for a subsistence homestead may not have a supply of pure water available because of surface or underground drainage. Public health authorities in the nearby city will test the water for purity or furnish the address of some State official who will do it. Although wells may be drilled at a reasonable cost in most localities, there is always some chance that a supply of good water will not be found near the surface.

In those sections of the United States where the rainfall is scant, it may be necessary to irrigate the crops during at least a part of the growing season. Under such conditions even more attention should be given to the water supply.

The location of the land with regard to community improvements, like roads, schools, churches, and electric-power lines, should also be considered. A part of the cost of some improvements, like paving and sidewalks, is often assessed against the adjoining property. This should be considered when deciding between two tracts of land, if only one has city improvements. The amount of the tax levy for recent years and the probable future taxes should be investigated.

In many cases a small tract of land with a house and outbuildings can be bought more cheaply than it would be possible to buy unimproved land and put up the buildings. But if the chief object is to have a place to raise a supply of food for the family, the quality of the soil should have greater weight than the state of repair of the buildings. In the New England and other eastern States uncleared land on the outskirts of cities is sometimes available at a very low price. Many city people have bought small tracts for home sites, but such land requires a great deal of labor to make it productive. Moreover, care must be taken on uncleared areas to keep rodents and other small-animal pests of agriculture sufficiently under control to insure a full crop.

Small acreages near cities are available for rent. These can usually be rented with the payment of rent on a monthly basis. A year's experience in renting such a place will not only make it possible to decide for oneself on the advantages and disadvantages of living on a subsistence homestead, but it will furnish an excellent basis of judgment as to the advantages and disadvantages of the particular property as compared with some other one located nearby.

If the purchaser hopes to increase his farming later, in order to have produce for sale, he should keep the possibilities of such increase in mind when buying.

VEGETABLE, POULTRY, AND FRUIT PRODUCTION

Enough vegetables and small fruits can be raised on one half to three quarters of an acre of good land to furnish a family of five with all they want during the summer and with plenty for canned, stored, and dried products for the winter. These small fruits and vegetables, together with a small poultry flock and a few fruit trees, are all that can be cared for properly by the ordinary family without a horse or garden tractor, if the man is chiefly employed in some other job during the growing season.

LAY-OUT FOR A SMALL ACREAGE

Figures 1 and 2 give suggested plans for using approximately 1 acre of land. Figure 1 shows a plan that is suitable in the North or Northern States as far west as there is sufficient rainfall. Figure 2 shows a plan adapted to the South or the old Cotton Belt. It is to be emphasized that these plans are merely suggestive. The topography and the quality of land vary so greatly in many localities that the plan for using any plot of land must be adapted to its specific conditions.

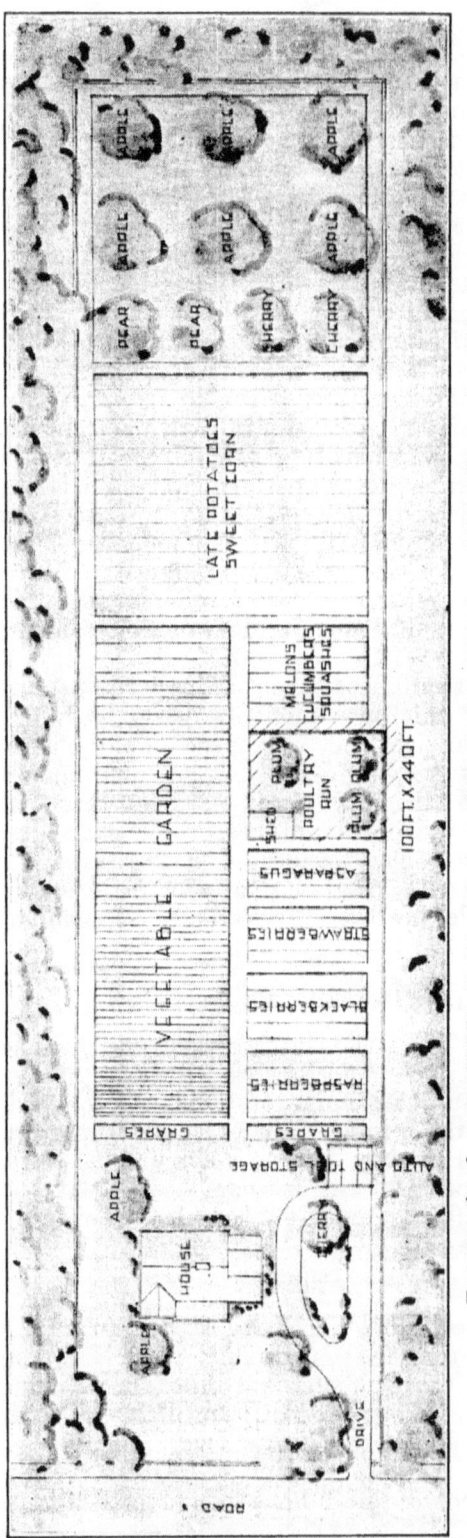

FIGURE 1.—A SUGGESTED PLAN FOR A 1-ACRE SUBSISTENCE HOMESTEAD IN THE NORTH.

Beauty and utility are combined in the lay-out of this tract containing 1.01 acres. In the area north of the Mason-Dixon line and east of the one hundredth meridian this plan provides for a year's supply of vegetables, small fruits, poultry products, early and late potatoes, and most of the necessary tree fruits for a family of five. This is all that a man who is employed elsewhere during the growing season can care for properly by hand with the help of his family.

A few important points are to be kept in mind in planning the home and grounds, regardless of locality. Although the chief object in securing a small acreage may be economy—growing food for the family and lowering the housing costs—beauty or sightliness should not be overlooked when planning the buildings, garden, and tree plantings. Success in changing from a city to a country type of living will depend more on the wife—on her ability and willingness to adapt herself to the new conditions and responsibilities—than on any other member of the family. Careful arrangement of the buildings and plantings will do much to make country living attractive to the family.

Economy of effort is important. The use of the land should be planned so that the work can be done with the least possible effort. This means that the vegetables and berries that need the most attention should be closest to the house. As more trips are made to the garden for small vegetables and berries than for late potatoes, sweet corn, and orchard fruit, the small vegetables and

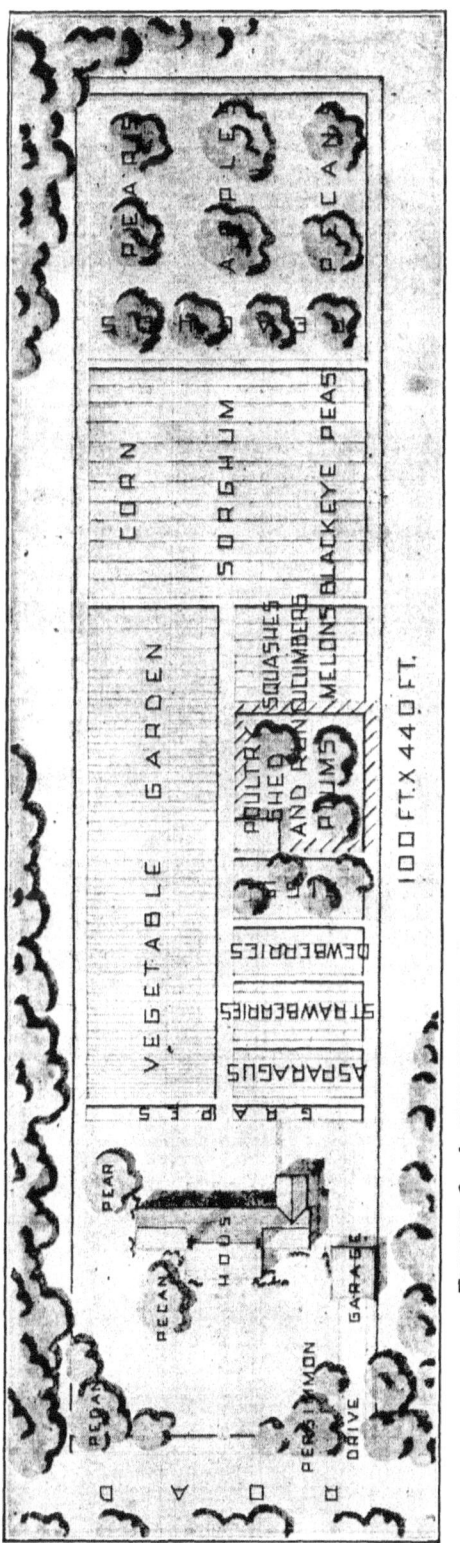

FIGURE 2.—A SUGGESTED PLAN FOR A 1-ACRE SUBSISTENCE HOMESTEAD IN THE SOUTH.

This lay-out differs from figure 1 in that it is adapted to that region of the United States often called the old Cotton Belt.

berries should be located nearer the kitchen. If the condition of the land permits, all the cultivated part should be located in one tract to facilitate the preparation of the seed beds and the cultivation. Since poultry requires attention at least twice a day, the chickens should be located reasonably near the house. Trees require the least care and, with the exception of those used for shade, should be located farthest from the house.

QUANTITY AND VARIETY OF GARDEN VEGETABLES AND SMALL FRUITS

Detailed plans for vegetable gardens in the North and South respectively are given in table 1. The amount of each vegetable crop to plant and the standard variety for the general region are suggested, as a guide for those who are not experienced. There may be other equally good or better varieties for any given locality or soil type within the region. The State agricultural experiment station and extension service or reliable garden-seed companies may be able to recommend varieties that are better adapted to specific local conditions.

To be most useful, the vegetable garden must provide a succession of crops throughout the growing season, and a supply for canning and storage for use during the other months. Varieties should be selected with these requirements in mind. With success in growing, the quantity of the various vegetables indicated in the tables will supply an adequate and balanced diet for the average family of five throughout the entire year.

Strawberries do well in most localities and bear fruit the second year after the plants are set out. Some of the better everbearing varieties will produce fruit throughout the fall of the first year. The Klondike and Missionary varieties are best for the Gulf coast region. The Southland, a new home-garden variety, is excellent for other parts of the South. Late summer or early fall is the proper time to set out strawberry plants in the South.

TABLE 1.—*Garden vegetables for a family of five*

IN THE NORTHERN STATES

Crop	Variety	50-foot rows	Succession crop	Distance between rows
		Number		*Inches*
Radishes	Scarlet Globe	1	Fall spinach	
Lettuce	New York and Simpson	1	....do	
Onions	Japanese	2	....do	
Beets	Detroit Dark Red	1		18
Carrots	Chantenay	2		
Swiss Chard	Lucullus	1		
Parsnips	Hollow Crown	1		
Salsify	Sandwich Island	1		
Peas	Alaska	1	Late beans	
	Little Marvel	1	....do	
	Thos. Laxton	1	....do	
	Telephone	2	....do	
Snap beans	Early Bountiful	1	Late cabbage	
	Tendergreen	1	....do	
	Currie Rust-Proof Wax	1	....do	30
	Stringless Green Pod	1	....do	
Lima beans	Henderson Bush	2		
	Fordhook Bush	2		
Early cabbage	Jersey Wakefield	2		
Broccoli	Italian Sprouting	1		
Early potatoes	Irish Cobbler or Triumph	8	Late cabbage	
Snap beans (2d and 3d planting)	Stringless Green Pod	2		
	Early Bountiful	2		
Tomatoes (early, staked)	Pritchard	2		
Tomatoes (not staked)	Marglobe	4		48
Early sweet corn	Golden Cross Bantam	5	Kale	
Medium sweet corn	Country Gentleman	5	Turnips	36
Late sweet corn	Stowell Evergreen	5		
Pole beans	Kentucky Wonder	1		42
	Pole lima	1		

IN THE OLD COTTON BELT

Spinach	Savoy	5	Swiss Chard	
Radishes	Scarlet Globe	1		
	White Icicle	1	Carrots	
Lettuce	White Boston	1		
	Curled Simpson	1	Beets	
Onions (sets)		2		18
Onions (plants)	Valencia	2	Fall lettuce	
Beets	Early Eclipse	1		
	Detroit Dark Red	1	Spinach	
Carrots	Chantenay	3	....do	
Early turnips		4	....do	
Mustard	Southern Curled	3	....do	
Early cabbage	Charleston Wakefield	3	Late beans	
Snap beans	Early Bountiful	2	....do	
	Stringless Black Valentine	2	....do	
	Rustproof	2	....do	36
Lima beans	Small bush	3		
Broccoli	Italian Sprouting	2		
Collards	Georgia	4		
Tomatoes (staked)	Marglobe	5		48
Tomatoes (not staked)	....do	4		
Early potatoes	Irish Cobbler or Triumph	5	Late turnips (broadcast)	36
Black Eye peas		4		
Sweetpotatoes		17		42
Okra	Perkins Mammoth	2		36
Pole beans	Kentucky Wonder	2		42

From North Carolina northward to the Canadian border the Premier or Howard 17 is one of the most popular strawberry varieties. Two good new varieties, the Fairfax and the Dorsett, are also well adapted to this region. For the northern Great Plains, the Howard 17, Dunlap, and Progressive are among the most popular varieties. The Progressive is an everbearing variety.

Strawberry plants can be set out in the spring in the Northern States and, if given proper care, will yield the second year. They do well in most localities. Some of the better everbearing varieties will produce fruit throughout the fall of the first year. Fifty plants for each member of the family are often recommended as a guide for planting. The strawberry bed should be so located that it can be changed and replanted every 2 years under most conditions.

Grapes bear well in most localities and are relatively easy to care for once the proper methods of pruning and training are learned. They usually reach practically full bearing in the third year after planting. In the Northern States the Concord, Niagara, and Moore's Early are the most popular varieties. In the Southeastern States, the Thomas and Scuppernong varieties are the most popular. About 10 plants set 10 feet apart in the row are plenty for an ordinary family. Grapes require a trellis and careful pruning each year for best results.

Raspberries, blackberries, and dewberries cannot be grown successfully in as large a part of the United States as grapes and strawberries. Dewberries winter kill in the Northern States but are excellent for the South. Raspberries and blackberries do not bear well in the far South. Raspberries, blackberries, and dewberries should bear the second year after planting in those sections of the country where they do well. About 50 to 100 plants of each planted 3 to 4 feet apart in the row should furnish plenty of berries for the ordinary family.

A small asparagus bed should also be found in each family garden and in the North a few hills of rhubarb.

Only a few inexpensive tools are necessary to care for the garden and berries. A good hoe, a garden rake, a spade or spading fork, a pair of pruning shears, and a trowel are all that are essential. Much hard work can be saved if a wheel hoe with a large wheel and a well-built wheel barrow can be bought. Other tools may be useful but are not necessary.

THE SMALL POULTRY FLOCK

Most families who are interested in raising their own vegetables are also interested in producing their own poultry and eggs. Studies in several States indicate that almost all part-time farmers keep a few hens, usually not over 25. A flock of 25 hens can be kept on very little land. They are fed on table scraps and some grain, and thus furnish eggs at low cost for home use. Their manure may be used on the garden land, thus reducing fertilizer cost. A few young chickens can be raised on a different small plot of land each year, in rotation with the garden and truck patch, or on the land planted to young fruit trees. In case the latter plan is used, the young growing trees must be protected.

The necessary permanent buildings and equipment for 25 hens and 40 young chickens would cost about $50 if built with home labor. Temporary buildings made of second-hand lumber and covered with roofing paper may be built for much less. The yearly expense for purchased grain for this number of chickens would be from $25 to $40. If they are well cared for, 25 hens are more than enough to supply the family with eggs throughout the year. In addition, approximately 20 young chickens weighing 3 pounds each and 12 hens weighing 4 to 6 pounds each would be available for meat. This is about 120 pounds of meat of a kind all families like.

There are great differences in the number of eggs produced by the same number of hens under different conditions. Commercial flocks average between 12 and 14 dozen eggs per hen, each year, but the average production in the United States is less than 7 dozen. With good care and housing, the pullets in the flock will lay all winter, but the spring months naturally bring the heaviest laying. It will probably take a few years of experience to get good fall and winter egg production. Eggs are usually lowest in price during the spring and highest in price during the fall and winter. During the heavy laying season in the spring the surplus eggs can be preserved in water glass for use in the winter. On request, the county agricultural agent or the home demonstration agent will furnish, without cost, instructions regarding the use of water glass.

Unless this plan is used the first year or two, it may be necessary to buy eggs in the fall and winter. As in the case of gardening, starting in a small way in egg production is advisable for the beginner. A dozen pullets may be enough for the first year. If the family is successful in getting good egg production from this number, they will have enough fresh eggs for their own use. If good production is not obtained the first year (and this would not be unusual) a larger flock would only mean a larger feed bill.

Losses in the raising of young chickens are likely to be heavy unless the chicks are fed properly and parasites and diseases controlled. To raise only a few chickens the first year will give the needed experience and will keep down the risk of heavy losses.

PRODUCTION OF TREE FRUITS ON SMALL ACREAGES

To grow tree fruits, especially winter apples, may be doubtful economy if the land is high priced and the family has enough cash income to buy these fruits. These trees do not come into bearing for several years; peaches take about 4 years, cherries and plums 4 to 5 years, and apples 6 to 8 years. During this time they must be cared for, sprayed, and pruned if they are to yield well at maturity. A well-rounded program of production for family subsistence, however, should include cherries, plums, peaches, pears, and apples in all localities where such trees bear well.

Bearing fruit trees should be sprayed several times each year, to kill the various insects and to combat the diseases that attack the trees and the fruit. This work is often neglected by those who have only a few trees, as it requires some special equipment, but unless this need is fully realized there is likely to be disappointment later.

A barrel mounted on a 2-wheel cart and fitted with a hand sprayer can be bought or built at a cost of not more than $30. This equipment can be used to spray the trees on 5 to 10 homesteads having 10 to 15 trees each. If the spraying equipment is owned in partnership the cost would be only $3 to $6 for each family.

FERTILIZERS

If the vegetables and other crops are to be cultivated entirely by hand, the intensive use of a small piece of land with heavy fertilization is more feasible and will give better results than the use of a larger area of land in medium or poor condition. Stable or barn-lot manure, when it can be obtained at a reasonable price, is the best garden fertilizer for most soils. A first application of 20 large wagonloads of partly rotted manure on a half-acre garden is not too much, if the land is lacking in organic matter and fertility. However, such manure is usually scarce and expensive near cities. The time to apply the manure will vary, but as a rule it should be spread just before the ground is plowed.

Commercial fertilizers can be used to advantage in many cases along with the manure from the poultry flock. An application at the rate of 600 to 1,200 pounds to the acre, when no manure is available, will usually prove satisfactory. A fertilizer that contains about 5 percent of nitrogen, 10 to 20 percent of phosphoric acid (usually in the form of superphosphate), and 5 or 6 percent of potash is about right for general garden crops. After the ground has been spaded or plowed, the fertilizer should be worked into the ground before the vegetables or other crops are planted.

INSECTS, DISEASES, AND OTHER HANDICAPS

Diseases, insects, rodents, and other pests attack the vegetables as well as the fruits and poultry. These pests, or poor seed, or unfavorable weather may cause a partial or total failure of any one crop or planting. Several plantings help to insure against total loss. A safe plan for the inexperienced is to plant only a small amount of each crop the first year or two. On the basis of the experience thus gained the family can decide which crops are the best for them, considering both what they are successful with and what the family needs.

Even if the first efforts are not successful, the particular crop or variety need not be condemned. Perhaps neighbors have been very successful with it. If so, it probably can be grown successfully if the right methods are used. The county agricultural agent, usually located at the county seat, will be able to give information on all such subjects without cost to the farmers. State agricultural experiment stations will send free bulletins about vegetable growing, insects and diseases, poultry raising, and other agricultural problems, on request. A list of free bulletins published by the Government, which are likely to be of interest to subsistence-homesteaders will be found on page 19.

CASH EXPENSES FOR AGRICULTURAL PRODUCTION AND RETURNS

Cash operating expenses in connection with such a program as outlined in the suggested 1-acre plan would be about as follows:

1 man and team—plowing and preparing the seed bed in the spring (5 hours)	$2.50 to $4
Seeds, plants, and bushes (after first year)	3.00 to 5
Fertilizer (300 to 600 pounds)	4.50 to 9
Insecticides	3.00 to 6
Feed for chickens (1,600 to 2,000 pounds of grain)	25.00 to 40
Total	38.00 to 64

The careful manager can sometimes reduce these cash outlays by exchanging tools with neighbors, by trading work, or by promising to trade products at the end of the season for items obtained earlier.

In return for the family's investment in the land, and its labor and cash expenses for the season, as indicated above, the family will get most of its supply of vegetables for the year, its entire supply of eggs and poultry for the year, and most of its fruit. The value of these vegetables and fruits has been variously estimated at from $70 to $150. If the 25 hens average 8 dozen eggs apiece, valued at 20 cents a dozen, the total value of the eggs produced would be $40; and 120 pounds of poultry meat at 25 cents a pound would be $30. This means that the total value of food from the 1-acre tract would be from $140 to $220.

It might be pointed out that an adequate diet at moderate cost for a very active family of five, as worked out by the United States Bureau of Home Economics, calls for only 85 dozen eggs. This indicates that about 100 dozen eggs would be available for sale if 25 hens are kept, but it would be at the season when egg prices are low, unless unusually progressive poultry practices are used.

WINTER VEGETABLE AND FRUIT SUPPLY FOR A FAMILY OF FIVE

The gardens and fruit trees suggested in the planting diagrams should provide ample supplies for use during the growing season, and also a generous quantity for winter needs. In the North fresh foods will be available for about 4 or 5 months. The southern gardens will produce during a longer period, although in some sections little can be grown during the hot, dry, midsummer months. Early in the year the family should make an estimate of the quantities of the various foods to be stored, canned, and otherwise preserved for use during the nonproductive months. The best method to use will depend upon the crops raised, the climate, and other local conditions.

Storing in cellars or pits is practicable for such relatively nonperishable crops as potatoes, carrots, beets, turnips, parsnips, onions, cabbage, apples, and pears. Sweetpotatoes, after a first curing, must be kept in a dry, warm, well-ventilated place; squash and pumpkin should also be stored in a dry, warm place.

Drying may be used to keep beans, peas, okra, corn, squash, and some fruits; 1 to 2 bushels of dried beans and peas and 15 to 30 pounds of dried fruit is a generous winter supply for a family of five.

Canning, in either glass jars or tin cans, is the best method of preservation for some foods. If proper equipment for canning cannot be bought by single families it may be possible to establish a community canning center where the equipment can be used cooperatively. The Department of Agriculture at Washington, D.C. will send a mimeographed leaflet on community canning centers, on request. A pressure cooker should be used for canning such vegetables as leafy greens, asparagus, beans, peas, okra, corn, or root vegetables. Unless a pressure cooker is available it is advisable to limit the canning to fruits, rhubarb, and acid vegetables, such as tomatoes, tomato combinations, sauerkraut, and beets in vinegar.

The two canning budgets that follow are suggested as general guides for families living in the North and South, respectively. More detailed canning plans based on the conditions peculiar to the individual States can be obtained from the extension services of the various State agricultural colleges or from the local home demonstration agent. The quantities suggested in the following budgets will provide 2 or 3 one-half-cup servings of canned fruits or vegetables for each member of the family for each day of the months when the garden is not producing. Used in connection with the stored and dried products, this amount of canned foods should be enough to meet the usual needs of a family of five. But it might be well to allow an additional 10 to 15 percent to care for guests, spoilage, or emergencies such as poor crops during the following season. As most properly canned food will keep well for at least 2 years, any that is unused may be carried over to use during the second year. It is best not to hold canned foods for longer than 2 years.

During the first few years a new homestead plot may not furnish enough fruit to supply the quantities suggested in the canning budgets. In some sections there may be wild fruits and berries to use. If enough fruit cannot be obtained, the quantities of the various canned vegetables should be increased somewhat.

Fruit and vegetable canning budget for family of five in the Northern States

[For use during 7 nonproductive months]

Tomatoes	quarts	100 to 150
Leafy greens (spinach, chard, etc.)	do	20 to 35
Other green vegetables (asparagus, string or lima beans, peas, okra, etc.)	quarts	20 to 35
Sauerkraut	do	15 to 20
Sweet corn	do	15 to 20
Soup mixtures	do	10 to 20
Fruits (peaches, pears, quinces, plums, grapes, cherries, berries, apples, apple sauce, etc.)	quarts	90 to 130
Fruit juices	do	15 to 25
Catsup, pickles, chow-chow, etc	pints	15 to 25
Jellies, jams, fruit butters, etc	do	15 to 25

Fruit and vegetable canning budget for family of five in the Southern States

[For use during 6 nonproductive months]

Tomatoes (if citrus fruits are available the quantity of canned tomatoes may be reduced)	quarts	75 to 125
Leafy greens (fresh greens are available for 12 months in many southern localities).		
Other green vegetables (asparagus, string or lima beans, peas, okra, etc.)	quarts	20 to 40
Sweet corn	do	15 to 25
Soup mixtures	do	15 to 25

Sauerkraut	quarts	10 to 15
Carrots and other vegetables	do	10 to 15
Fruits (peaches, pears, plums, figs, grapes, berries, cherries, etc.)	quarts	75 to 110
Fruit juices	do	15 to 25
Catsup, pickles, chow-chow, etc	pints	15 to 25
Jellies, jams, fruit butters, etc	do	15 to 25

FEED AND LIVESTOCK PRODUCTION ON A SUBSISTENCE HOMESTEAD

If horse or mechanical power is available at a reasonable cost the farm plans can be materially changed to advantage. The garden and truck patch may be laid out in long rows, 3 feet apart, and can be cultivated with power throughout the growing season. This will greatly reduce the hand labor and will permit the use of a larger acreage.

Figure 3 shows a suggested plan for fruit and vegetable production where power is available. Approximately 2 acres of land are included in this plan. Unless some arrangement can be made to secure power cultivation at reasonable cost this plan will not be feasible. To keep a horse or garden tractor for use on such a small piece of cultivated land is questionable economy. A half-acre orchard may not be considered desirable since fruit cannot be gathered for several years. In that case the ground might be used to grow corn or other feed crops for the poultry.

If an orchard is planted as indicated, during the first few years while the trees are young, many of the garden vegetables can be raised in the space between the trees. This would leave some of the other land for growing feed for the poultry.

The one fourth acre sown to legumes in figure 3, if planted to the appropriate crops, may be used in growing the young chickens.

THE FAMILY COW

Studies indicate that a family of five should have from 1,200 to 1,500 quarts of milk and 90 to 150 pounds of butter a year. One good cow can supply these needs most of the time. From the standpoint of an adequate diet for children in families that have very low incomes, keeping a cow would seem to be more valuable than raising vegetables or fruits. But the keeping of a cow by inexperienced people, on a small piece of land has many disadvantages which may make it questionable.

A high-producing dairy cow is a sensitive animal, responding to good care, but quick to give less milk on receiving poor or improper care. Milking, feeding, and watering require regular attention twice each day. But if a family is willing to undertake the regular care of a cow and has a natural knack for taking care of animals it should have no serious difficulties in obtaining a reasonably satisfactory quantity of milk.

Although one good cow, well cared for, will give over 7,000 pounds of milk (the quantity necessary to supply the milk and butter for the family of five), the average production in the United States is only about 4,500 pounds per cow. As the usual lactation period for a cow is 10 or 11 months, at best, milk and butter would have to be bought during part of the year. It is reasonable to estimate that, with ordi-

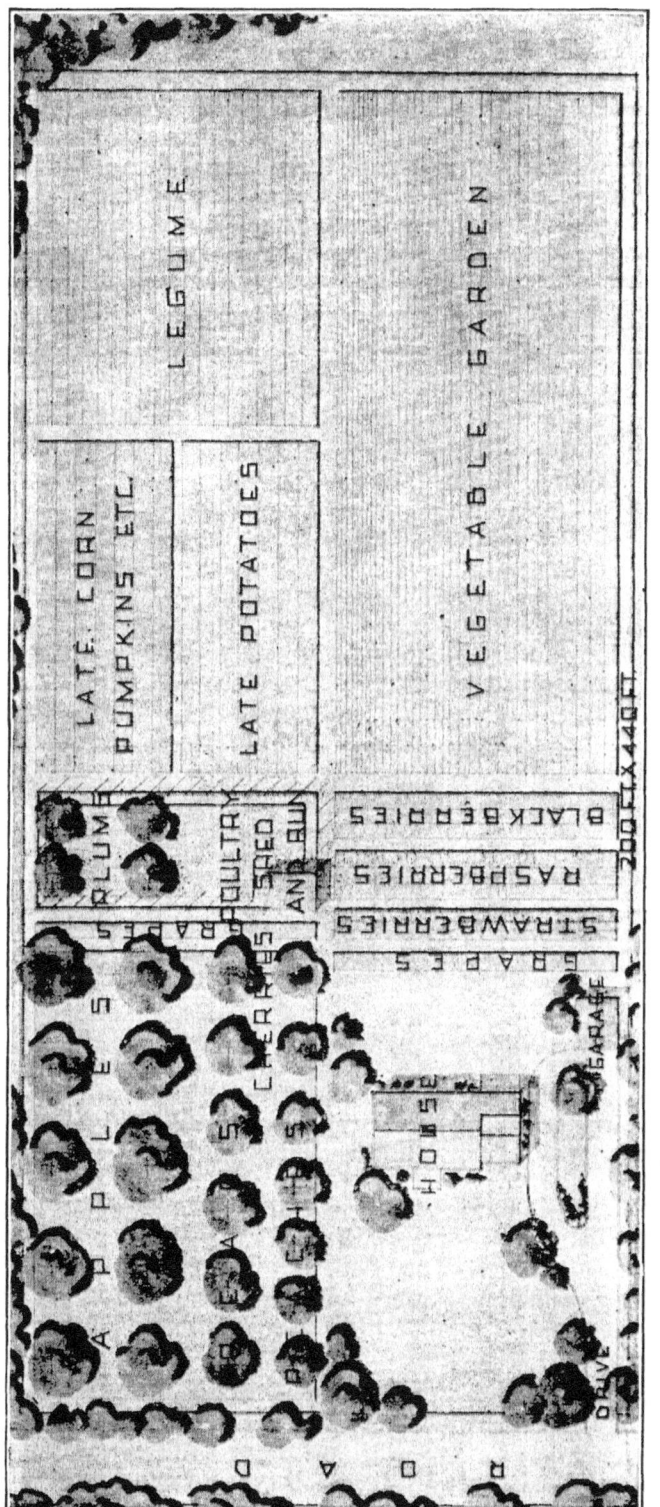

FIGURE 3.—A SUGGESTED PLAN FOR A 2-ACRE SUBSISTENCE HOMESTEAD

Cultivation with horse or tractor power requires wider rows and a larger garden. It also makes it possible to care for a larger acreage. Alternate uses of the space allotted for an orchard and for the rotation of crops are: as pasture for a cow, pasture for milk goats, or pasture for pigs, or for the growing of feed grains for poultry.

nary care, a cow will furnish both the milk and butter for a family of five for 4 months of the year. For another 6 or 7 months there will be plenty of milk, but the butter will have to be bought. Both milk and butter would have to be bought for the remaining 1 or 2 months. If a cow is kept, it may be more economical to sell the extra milk to neighbors and buy butter, rather than try to make butter. The money from sales of milk at retail prices during the first part of the lactation period would not only buy the butter during this period but would largely pay for the necessary purchases of milk during the period when the cow is dry. The question of whether or not to keep a cow may turn on the possibility of selling the extra milk to neighbors at retail prices.

In the Northeastern and Midwestern States, 1 to 2 acres are necessary to pasture a cow. If the land on a 2-acre tract is very productive and no orchard is wanted, enough pasture and green crops could be grown to feed a cow during the summer. A better balanced plan of farm production for family subsistence purposes, however, would be attained by adding 2 acres of pasture to the 2-acre plot suggested above. Figure 4 shows how this might be done, with the pasture arranged so that the cow will come up close to the house for watering, feeding, and milking.

Good summer pasture, supplemented by roughage from the garden, will reduce to a minimum the grain to be fed to the dairy cow during summer months. During the winter in the Northern States a cow will need about 2½ tons of hay, costing from $20 to $38, and from 1,000 to 2,000 pounds of grain, costing from $10 to $30. A shed, built in connection with the poultry house or some other outbuilding, large enough to keep a cow and some feed would cost from $50 to $150. In the South the milder climate makes a warm building unnecessary, but some form of shelter should be provided even there.

MILK GOATS

If for any reason a cow will not be kept, milk goats might be considered in those communities where breeding stock is available. In the southwestern and western parts of the United States in particular, a number of the families on small acreages keep a milk goat or two to supply milk for the family. An ordinary milk goat gives from 1½ to 2 quarts of milk a day and needs only about one sixth as much feed as a cow. Three to five does would be necessary to furnish an ample supply of milk throughout the year for a family of five.

There are a number of things to be learned before buying a milk goat. Farmers' Bulletin 920 on milk goats gives some valuable general information and will be sent free by the United States Department of Agriculture on request. In general, people in this country do not know much about milk goats, but in some communities there may be neighbors who have had experience in keeping goats who can give advice and information.

PORK FOR FAMILY USE

A family of five requires from 400 to 600 pounds of meats and cooking fat a year. This quantity can be produced in the form of pork and lard by growing and fattening three pigs. But most

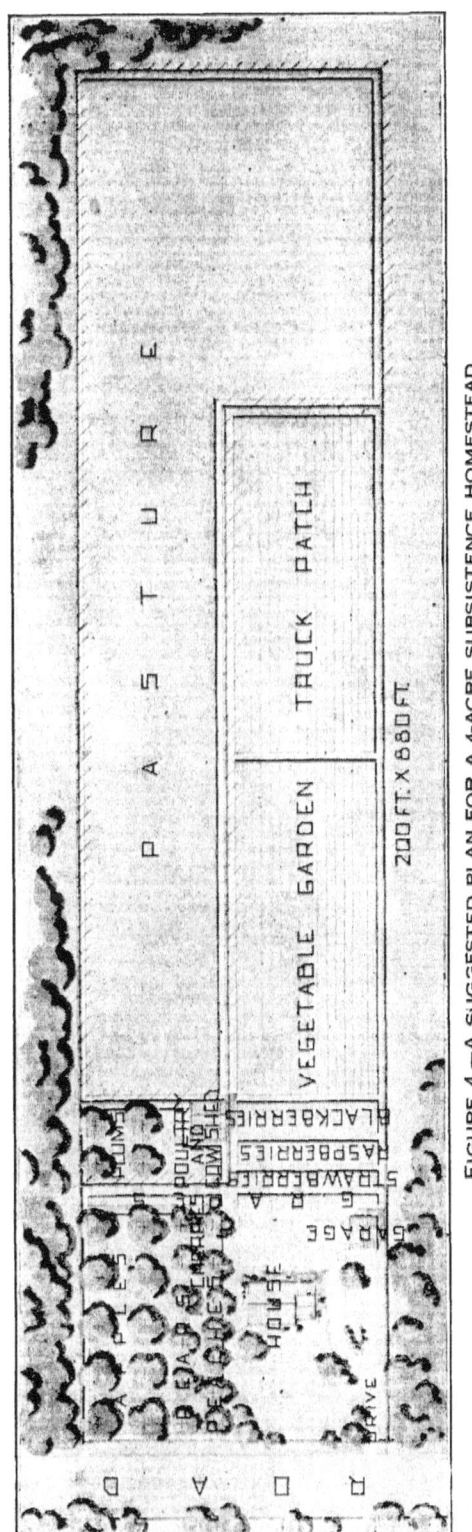

FIGURE 4.—A SUGGESTED PLAN FOR A 4-ACRE SUBSISTENCE HOMESTEAD

The addition of 2 acres of pasture to the plan suggested in figure 3 will provide ample pasture for a cow in those sections of the United States where grass grows well.

families will not wish to depend on hogs alone for their meat, even though they also have eggs and poultry from their own flock.

In some States and communities there are regulations that prohibit the raising of pigs close to neighbors. In any case, pigs should be kept some distance from any house, even though water and feed must be carried to them.

Two or three pigs can be kept in a small pen and fed table scraps and some grain. Thus they grow into 500 to 700 pounds of live pork at a relatively low cost if the grain can be raised or bought economically. Pigs can be bought as weanlings in most communities for from $3 to $5 each. Pigs immunized against cholera should be bought, particularly if table scraps are to be fed. A pig will eat from 600 to 1,000 pounds of grain costing $6 to $15, while growing to a weight of 200 pounds. Savings of 10 to 20 percent on feed costs may be expected if one fourth to one half of an acre of good pasture can be provided. Shade is very important for pigs in the summer. Plenty of fresh water is also essential. A comparison of the cost of small pigs plus the cost of grain for feed on the one hand and the price of dressed pork on the other, should be made. This, and the effort and risk involved, should be considered carefully before a decision is made. Studies of part-time farmers show that only one fourth to one third of these men (mostly on the larger acreages) keep cows and even fewer keep pigs. Evidently most of them find it more economical or easier to buy their milk and meat.

Manure from the animals is valuable for the garden and reduces the cash expenses for fertilizer. Much of the cow manure would be used on the pasture; but even so, fertilizer requirements for the cultivated land should be reduced by 50 to 70 percent when 25 hens, a cow, and pigs are kept.

FEED FOR LIVESTOCK ON SMALL ACREAGES

Many people who want to raise as much of the family's food supply as possible with the lowest cash cost, plan to keep poultry, a cow or two, and pigs, and to raise the necessary feeds. It takes about 1½ acres of land to raise the necessary corn and wheat for 25 hens and 40 young chickens. In addition to 2 acres of pasture for a cow, approximately 1¾ acres are necessary to raise the hay and 1¼ acres to raise the grain consumed by the cow during the year. This makes a total of 5 acres for one cow; if two cows are kept this acreage should be doubled. One and one half acres should produce enough grain to fatten three pigs.

Using 6 acres of land for raising feed in addition to 1 acre of garden and truck crops would require the work of a man and team 15 to 25 days during the growing and harvesting season. If a one-horse outfit were used, 30 to 50 days would be required. This is too small an amount of work for one horse if the overhead cost is to be kept low. On the other hand, to hire a man and team 15 to 25 days at the usual rates means a considerable cash expense.

A horse requires about the same quantity of feed and pasture as a cow. If a horse is to be kept, 5 more acres should be obtained. It might be possible for two or more families to own a horse or team in partnership and thus reduce the cost.

Therefore, if a family plans to do the work by hand an intensive use of a relatively small piece of land will probably be more satisfactory than spreading the effort over a larger area. Unless a cow or pigs are kept, 1 acre of good land is enough under such circumstances. If a cow is kept and it is planned to buy the winter roughage and grain, 2 additional acres of good pasture land would be enough. A man employed elsewhere, working only a few hours a day on his place during the growing season, with the help of his family can care for the vegetable garden, small fruits, a few fruit trees, and a cow without any difficulty.

If mechanical power or horsepower is available at low cost, the vegetables can be grown in wider rows and cultivated with a horse or garden tractor. This makes it possible to put to good use a larger acreage. But it is difficult to have horse cultivation at low cost on a very small acreage. Large families with small incomes, who have considerable free time during the growing season may find it economical to keep a horse, 1 or 2 cows, and some pigs, and raise the farm-grown feeds for the livestock in addition to the vegetables and fruits. At least 15 acres of good land should be acquired in such cases. A careful study should be made of all sides of the question before a family decides to undertake so much farm work for family living purposes. Growing feeds on the farm in such small quantities and the cost of keeping a horse when it is used only a small part of the time mean relatively high costs and low net returns, as compared with the returns from industrial employment, if that is available.

POSSIBILITIES OF A SMALL WOOD LOT

The yearly fuel bill is always difficult for families with small incomes. More fuel is used in country homes where there is no gas or electricity for cooking. If land can be obtained which includes a few wooded acres, the family's wood supply can be provided with almost no additional cash cost. Cutting can be done in the winter or whenever there is extra time, and if the trees to be cut are carefully selected, the supply of timber will continue throughout the owner's lifetime. Perhaps some exchange of work could be arranged with an owner of a team, in order to have the wood hauled to the house.

If the farmer does not buy any timberland but there is considerable timber in the community, he may be able to get the privilege of cutting his fuel supply from a neighbor's woods for a very small sum.

LIMITATIONS OF SMALL ACREAGES AS A MEANS OF SELF-SUPPORT

Letters coming from townspeople show that more often they hear about the best results from farming than about the poorest results; it has therefore seemed best to caution the reader frequently not to regard subsistence farming too optimistically. No real service is rendered in holding out rosy possibilities when the probabilities are slight that such results will be realized by most people. On the other hand it is not intended to discourage those townspeople who are handicapped by lack of capital and are getting only a small income, if they have an honest wish to better their conditions by raising most of their food supply even though it means some trouble and much work.

The work may be hard and the results not always up to expectations; but if the family has no better possibility almost any arrangement to obtain the use of a piece of land should be better than continued idleness or full support from charity or relief funds.

It cannot be overemphasized, however, that a program of farm production as here outlined, even though all the livestock feed is raised, does not make the family self-maintaining. Cash farm expenses must be met, such as the purchase of seeds and feeds that cannot be raised economically, taxes, and repairs of equipment. Family living expenses for clothes, school supplies, and medical care mean cash expenditures. Part-time farming studies do not throw much light on the minimum cash income necessary to meet these expenses. The average cash income reported for those groups of part-time farmers whose financial relations were studied varied from $400 to $900 in most cases.

A number of people, after gaining farm experience, will find that they can raise some products for sale at a profit. A commercial poultry business large enough to employ a man full time and bring in an adequate income can be developed on as little as 2 acres if conditions are right.

PRODUCTION FOR HOME USE ON LARGER ACREAGES

Many people in towns who have little hope of further employment, because of age or for other reasons, would like to get a larger acreage of cheap land on which they can become independent for the rest of their lives. They are chiefly interested in producing for home use; they are interested in producing for sale only enough to furnish the few necessities of life not obtained on the farm. Usually their capital and experience are so limited that cheapness of land is their chief concern. They are naturally attracted by advertisements describing farms that can be bought for a fraction of the cost of the improvements on them.

As a matter of fact, a great deal of farm land in the United States is not productive enough to be of value in growing market crops and livestock. This is especially true in the southern Appalachian region, the Ozarks, the New England States, and the cut-over areas of the Southern and Great Lake States. Many farms in these areas have very low producing possibilities, and the families on them grow crops and livestock almost entirely for their own use.

SELF-SUFFICING FARMS

The 1930 agricultural census, in its study of types of farming, classified all farms as self-sufficing where 50 percent or more of the value of the farm products was consumed by the family. This group of farms, 498,019 in 1929, compares with the type of farming many townspeople propose to engage in. These self-sufficing farms are most common in the southern Appalachian region. Figures from a study of 151,000 of these self-sufficing farms in this region show how meager a living those people really had.

Most of the farms were from 20 to 100 acres in size. The average value was $2,029. The value of tools and machinery per farm was only $74. Not all of the farms had horses; only a little over one half of them kept milk cows; and about one half of them kept hogs. The total value of the farm products sold, traded, or used by the operator's family, in 1929, was $464, of which $323 was used by the operator's family.

INDIVIDUAL FARMS VARY IN PRODUCTIVITY

Studies indicate that the opportunities or likelihood of making a living on some of the farms in these poorer areas is very limited. A full set of buildings is no indication of a productive farm. Many abandoned farms, several hundred acres in size, have failed to yield a reasonable living under any type of farming. Many families living in these areas have another source of income, such as cutting wood for sale, road work, or coal mining, which supplements their living obtained from the farm.

Natural productivity of the soil varies greatly. To the inexperienced, good and poor soils in these regions look alike. The county agricultural agent located at the county seat will be able to appraise the relative productivity of the various farms in his county. Neighbors who have lived in the community for years should be consulted. Inquiry as to how they are farming and the results they are obtaining on their own farms, as well as the results to be expected on nearby farms for sale, may bring valuable information.

Social considerations should form an important part in making a decision. Good schools and churches and desirable associates for the growing children are always considered by responsible parents when buying a home whether in town or country. In general, the communities on poor land are not likely to be able to have good schools and churches. If there are no growing children in the family less consideration need be given this question, and if money is extremely limited it may be impossible to do much about it. But these social problems should not be overlooked.

Buying a farm entirely by correspondence is especially full of dangers. A thorough investigation before buying in unfamiliar areas will prevent many mistakes. Renting for a time before buying gives a family a chance to learn the advantages and disadvantages of any particular farm.

FARMERS' BULLETINS OF INTEREST

The following Farmers' Bulletins published by the United States Department of Agriculture deal with many of the problems encountered in agricultural production for family subsistence purposes. They are available for distribution on request.

F.B. 1673. The Farm Garden.
F.B. 1371. Diseases and Insects of Garden Vegetables.
F.B. 1508. Poultry Keeping in Back Yards.
F.B. 1652. Diseases and Parasites of Poultry.
F.B. 1610. Dairy Farming for Beginners.
F.B. 920. Milk Goats.
F.B. 879. Home Storage of Vegetables.
F.B. 1088. Selecting a Farm.
F.B. 1746. Subsistence Farm Gardens.
F.B. 1753. Livestock on Small Farms.
F.B. 1762 Home Canning of Fruits, Vegetables, and Meats.
F.B. 1800. Home-made Jellies, Jams, and Preserves.

ORGANIZATION OF THE UNITED STATES DEPARTMENT OF AGRICULTURE WHEN THIS PUBLICATION WAS LAST PRINTED

Secretary of Agriculture	HENRY A. WALLACE.
Under Secretary	CLAUDE R. WICKARD.
Assistant Secretary	GROVER B. HILL.
Director of Information	M. S. EISENHOWER.
Director of Extension Work	M. L. WILSON.
Director of Finance	W. A. JUMP.
Director of Personnel	ROY F. HENDRICKSON.
Director of Research	JAMES T. JARDINE.
Director of Marketing	MILO R. PERKINS.
Solicitor	MASTIN G. WHITE.
Land Use Coordinator	M. S. EISENHOWER.
Office of Plant and Operations	ARTHUR B. THATCHER, Chief.
Office of C. C. C. Activities	FRED W. MORRELL, Chief.
Office of Experiment Stations	JAMES T. JARDINE, Chief.
Office of Foreign Agricultural Relations	LESLIE A. WHEELER, Director.
Agricultural Adjustment Administration	R. M. EVANS, Administrator.
Bureau of Agricultural Chemistry and Engineering.	HENRY G. KNIGHT, Chief.
Bureau of Agricultural Economics	H. R. TOLLEY, Chief.
Agricultural Marketing Service	C. W. KITCHEN, Chief.
Bureau of Animal Industry	JOHN R. MOHLER, Chief.
Commodity Credit Corporation	CARL B. ROBBINS, President.
Commodity Exchange Administration	J. W. T. DUVEL, Chief.
Bureau of Dairy Industry	O. E. REED, Chief.
Bureau of Entomology and Plant Quarantine.	LEE A. STRONG, Chief.
Farm Credit Administration	A. G. BLACK, Governor.
Farm Security Administration	W. W. ALEXANDER, Administrator.
Federal Crop Insurance Corporation	LEROY K. SMITH, Manager.
Federal Surplus Commodities Corporation	MILO R. PERKINS, President.
Food and Drug Administration	WALTER G. CAMPBELL, Chief.
Forest Service	EARLE H. CLAPP, Acting Chief.
Bureau of Home Economics	LOUISE STANLEY. Chief.
Library	CLARIBEL R. BARNETT, Librarian.
Division of Marketing and Marketing Agreements.	MILO R. PERKINS; In Charge.
Bureau of Plant Industry	E. C. AUCHTER, Chief.
Rural Electrification Administration	HARRY SLATTERY, Administrator.
Soil Conservation Service	H. H. BENNETT, Chief.
Weather Bureau	FRANCIS W. REICHELDERFER, Chief.

For sale by the Superintendent of Documents, Washington, D. C.   Price 5 cents

U. S. DEPARTMENT OF AGRICULTURE.

FARMERS' BULLETIN No. 255.

THE HOME VEGETABLE GARDEN.

BY

W. R. BEATTIE,
Assistant Horticulturist, Bureau of Plant Industry.

WASHINGTON:
GOVERNMENT PRINTING OFFICE.
1906.

LETTER OF TRANSMITTAL.

U. S. DEPARTMENT OF AGRICULTURE,
BUREAU OF PLANT INDUSTRY,
OFFICE OF THE CHIEF,
Washington, D. C., April 12, 1906.

SIR: I have the honor to transmit and to recommend for publication as a Farmers' Bulletin the accompanying paper on "The Home Vegetable Garden," prepared by Mr. W. R. Beattie, Assistant Horticulturist.

This bulletin supersedes Farmers' Bulletin No. 94, "The Vegetable Garden."

Respectfully,

B. T. GALLOWAY,
Chief of Bureau.

Hon. JAMES WILSON,
Secretary of Agriculture.

CONTENTS.

	Page.
Introduction	5
Location of the garden	6
Plan and arrangement of the garden	6
Kind of cultivation to be employed	8
Location of crops	8
Succession of crops	9
Preparation of the soil	9
Drainage	9
Plowing	9
Smoothing and pulverizing the soil	10
Special preparation	10
Fertilizers	11
Barnyard manure	11
Commercial fertilizers	11
Seeds and plants for the garden	12
Early plants in hotbeds	12
Early plants in cold frames	15
The seed bed	15
Seed sowing	15
Care of the seed bed	16
The handling of plants	16
Hardening off	16
Importance of thinning	17
Effects of transplanting	17
Special methods of transplanting	18
Setting in the open ground	18
Time of planting	19
Protection of plants	19
Protection from heat	20
Protection from cold	20
Cultivation of garden crops	21
Tools for use in the garden	21
Irrigation of garden crops	22
Precautions to avoid attacks of insects and diseases	23
Cultural hints for garden crops	24
Artichoke (Globe), artichoke (Jerusalem), asparagus	24
Beans, beets, Brussels sprouts	26, 27
Cabbage, cardoon, carrot, cauliflower, celeriac, celery, chervil, chicory, chive, citron, collards, corn salad, corn (sweet), cress, cucumber	28-32
Dandelion	33
Eggplant, endive	33
Garlic	34
Horse-radish	34
Kale (or borecole), kohl-rabi	34

255

Cultural hints for garden crops—Continued.	Page.
Leek, lettuce	35
Melon—muskmelon; melon—watermelon; mustard	35, 36
New Zealand spinach	36
Okra (or gumbo), onions	36, 37
Parsley, parsnip, peas, peppers, physalis, potato (Irish), potato (sweet), pumpkin	38–42
Radish, rhubarb, ruta-baga	42, 43
Salsify (or vegetable oyster), spinach, squash	43, 44
Tomato, turnip	44, 45
Vegetable marrow	45
Gardener's planting table	46

ILLUSTRATIONS.

Fig.		Page
1.	Plan of a half-acre garden	7
2.	Plan of a city-lot or back-yard garden	8
3.	Cross section of land bedded up for early crops	10
4.	Cross section of land ridged up for early crops	10
5.	Cross section of land showing trenches employed in the cultivation of celery and similar crops	11
6.	Flat, or tray, for starting plants or transplanting	12
7.	Hotbed, showing frame and sash	13
8.	Cross section of temporary hotbed	13
9.	Cross section of permanent hotbed	13
10.	Cross section of pipe-heated hotbed	14
11.	Cross section of permanent hotbed with enlarged pit	14
12.	Celery plants, showing effect of transplanting on root system	17
13.	Berry box used for starting and transplanting early plants	18
14.	Cross section of land illustrating the use of the dibble in setting plants	19
15.	Board used for protection of plants	20
16.	Small-tooth horse cultivator	21
17.	Spading fork	21
18.	Dibbles used for transplanting	21
19.	Transplanting trowel	22
20.	Onion hoe	22
21.	Hand weeder	22
22.	Thinning or weeding hook	22
23.	Wheel hoe	22
24.	Cross section of soil showing arrangement of tiles for subirrigation	23
25.	Globe or bur artichoke	24
26.	Asparagus plant	25
27.	Chive	31
28.	Device for protecting young cucumber plants	32
29.	Kohl-rabi	34
30.	Onions	37
31.	Cross section of Potato or Multiplier onion	37
32.	Top or Tree onion, producing bulblets on top of stem	37
33.	Parsnips	38
34.	Spinach plant in proper condition for cutting	44

B. P. I.—211.

THE HOME VEGETABLE GARDEN.

INTRODUCTION.

Perhaps the most characteristic feature of our northern and eastern farms is the home vegetable garden. Even where no orchard has been planted, and where the ornamental surroundings of the home have been neglected, a fairly well-kept garden in which are grown a number of the staple kinds of vegetables is generally to be found. In many cases the principal interest in the garden is manifested by the women of the household and much of the necessary care is given by them. A small portion of the garden inclosure is generally devoted to the cultivation of flowers, and a number of medicinal plants are invariably present. Throughout the newer parts of the country one finds that the conditions governing the maintenance and use of the vegetable garden are somewhat different, and, while a number of vegetable crops may be grown somewhere on the farm, there is wanting that distinction so characteristic of the typical New England kitchen garden.

It would be impossible to make an accurate estimate of the value of crops grown in the kitchen gardens of the United States, but from careful observation the statement can safely be made that a well-kept garden will yield a return ten to fifteen times greater than would the same area and location if devoted to general farm crops. A half acre devoted to the various kinds of garden crops will easily supply a family with $100 worth of vegetables during the year, while the average return for farm crops is considerably less than one-tenth of this amount. A bountiful supply of vegetables close at hand where they may be secured at a few moments' notice is of even more importance than the mere money value.

Fresh vegetables from the home garden are not subjected to exposure on the markets or in transportation and are not liable to become infected in any way. Many of the products of the garden lose their characteristic flavor when not used within a few hours after gathering. By means of the home garden the production of the vegetable supply for the family is directly under control, and in many cases is the only way whereby clean, fresh produce may be secured. The home vegetable garden is worthy of increased attention, and a greater number and variety of crops should be included in the garden.

Suggestions are herein given as to the location of the garden, the soil and its preparation, fertilizers, seeds, and plants, with brief cultural methods for a number of the more important crops.

LOCATION OF THE GARDEN.

The question of the proximity to the house or other buildings is of great importance when locating the garden. In old homesteads the garden was generally located directly adjacent to the house, requiring but a few steps from the kitchen to reach the extreme parts of the garden. The work of caring for a garden is usually done at spare times, and for this reason alone the location should be near the dwelling. In case the site chosen for the garden should become unsuitable for any cause it is not a difficult matter to change the location. Many persons prefer to plant the garden in a different location every five or six years.

The lay of the land has considerable influence upon the time that the soil can be worked, and a gentle slope toward the south or southeast is most desirable for the production of early crops. It is an advantage to have protection on the north and northwest by either a hill, a group of trees, evergreens, a hedge, buildings, a tight board fence, or a stone wall to break the force of the wind.

Good natural drainage of the garden area is of prime importance. The land should have sufficient fall to drain off surplus water during heavy rains, but the fall should not be so great that the soil will be washed. The surface of the garden should not contain depressions in which water will accumulate or stand. Waste water from surrounding land should not flow toward the garden, and the fall below should be such that there will be no danger of flood water backing up. The garden should not be located along the banks of a creek or stream that will be liable to overflow during the growing season.

A good fence around the garden plot is almost indispensable, and it should be a safeguard against all farm animals, including poultry, and should be close enough to keep out rabbits. A tight board fence will accomplish this result and also serve as a wind-break.

PLAN AND ARRANGEMENT OF THE GARDEN.

It would be difficult to give a plan or specific arrangement for a garden that would suit all demands, and such a plan must be devised by each individual grower. Suggestive arrangements, however, are here presented, with the idea that they can readily be changed to suit local conditions.

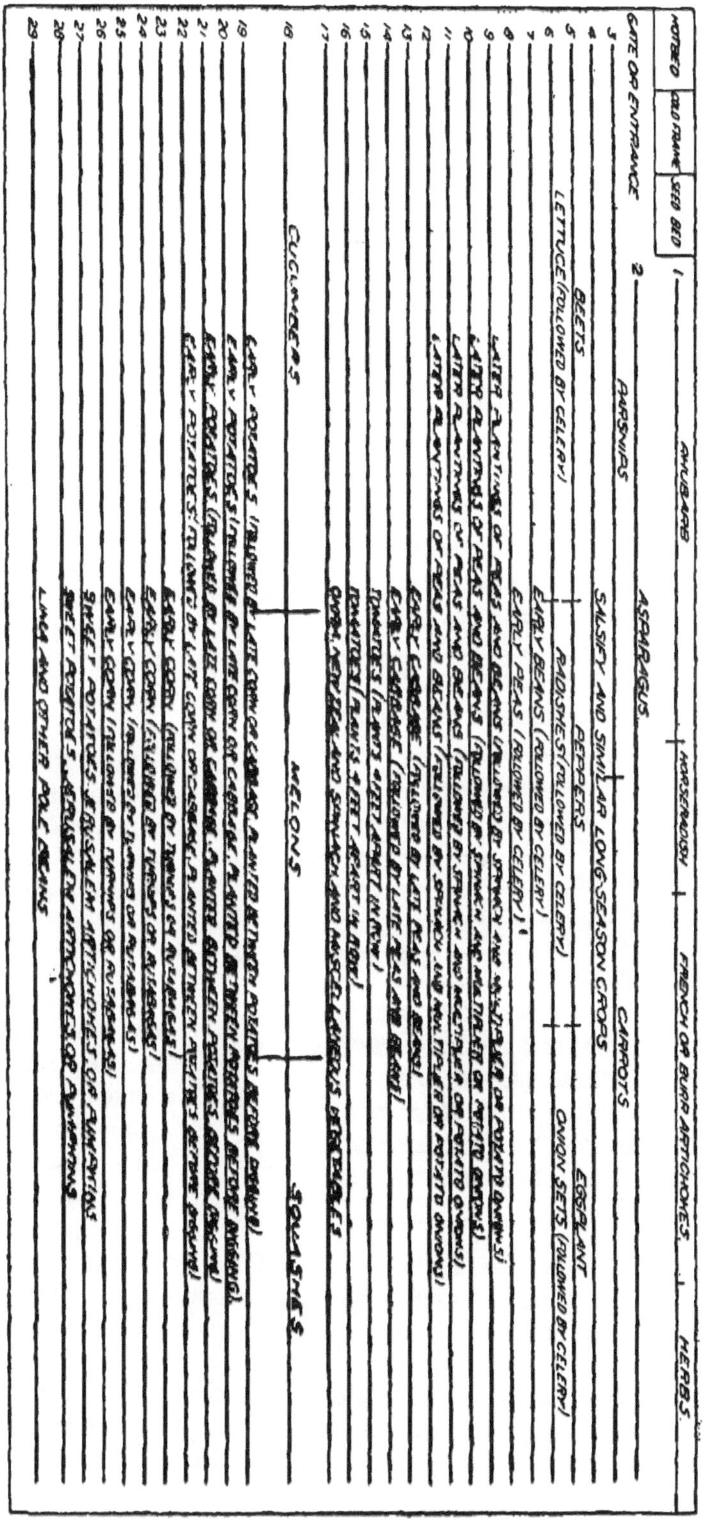

FIG. 1.—Plan of a half-acre garden. Length, 220 feet; width, 100 feet.

KIND OF CULTIVATION TO BE EMPLOYED.

The first consideration in planning the arrangement of a garden is the kind of cultivation that is to be employed. Where the work is to be done mainly by means of horse tools the arrangement should be such as to give the longest possible rows, and straight outlines should be followed. The garden should be free from paths across the rows, and turning spaces should be provided at the ends. (Fig. 1.) For hand cultivation the arrangement can be quite different, as the garden may be laid off in sections, with transverse walks, and the rows can be much closer for most crops. (Fig. 2.) Horse cultivation is recommended whenever possible, as it very materially lessens the labor and cost of caring for the crops.

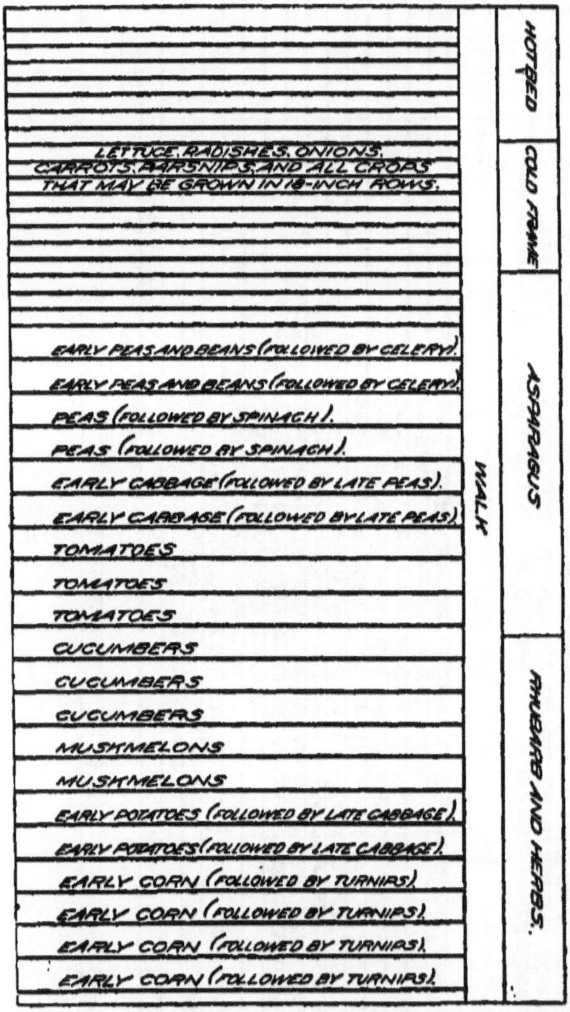

FIG. 2.—Plan of a city-lot or back-yard garden. 50 by 90 feet.

LOCATION OF CROPS.

The second matter for consideration is the location of permanent crops, such as asparagus and rhubarb, and if any of the small fruits, such as raspberries, currants, and gooseberries, are to be planted within the garden inclosure, they should be included with the permanent crops. The area devoted to the hotbed, cold frame, and seed bed should be decided upon, but these may be shifted more or less from year to year or located in some convenient place outside of the garden.

Where there is any great variation in the composition of the soil in different parts of the garden it will be advisable to take this into consideration when arranging for the location of the various crops. If a part of the land is low and moist, such crops as celery, onions, and late cucumbers should be placed there. If part of the soil is high, warm, and dry, that is the proper location for early crops and those that need quick, warm soil.

SUCCESSION OF CROPS.

In planning the location of the various crops in the garden, due consideration should be given to the matter of succession in order that the land may be occupied at all times. As a rule it would not be best to have a second planting of the same crop follow the first, but some such arrangement as early peas followed by celery, or early cabbage or potatoes followed by late beans or corn, and similar combinations, are more satisfactory. In the South as many as three crops may be grown one after the other on the same land, but at the extreme north, where the season is short, but one crop can be grown, or possibly two by some such combination as early peas followed by turnips.

PREPARATION OF THE SOIL.

Where there is considerable choice in the location of the garden plot, it is often possible to select land that will require very little special preparation. On the other hand, it may be necessary to take an undesirable soil and bring it into suitable condition, and it is generally surprising to note the change that can be wrought in a single season.

DRAINAGE.

There are very few soils that are not improved by some form of drainage. Heavy clay soils are benefited most by drainage, but sandy soils having a clay subsoil are made warmer and greatly improved by having the excess soil water removed quickly.

PLOWING.

Autumn is the time for plowing hard or stiff clay soils, especially if in a part of the country where freezing takes place, as the action of the frost during the winter will break the soil into fine particles and render it suitable for planting. Sandy loams and soils that contain a large amount of humus may be plowed in the spring, but the work should be done early in order that the soil may settle before planting. In the Southern States, where there is not sufficient frost to mellow the soil, this process must be accomplished by means of frequent cultivations, in order that the air may act upon the soil particles. It is desirable to plow the garden early, at least a few days sooner than for general field crops.

Sandy soils will bear plowing much earlier than heavy clay soils. The usual test is to squeeze together a handful, and if the soil adheres in a ball it is too wet for working. In the garden greater depth of plowing should be practiced than for ordinary farm crops, as the roots of many of the vegetables go deeply into the soil. Subsoiling will be found advantageous in most cases, as the drainage and general movement of the soil moisture will be improved thereby.

Hand spading should be resorted to only in very small gardens or where it is desirable to prepare a small area very thoroughly.

SMOOTHING AND PULVERIZING THE SOIL.

After plowing, the next important step is to smooth and pulverize the soil. If the soil be well prepared before planting, the work of caring for the crops will be very materially lessened. It is not sufficient that the land be smooth and fine on top, but the pulverizing process should extend as deep as the plowing. Some gardeners prefer to thoroughly cut the land with a disk harrow before plowing, so that when it is turned by the plow the bottom soil will be fine and mellow. After the plow the disk or cutting harrow is again brought into play and the pulverizing process completed. If the soil is a trifle too dry and contains lumps, it may

FIG. 3.—Cross section of land bedded up for early crops.

be necessary to use some form of roller or clod crusher to bring it down. For smoothing the surface and filling up depressions a float or drag made from planks or scantlings will be found serviceable.

SPECIAL PREPARATION.

For growing certain crops it has often been found advisable to prepare the ground in a special manner. Such crops as beets, radishes, and onions are sometimes grown on beds 6 to 10 feet in width and raised 6 to 8 inches, with narrow walks between, as shown in figure 3. From Baltimore southward cabbage, cauliflower, and similar crops are frequently grown on top

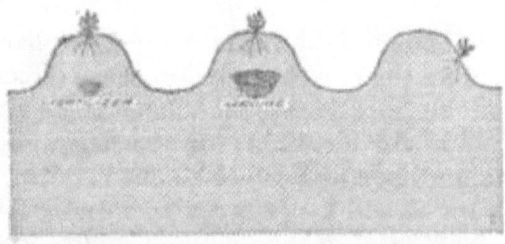

FIG. 4.—Cross section of land ridged up for early crops.

or on the side of ridges. When the plants are set on top of the ridge, better drainage for the roots is secured. When set on the south side of the ridge, greater warmth and earlier maturity will be secured, and when planted on the north side, the growth is retarded. The ridging method is illustrated by figure 4. For growing celery and a few similar crops it has often been found advisable to place the plants in furrows

FIG. 5.—Cross section of land showing trenches employed in the cultivation of celery and similar crops.

or slight trenches in order that the soil removed may be available for working in around the plants as they mature. (Fig. 5.)

FERTILIZERS.

The kind of fertilizer employed has a marked influence upon the character and quality of the vegetables produced. For the garden only those fertilizers that have been carefully prepared should be used. Fertilizers of organic composition, such as barnyard manure, should have passed through the fermenting stage before being used. The use of night soil generally is not to be recommended, as its application, unless properly treated for the destruction of disease germs, may prove dangerous to health.

BARNYARD MANURE.

For garden crops there is no fertilizer that will compare with good, well-rotted barnyard manure. In localities where a supply of such manure can not be secured it will be necessary to depend upon commercial fertilizers, but the results are rarely so satisfactory. In selecting manure for the garden, care should be taken that it does not contain any element that will be injurious to the soil. An excess of sawdust or shavings used as bedding will have a tendency to produce sourness in the soil. Chicken, pigeon, and sheep manures rank high as fertilizers, their value being somewhat greater than ordinary barnyard manures, and almost as great as some of the lower grades of commercial fertilizers. The manure from fowls is especially adapted for dropping in the hills or rows of plants.

COMMERCIAL FERTILIZERS.

Commercial fertilizers are sold under a guaranteed analysis, and generally at a price consistent with their fertilizing value. No definite rule can be given for the kind or quantity of fertilizer to be applied, as this varies with the crop and the land. At first the only safe procedure is to use a good high-grade fertilizer at the rate of from 1,000 to 2,000 pounds to the acre and note the results. Market gardeners frequently apply as much as 2,500 pounds of high-grade fertilizer per acre each year.

For further information on this subject, see Farmers' Bulletins Nos. 77 on The Liming of Soils, 192 on Barnyard Manure, and 222, Experiment Station Work, XXVIII, which contains a chapter on the Home Mixing of Fertilizers.

SEEDS AND PLANTS FOR THE GARDEN.

The supply of seeds for the garden should be secured some time in advance of the planting season. During the winter months send for the catalogue of some seedsman in your part of the country and make a selection of the kinds and quantities of seeds that you desire to plant. Garden seeds can frequently be secured of some local dealer who handles them in conjunction with other goods. Many of the garden seeds lose their vitality after one year's time, and old seeds should, as a rule, not be relied upon.

FIG. 6.—Flat, or tray, for starting plants or transplanting.

Throughout the Northern States it is desirable to start plants of certain crops before the danger of frost has passed. The simplest method of starting a limited number of early plants is by means of a shallow box placed in a south window of the dwelling. (Fig. 6.) After the plants appear, the box should be turned each day to prevent the plants drawing toward the light.

EARLY PLANTS IN HOTBEDS.

The most common method of starting early plants in the North is by means of a hotbed. The hotbed consists of an inclosure covered with sash and supplied with some form of heat, usually fermenting stable manure, to keep the plants warm and in a growing condition. As a rule, the hotbed should not be placed within the garden inclosure, but near some frequently used path or building where it can receive attention without interfering with other work. The hotbed should always face to the south, and the south side of either a dwelling, barn, tight board fence, hedge, or anything affording similar protection, will furnish a good location.

In the North the hotbed should be started in February or early in March, in order that such plants as the tomato and early cabbage may be well grown in time to plant in the open ground. There are two or three forms of hotbeds that are worthy of description, and the plans suggested may be modified to suit local conditions.

A temporary hotbed, such as would ordinarily be employed on the farm, is easily constructed by the use of manure from the horse stable as a means of furnishing the heat. Select a well-drained location,

FIG. 7.—Hotbed, showing frame and sash.

where the bed will be sheltered, shake out the manure into a broad, flat heap, and thoroughly compact it by tramping. The manure heap should be 8 or 9 feet wide, 18 to 24 inches deep when compacted, and of any desired length, according to the number of sash to be employed. The

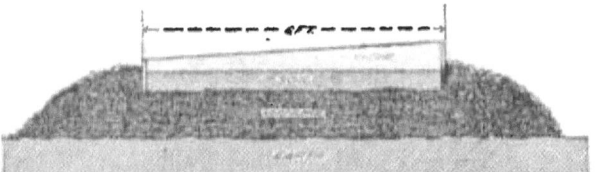

FIG. 8.—Cross section of temporary hotbed.

manure for hotbed purposes should contain sufficient litter, such as leaves or straw, to prevent its packing soggy, and should spring slightly when trodden upon.

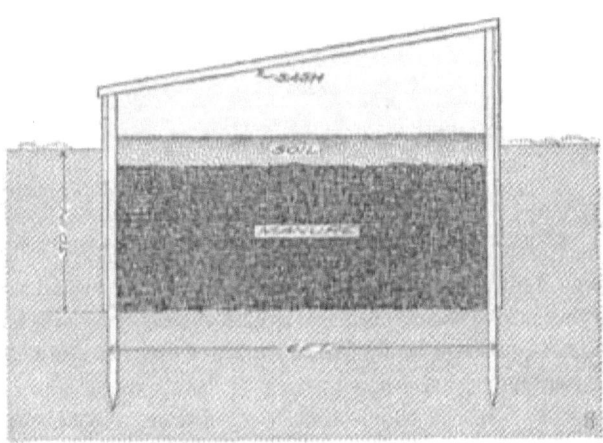

FIG. 9.—Cross section of permanent hotbed.

After the manure has been properly tramped and leveled, the frames to support the sash are placed in position facing toward the south. These frames are generally made to carry 4 standard hotbed sash, and the front board should be 4 to 6 inches lower than the back, in order that water will drain from the glass. When the frame is in position upon the manure, the surface hotbed will appear as shown in figures 7 and 8. Three to five inches of good garden loam or specially prepared soil is spread evenly over the area inclosed by the frame, the sash put on, and the bed allowed to heat. At first the temperature of the bed will run quite high, but no seeds should be planted until the soil temperature falls to 80° F., which will be in about three days.

Hotbeds having more or less permanence may be so constructed as to be heated either with fermenting manure, a stove, a brick flue, or by means of radiating pipes supplied with steam or hot water from a dwelling or other heating plant. For a permanent bed in which fermenting manure is to supply the heat, a pit 24 to 30 inches in depth should be provided. The sides and ends of the pit may be supported by brick walls or by a lining of 2-inch plank held in place by stakes. Figures 9, 10, and 11 illustrate different methods of constructing permanent hotbeds.

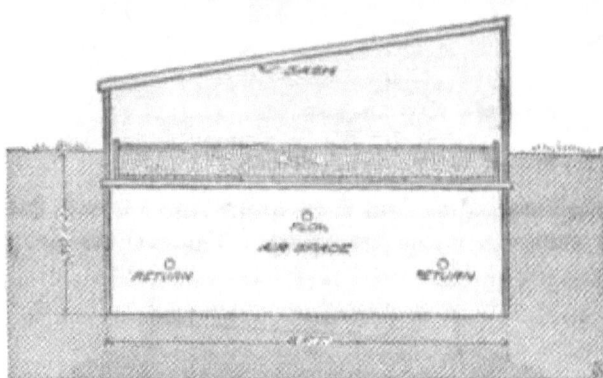

FIG. 10.—Cross section of pipe-heated hotbed.

Standard hotbed sash are 3 by 6 feet in size, and are usually constructed of white pine or cypress. As a rule, hotbed sash can be purchased cheaper than they can be made locally, and are on sale by seedsmen and dealers in garden supplies. In the colder parts of the country, in addition to glazed sash

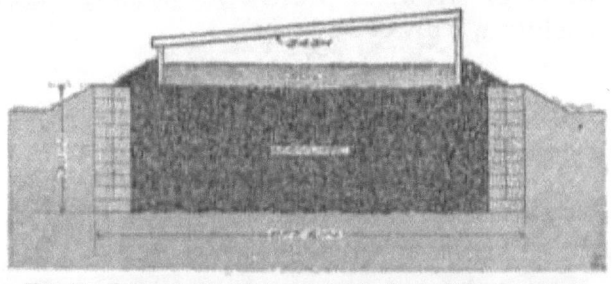

FIG. 11.—Cross section of permanent hotbed with enlarged pit.

either board shutters, straw mats, burlap, or old carpet will be required as a covering during cold nights. It is also desirable to have a supply of straw or loose manure on hand to throw over the bed in case of extremely cold weather.

During bright days the hotbed will heat very quickly from the sunshine on the glass and it will be necessary to ventilate during the early morning by slightly raising the sash on the opposite side from the wind. Care should be taken in ventilating to protect the plants from a draft of cold air. Toward evening the sash should be closed in order that the bed may become sufficiently warm before nightfall.

Hotbeds should be watered on bright days and in the morning only. Watering in the evening or on cloudy days will have a tendency to chill the bed and increase the danger from freezing. After watering, the bed should be well ventilated to dry the foliage of the plants and the surface of the soil, to prevent the plants being lost by damping-off fungus or mildew.

EARLY PLANTS IN COLD FRAMES.

The construction of cold frames is the same as for temporary hotbeds except that no manure or other heating material is provided. The frames used are similar to those shown in figure 7. Cold frames are covered by means of ordinary hotbed sash, or cotton cloth may be substituted for the sash. In the North the use of the cold frame is for hardening off plants that have been started in the hotbed, preparatory to setting them in the garden. In the South, where the weather is not so severe, the cold frame is made to take the place of the hotbed in starting early plants. The same methods of handling recommended for a hotbed should apply to a cold frame, and thorough ventilation should be maintained.

THE SEED BED.

In the broadest sense the entire garden is a seed bed, as the seeds of many of the crops are planted where they are to grow. As the term "seed bed" is used here it refers to some specially prepared place for starting plants, from which they may be transplanted to their permanent positions in the garden. The location of an outdoor seed bed should be such that it may be conveniently reached for watering, and it should be naturally protected from drying winds.

Good soil for a seed bed consists of one part of well-rotted manure, two parts of good garden loam or rotted sods, and one part of sharp, fine sand. The manure should be thoroughly rotted, but it should not have been exposed to the weather and the strength leached out of it. The addition of leaf mold or peat will tend to make the soil better adapted for seed-bed purposes. Mix all the ingredients together in a heap, stirring well with a shovel, after which the soil should be sifted and placed in boxes or in the bed ready for sowing the seed.

Weed seeds and the spores of fungous diseases that are present in the soil for a seed bed may be killed by placing the soil in pans and baking it for an hour in a hot oven.

SEED SOWING.

Garden seeds should always be sown in straight rows regardless of where the planting is made. If a window box is employed for starting early plants in a dwelling, the soil should be well firmed and then laid off in straight rows about 2 inches apart. The same method holds good for planting seeds in a hotbed, cold frame, or bed in the garden, except that the rows should be farther apart than in the window box. By planting in straight rows the seedlings will be more uniform in size and shape, and thinning and cultivating will be more easily accomplished. In all cases where the soil of the seed bed is not too wet it should be well firmed or pressed down before laying off and marking for sowing the seeds. After the seeds are sown and covered, the surface should again be firmed by means of a smooth board.

No definite rule can be given for the depth to which seeds should be planted, for the depth should vary with the kind of seed and with the character and condition of the soil. In heavy clay and moist soils the covering should be lighter than in sandy or dry soils. In all cases the depth should be uniform, and when planting seeds in boxes or a bed the grooves in which the seeds are planted should be made with the edge of a thin lath.

CARE OF THE SEED BED.

The seed bed should never be allowed to become dry, but great care should be taken that too much water is not applied. Plants require the action of air upon their roots and an excess of water in the soil will exclude the air. Too frequent and heavy waterings will cause the damping-off of the seedlings.

THE HANDLING OF PLANTS.

Successful transplanting of indoor-grown plants to the garden or field depends largely upon their proper treatment during the two weeks preceding the time of their removal. Spindling and tender plants will not withstand the exposure of the open ground so well as sturdy, well-grown plants, such as may be secured by proper handling.

HARDENING OFF.

Plants grown in a house, hotbed, or cold frame will require to be hardened off before planting in the garden. By the process of hardening off, the plants are gradually acclimated to the effects of the sun and wind so that they will stand transplanting to the open ground. Hardening off is usually accomplished by ventilating freely and by reducing the amount of water applied to the plant bed. The plant bed should not become so dry that the plants will wilt or be seriously checked in their growth. After a few days it will be possible to leave the plants uncovered during the entire day and on mild nights. By the time the plants are required for setting in the garden they should be thoroughly acclimated to outdoor conditions and can be transplanted with but few losses.

IMPORTANCE OF THINNING.

Where plants are not to be transplanted twice, but remain in the plant bed until required for setting in the garden, it may be necessary to thin them somewhat. This part of the work should be done as soon as the plants are large enough to pull, and before they begin to "draw" or become spindling from crowding.

When thinning plants in the plant bed it should be the aim to remove the centers of the thick bunches, leaving the spaces as uniform as possible. When thinning the rows of seedlings in the garden the best plants should be allowed to remain, but due consideration should be given to the matter of proper spacing. Failure to thin plants properly will invariably result in the production of an inferior crop.

EFFECTS OF TRANSPLANTING.

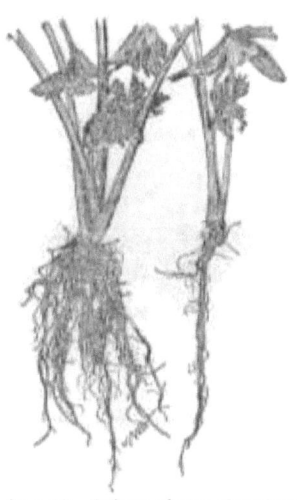

FIG. 12.—Celery plants, showing effect of transplanting on root system.

At the North, where the growing season is short, it is necessary to transplant several of the garden crops in order to secure strong plants that will mature within the limits of the growing season. In the Southern States the season is longer, and transplanting, while desirable, may not be necessary, as many crops that must be started indoors at the North can be planted in the garden where they are to remain. Transplanting should be done as soon as the seedlings are large enough to handle, and again when the plants begin to crowd one another.

Aside from producing more uniform and hardy plants, the transplanting process has several other very marked influences. Certain crops which are grown for their straight roots are often injured by having their roots bent or broken in transplanting. On the other hand, such plants as celery, which at first have a straight root and are grown for their tops, are greatly benefited by transplanting. Figure 12 shows two celery plants from the same seeding, the one on the left having been transplanted and the one on the right allowed to remain in the seed bed until time for planting in the garden. In all cases transplanting has a tendency to increase the number of small roots, and these are the main dependence of the plant at the time it is set in the open ground.

SPECIAL METHODS OF TRANSPLANTING.

A large number of garden crops, including melons, cucumbers, and beans, do not transplant readily from the seed bed to the open ground, and some special means for handling the plants must be employed where extra early planting is desired. A common practice among gardeners is to fill pint or quart berry boxes with good soil and plant a single hill in each box, as shown in figure 13.

Another method is to cut sods into pieces about 2 inches thick and 6 inches square and place them, root side upward, on the greenhouse bench or in the hotbed, the hills being planted in the loamy soil held in place by the roots of the grass. When the weather becomes sufficiently warm, and it is desired to set the plants in the garden, the berry boxes or pieces of sod are placed on a flat tray and carried to the place where the planting is to be done. Holes of sufficient size and depth are dug and the boxes or sods are simply buried at the points where it is desired to have the hills of plants. The boxes should be placed a little below the surface and fine earth worked in around the plants. If it is thought desirable, the bottoms of the boxes may be cut away when set in the garden.

FIG. 13.—Berry box used for starting and transplanting early plants.

SETTING IN THE OPEN GROUND.

A few hours before removing plants from the seed bed or plant bed they should be well watered and the water allowed to soak into the soil. This will insure a portion of the soil adhering to the roots and prevent the plants from wilting. If the plants have been properly thinned or transplanted it is often possible to run a knife or trowel between them, thus cutting the soil into cubes that are transferred with them to the garden.

Where the soil does not adhere to the roots of the plants it is well to puddle them. In the process of puddling, a hole is dug in the earth near the plant bed, or a large pail may be used for the purpose, and a thin slime, consisting of clay, cow manure, and water, is prepared. The plants are taken in small bunches and their roots thoroughly coated with this mixture by dipping them up and down in the puddle a few times. Puddling insures a coating of moist earth over the entire root system of the plant, prevents the air from reaching the rootlets while on the way to the garden, and aids in securing direct contact between the roots and the soil.

Previous to setting out plants, the land should be worked over and put in good condition, and everything should be ready for quick operations when a suitable time arrives. The rows should be measured off, but it is well to defer making the furrows or digging the holes until ready to plant, in order to have the soil fresh. The time best suited for transferring plants from the plant bed to the open ground is when there is considerable moisture in the air and clouds obscure the sun, and if the plants can be set before a shower there will be no difficulty in getting them to grow. During seasons when there is very little rain at planting time, or in irrigated regions, evening is the best time to set the plants.

It is possible to set plants in quite dry soil, provided the roots are puddled and the earth well packed about them. When water is used in setting plants it should be applied after the hole has been partially filled, and the moist earth should then be covered with dry soil to prevent baking. Where water is available for irrigation it will be sufficient to puddle the roots and then irrigate after the plants are all in place.

FIG. 14.—Cross section of land illustrating the use of the dibble in setting plants. Improperly set plant on left.

Plants should be set a trifle deeper in the garden than they were in the plant bed. The majority of plants require to be set upright, and where the dibble is used for planting care should be taken that the soil is well pressed around the roots and no air spaces left. (Fig. 14.)

TIME OF PLANTING.

No definite rule can be given regarding the time for planting seeds and plants in the garden, for the date varies with the locality and the time that it is desired to have the crop mature. A little practice will soon determine when and how often sowings should be made in order to escape frost and mature the crop at a time when it will be most useful. Certain crops will not thrive during the heated part of the summer, and their time of planting must be planned accordingly.

PROTECTION OF PLANTS.

Some plants require protection from the direct rays of the sun in summer or from cold in winter, and there are many that need special protection while they are quite small. Seedlings of many of the garden crops are unable to force their way through the crust formed on the soil after heavy rains, and it is necessary either to break the crust with a steel rake or soften it by watering.

PROTECTION FROM HEAT.

In parts of the country where the sunshine is extremely hot during a part of the summer, some plants, especially those that are grown for salad purposes, are benefited by shading. Shading is often used in the care of small plants when they are first transplanted.

Where boards are available they can be used for protecting plants that have been set in rows in the garden by placing them on the south side of the row at an angle that will cast a shadow over the plants, and holding them in place by short stakes driven in the ground, as shown in figure 15. Laths, wooden slats, cotton cloth, or shaded sash are frequently used to protect plant beds from the heat of summer.

FIG. 15.—Board used for protection of plants.

PROTECTION FROM COLD.

For protecting plants from cold in winter several kinds of materials are used, such as boards, cloth, pine boughs, straw, manure, or leaves. There are a number of crops of a tropical nature that may be grown far north, provided they are properly protected during the winter.

Several of the annual crops can be matured much earlier in the spring if they are planted in the autumn and protected during the winter. Plants of this kind can often be protected by means of boards set at an angle on the north side of the row instead of on the south, as shown in figure 15. A mulch of manure, straw, or leaves forms a good protection, but care should be taken that the mulch does not contain seeds of any kind or serious trouble will attend the further cultivation of the crop. Plants are like animals in that they require air, and care should be exercised in putting on the winter covering not to smother them. Coarse, loose materials are better for a winter covering than fine, easily compacted substances.

CULTIVATION OF GARDEN CROPS.

Frequent shallow cultivation should be employed for most garden crops, and during dry weather the depth should not exceed 2 inches. By keeping the surface soil well stirred what is termed a "dust mulch" is formed, and while this layer of finely divided soil will become quite dry it prevents the escape of moisture through the pores of the soil. A mulch consisting of fine manure, clippings from the lawn, or any similar material, spread to a distance of 10 or 12 inches around the plants will preserve the moisture; but the mulch should not be so heavy as to exclude the air.

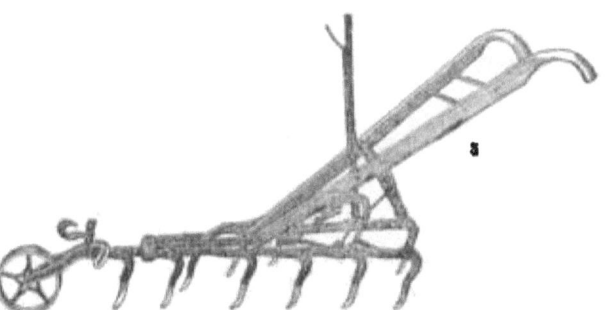

FIG. 16.—Small-tooth horse cultivator.

A crust forming over the soil after a rain or watering is detrimental to plant growth and should be broken up as soon as the land can be worked. To determine when the soil is sufficiently dry for cultivation, apply the usual test of squeezing in the hand. Sandy soils can be worked much sooner than clay soils after a rain. Too much importance can not be placed upon the matter of thorough cultivation of the garden, and if the work is promptly and properly done there will be little difficulty in controlling weeds.

TOOLS FOR USE IN THE GARDEN.

There are a number of one-horse cultivators that are especially adapted for work in the garden. These may be provided with several sizes of teeth and shovels, and are easily transformed for various kinds of work (fig. 16). In working the crops while they

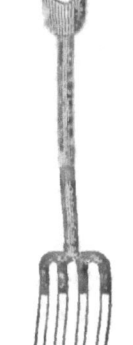

FIG. 17.—Spading fork.

FIG. 18.—Dibbles used for transplanting.

are small the harrow or smaller teeth may be used, and later when the plants become larger the size of the shovels may be increased. Many gardeners, however, prefer to use the harrow teeth at all times.

When it is desirable to ridge up the soil around a crop, the wings, or hillers, may be put on either side of the cultivator. A one-horse turning plow is useful for running off rows or throwing up ridges similar to those shown in figure 4, page 10. Aside from the horse

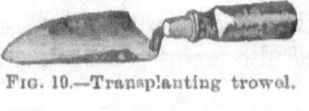

Fig. 10.—Transplanting trowel.

Fig. 20.—Onion hoe.

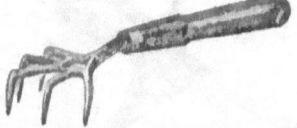

Fig. 21.—Hand weeder.

Fig. 22.—Thinning or weeding hook.

tools in general use on the farm, there are only one or two cultivators that will be required for the garden, and these are not expensive.

The outfit of hand tools for the garden should include a spade, a

Fig. 23.—Wheel hoe.

spading fork (fig. 17), a cut-steel rake, a 10-foot measuring pole, a line for laying off rows, a standard hoe, a narrow hoe, dibbles (fig. 18), a trowel (fig. 19), an assortment of hand weeders (figs. 20 to 22), a watering can, a wheelbarrow, and if the work is to be done largely by hand the outfit should also include some form of wheel hoe, of which there are a number on the market (fig. 23).

IRRIGATION OF GARDEN CROPS.

Throughout the portions of the country where rains occur during the growing season it should not be necessary to irrigate in order to produce the ordinary garden crops. In arid regions, where irrigation must be depended upon for the production of crops, the system best adapted for use in that particular locality should be employed in the garden. Wherever irrigation is practiced the water should not be applied until needed, and then the soil should be thoroughly soaked.

After irrigation, the land should be cultivated as soon as the surface becomes sufficiently dry, and no more water should be applied until the plants begin to show the need of additional moisture. Constant or excessive watering is very detrimental in every case. Apply the water at any time of the day that is most convenient and when the plants require it.

By the subirrigation method of watering, lines of farm drain tiles or perforated pipes are laid on a level a few inches below the surface of the soil. This system is especially adapted for use in back-yard gardens where city water is available and where the area under cultivation is small. Subirrigation is expensive to install, as the lines of tiles should be about 3 feet apart, or one line for each standard row.

FIG. 24.—Cross section of soil showing arrangement of tiles for subirrigation.

By connecting the tiles at one end by means of a tile across the rows the water may be discharged into the tiles at one point from a hose, and will find its way to all parts of the system, entering the soil through the openings. A cross section of soil showing the proper arrangement of tiles is shown in figure 24.

For further information on irrigation see Farmers' Bulletin No. 138, entitled "Irrigation in Field and Garden."

PRECAUTIONS TO AVOID ATTACKS OF INSECTS AND DISEASES.

In the control of insects and diseases that infest garden crops it is often possible to accomplish a great amount of good by careful sanitary management. In the autumn, after the crops have been harvested, or as fast as any crop is disposed of, any refuse that remains should be gathered and placed in the compost heap, or burned if diseased or infested with insects. Several of the garden insects find protection during the winter under boards and any loose material that may remain in the garden. Dead vines or leaves of plants are frequently covered with spores of diseases that affect those crops during the growing season, and these should be burned, as they possess very little fertilizing value.

For information on garden insects and their control address the Bureau of Entomology of this Department.

The diseases of garden crops are too numerous for attention in a publication of this nature. Specific information can be secured by addressing the Chief of the Bureau of Plant Industry of this Department.

CULTURAL HINTS FOR GARDEN CROPS.

ARTICHOKE, GLOBE.

Deep, rich sandy loam, with a liberal supply of well-rotted manure, is best suited for growing artichokes. Plant the seeds as soon as the soil is warm in the spring, and when the plants have formed three or four leaves they may be transplanted to rows 3 feet apart and 2 feet apart in the row. The plants do not produce until the second season, and in cold localities some form of covering will be necessary during the winter. This crop is not suited for cultivation north of the line of zero temperature.

Fig. 25.—Globe or bur artichoke.

After the bed is once established the plants may be reset each year by using the side shoots from the base of the old plants. If not reset the bed will continue to produce for several years, but the burs will not be so large as from new plants. The bur, or flower bud, as shown in figure 25, is the part used, and the burs should be gathered before the blossom part appears. If they are removed and no seed is allowed to form, the plants will continue to produce until the end of the season.

The heads, or burs, of the French artichoke are prepared for the table by boiling, and served with melted butter or with cream dressing.

ARTICHOKE, JERUSALEM.

The Jerusalem artichoke will grow in any good garden soil, and should be planted 3 to 4 feet apart each way, with three or four small tubers in a hill. If large tubers are used for planting they should be cut the same as Irish potatoes. Plant as soon as the ground becomes warm in the spring and cultivate as for corn. A pint of tubers cut to eyes will plant about thirty hills. The tubers will be ready for use in October, but may remain in the ground and be dug at any time during the winter.

The tubers are prepared by boiling until soft, and are served with butter or creamed. They are also used for salads and pickles.

The Jerusalem artichoke is not of great importance as a garden vegetable, and the plant has a tendency to become a weed.

ASPARAGUS.

Asparagus should have a place in every home vegetable garden where it will thrive. This crop can be grown on almost any well-drained soil, but will do best on a deep, mellow, sandy loam. There is little possibility of having the land too rich, and liberal applications of partly rotted barnyard manure should be made before the plants are set. The seeds of asparagus may be sown during the early spring in the rows where the plants are to remain and the seedlings thinned to stand 14 inches apart in the row at the end of the first season. It is usually more satisfactory to purchase two-year-old roots from some seedsman or dealer. (Fig. 26.) The price of good roots is generally about $1.25 per hundred, and one to two hundred plants will be found sufficient to supply the ordinary family. The roots should be transplanted during the late autumn or early spring.

Before setting out the plants the land should be loosened very deeply, either by subsoil plowing or deep spading. It is a good plan to remove the topsoil and spade manure into the subsoil to a depth of 14 or 16 inches; then replace the topsoil and add more manure. There are two methods of setting an asparagus bed, depending entirely upon the kind of cultivation to be employed in the garden. If horse tools are to be used, the plants should be set in rows $3\frac{1}{2}$ feet apart and 14 inches apart in the row. On the other hand, if the garden space is limited the plants should be set in a solid bed, 1 foot apart each way, and cultivated by hand. In setting asparagus the crowns should be covered to a depth of 4 or 5 inches.

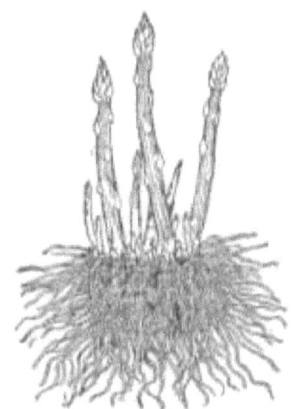

FIG. 26.—Asparagus plant.

At the North it will be desirable to mulch the asparagus bed during the winter with 3 or 4 inches of loose manure or straw. In the South the covering during the winter will not be necessary, but the bed should receive a dressing of manure or fertilizer at some time each year, preferably in the autumn.

The part of the asparagus used as a vegetable is the young shoots that are thrown up during the early spring. The shoots are removed when about 4 or 5 inches in length by cutting slightly below the surface of the ground, but care should be taken that the knife is not thrust at an angle or the crowns will be injured. If so desired, the shoots may be blanched by ridging up over the rows with loose, sandy soil or by allowing the mulch to remain and the shoots to make their way through it, but unblanched asparagus always has a better flavor than blanched, is more easily produced, and is most satisfactory for home use. Too heavy mulching has a tendency to retard the growth of the shoots by keeping the ground cold until late in the spring.

No shoots should be removed the first year the plants are set in the permanent bed, and the period of cutting should be short the second year. After the second year the plants become well established, and with proper fertilizing and care the bed will last indefinitely. During the cutting season all of the shoots should be removed, as the roots will cease to throw up shoots as soon as one is allowed to mature. When the shoots become tough and stringy, or are no longer desired for use, the cutting should cease and the tops should be allowed to grow during the summer. Late in the autumn, when the tops become dead, they can be removed and burned, the soil between the rows cultivated, and a fertilizer or mulch applied. For full information, see Farmers' Bulletin No. 61, entitled "Asparagus Culture."

There are several methods of preparing asparagus shoots for the table, the more common of which are as follows:

(1) Boil the shoots until tender in water to which a small quantity of salt has been added; serve while hot, as greens, with a little butter, vinegar, salt, and pepper.

(2) Boil as above and serve either with plain butter or creamed. The shoots can be cooked entire or cut into short pieces, and when creamed they are frequently served on toast.

BEANS.

Beans thrive best in a rather warm sandy loam, but may be grown on almost any kind of soil. For the best results the soil should not be too rich in nitrogenous matter, or the plants will run to foliage and stems at the expense of the crop of pods. Heavy clay soils are not well adapted to bean culture, owing to the tendency of the soil to bake and prevent the seedlings from coming up evenly. The bean does not draw heavily upon the soil and is suitable for rotation with other garden crops.

Beans will not withstand frost, and the first plantings in the spring are frequently lost in this manner. It is very little trouble, however, to make a planting of beans, and the first planting should be made as soon as the ground is reasonably warm; this to be followed by a second and a third planting at intervals of about a week or ten days. It sometimes happens that the first planting will be killed by frost, and that the second will come through the ground immediately after the frost and mature several days ahead of those planted to replace the ones that were killed.

There are several classes of edible beans, including both climbing and bush sorts, all of which are valuable as foods and of great commercial importance. The various types and varieties of beans are too numerous for discussion here, and a few cultural hints only will be given.

In the cultivation of beans, the general rules for the care of garden crops should be adhered to, and frequent shallow stirring of the soil practiced. For a constant supply of bunch or snap beans successive plantings should be made, the final planting being made about eight weeks before time for frost in the autumn. In the South, plantings should be made as soon as the ground begins to warm, and continue until hot weather sets in. Toward the end of summer one or two plantings should be made for a fall crop.

For the production of bunch dry beans, such as Red Kidney, White Kidney, or White Marrow, plantings may be made almost any time during the first half of the summer. This class of bean is generally planted as late as possible to have the crop ripen just before early frost in the autumn. Bunch beans are generally planted in rows 30 inches apart, and the plants allowed to stand singly 3 or 4 inches apart, or they are planted in hills of 3 to 5 plants each, 12 to 15 inches apart. Good results may be obtained from planting Kidney or Marrow beans in the cornfield alongside the hills after the corn has been cultivated once or twice.

Pole beans require a somewhat richer soil than the bunch type, and should be planted in hills 3 by 4 or 4 by 4 feet, and, as the name implies, they require a pole or some similar support. Plant the seed during the early summer. Several varieties of climbing bean may be planted in the cornfield and allowed to climb upon the hills of corn. The old-fashioned corn bean belongs to this type.

The Lima bean, both pole and bush, forms one of the most desirable products of the garden. This crop thrives best when the soil is quite rich; in fact, good Lima beans can not be grown in poor soil. They should not be planted until the soil becomes thoroughly warm. Place the seed in hills, 8 or 10 to the hill, and after the plants become established thin to 4 or 5. The hills should be 4 or 5 feet apart for the pole varieties and 2 or 3 feet apart for the dwarf or bunch varieties. It is a good plan to make up the hill with a little additional manure well mixed with the soil. Cover the beans about $1\frac{1}{2}$ inches, placing them with the eye downward.

When planting beans of any kind, the seed should not be covered to a greater depth than 2 inches when the soil is moderately dry, and if the soil is wet, the covering should be very slight.

For additional information the reader is referred to Farmers' Bulletin No. 121, entitled "Beans, Peas, and Other Legumes as Food."

BEETS.

The red garden beet may be grown in any good soil, but rich sandy loam will give the best results. Sow the seeds in the spring as soon as danger of frost has passed. Beets should be planted in drills 12 to 18 inches apart, and when the plants are well up they should be thinned to 4 or 5 inches in the row. If desirable to plant in rows 3 feet apart for horse cultivation, the seeds may be sown in a double drill with 6 inches between, leaving 30 inches for cultivation. Two ounces of beet seed are required to plant 100 feet of row, or 5 pounds to the acre. As a rule each seed ball contains more than one seed, and this accounts for beets coming up very thickly. The seed should be covered to a depth of about 1 inch. For a succession of young beets during the summer, plantings should be made every four or five weeks during the spring months. Beets intended for winter storage should not be sown until late in the summer, the crop being harvested and stored in the same manner as turnips. Sugar beets are often substituted for the ordinary garden beet, especially for winter use.

Beets are used for pickles, or boiled, sliced, and fried in butter, adding a little vinegar just before removing from the fire. The young plants are used for greens.

BORECOLE. (See KALE.)

BRUSSELS SPROUTS.

This crop is closely related to cabbage and cauliflower, and may be grown in the same manner. Instead of a single head, Brussels sprouts form a large number of small heads in the axils of the leaves.

As the heads begin to crowd, the leaves should be broken from the stem of the plant to give them more room. A few leaves should be left at the top of the stem where the new heads are being formed. Brussels sprouts are more hardy than cabbage, and in mild climates may remain in the open ground all winter, the heads being removed as desired. For winter use in cold localities, take up plants that are well laden with heads and set them close together in a pit, cold frame, or cellar, with a little soil around the roots. The uses of Brussels sprouts are similar to those of cabbage, but they are considered to be of a superior flavor.

BUR ARTICHOKE. (See ARTICHOKE, GLOBE.)

CABBAGE.

For early spring cabbage in the South, sow the seeds in an outdoor bed and transplant to the garden before January 1. In the North, plant the seeds in a hotbed during February and set the plants in the open ground as early as the soil can be worked. For a late crop in the North, plant the seeds in a bed in the open ground in May or June and transplant to the garden in July. Early cabbages require a rich, warm soil in order that they may mature early. For late cabbages the soil should be heavier and more retentive of moisture and not so rich as for the early crop, as the heads are liable to burst. Cabbages should be set in rows 30 to 36 inches apart and 14 to 18 inches apart in the row. Where the plants are set out in the autumn and allowed to remain in the ground over winter, they are usually placed on top of ridges, as shown in figure 4, page 10. Early cabbage must be used soon after it has formed solid heads, as it will not keep during hot weather.

Late cabbage may be buried in pits or stored in cellars or specially constructed houses. The usual method of storing cabbage is to dig a trench about 18 inches deep and 3 feet wide and set the cabbage upright, with the heads close together and the roots bedded in soil. As cold weather comes on, the heads are covered slightly with straw and then 3 or 4 inches of earth put on. Slight freezing does not injure cabbage, but it should not be subjected to repeated freezing and thawing. If stored in a cellar or building, the heads are generally cut from the stems and stored on slatted shelves or in shallow bins. While in storage, cabbage should be well ventilated and kept as cool as possible without freezing.

CANTALOUPE. (See MELON—MUSKMELON.)

CARDOON.

The cardoon is a thistle-like plant, very similar in appearance to the Globe artichoke, but is grown as an annual. The seeds are sown in early spring in a hotbed or cold frame and the plants transplanted later to the open ground. The cardoon should be planted in rows 3 feet apart and 18 inches apart in the row on rich soil, where it can secure plenty of moisture and make rapid growth. Toward autumn the leaves are drawn together and the center blanched in the same manner as endive. If intended for winter use, the leaves are not blanched in the garden, but the plants are lifted with considerable earth adhering to the roots and stored closely in a dark pit or cellar to blanch.

The blanched leaf stems are used for making salads, soups, and stews.

CARROT.

The culture of the carrot is practically the same as the parsnip, except that carrots are not thinned so much and are allowed to grow almost as thickly as planted. Carrots should be dug in the autumn and stored the same as parsnips or turnips. Any surplus can be fed sparingly to horses, mules, or cattle.

The roots of the carrot are used at all times of the year, mostly in soups, but they may be boiled and served with butter or creamed.

CAULIFLOWER.

Cauliflower requires a rich, moist soil, and thrives best under irrigation. Cauliflower will not withstand as much frost as cabbage. The culture is the same as for cabbage until the heads begin to develop, after which the leaves may be tied together over the heads in order to exclude the light and keep the heads white.

The tender heads of cauliflower are boiled and served with butter, or creamed, and are also used for pickling.

CELERIAC.

A large-rooted form of celery used for cooking only. Cultivate the same as celery, but banking or blanching is not required. The roots may remain in the ground until wanted for use, provided a light covering be applied to prevent freezing.

CELERY.

For the North sow the seed in a hotbed or cold frame and transplant to the open ground. Celery plants are generally improved by transplanting twice. In the South the plants are not started until late in the summer and the crop is matured during the early winter. Celery seeds are very small and are slow in germinating, and the temperature of the seed bed should be kept low. The seed bed should be especially well prepared and the seeds should not be covered to a greater depth than one-eighth of an inch. Watering should be attended to very carefully and the bed should not dry out. After the plants are up care should be taken that the bed does not become too wet and the plants damp off. Five hundred plants will be sufficient for the ordinary family, and they should be set 6 inches apart in rows 3 to 5 feet apart.

Celery requires a deep, rich, moist soil, with plenty of well-rotted barnyard manure or fertilizer and frequent shallow cultivation. In the garden celery may be planted after some early crop, such as lettuce, radishes, peas, or beans. As soon as the plants attain considerable size the leaves should be drawn up and a little soil compacted about the base of the plant to hold it upright. If the blanching is done with earth, care should be taken that the hearts of the plants do not become filled. Boards, paper, drain tiles, or anything that will exclude the light may be used for blanching, but earthing up will produce the finest flavor.

Celery may be kept for winter use by banking with earth and covering the tops by means of leaves or straw to keep it from freezing, or it may be dug and removed to a cellar, cold frame, vacant hotbed, or pit, and reset close together, with the roots bedded in earth. While in storage celery should be kept as cool as possible without freezing.

The blanched stems of celery are eaten in the raw state, and both the stems and enlarged roots are stewed and creamed. Celery seed is used for flavoring soups and pickles.

For further information on celery read Farmers' Bulletin No. 148, entitled "Celery Culture."

CHERVIL.

Under the name of chervil two distinct plants, known as salad chervil and the turnip-rooted chervil, are cultivated. The seeds of the salad chervil are sown in spring and the crop will thrive on any good garden soil. The seeds of the turnip-rooted chervil should be sown in the early autumn, but they will not germinate until the following spring.

The edible part of this plant is the root, which somewhat resembles the carrot and is used in the same manner. The leaves are used the same as parsley for garnishing and in flavoring soups.

CHICORY.

Chicory is grown for two or three purposes. The root of this plant is the common adulterant of coffee, and large quantities are used for this purpose. The commercial growing of chicory is confined to a few sections, as the crop will not thrive on every kind of soil.

A deep, rich loam, without excessive amounts of clay or sand, is desirable, and soil that is not too rich in nitrogenous matter is best suited to the production of roots.

The roots of chicory are frequently placed in soil under a greenhouse bench or in a warm cellar and covered with a foot or more of straw, or with a light covering of straw and then several inches of warm manure. Under this covering the leaves will be formed in a solid head, which is known on the market as witloof.

Chicory has run wild in some parts of the country and is considered a bad weed. The handsome blue flowers of the chicory, which are borne the second season, are very attractive.

As a pot herb chicory is used like spinach, but the leaves should be boiled in two waters to remove the bitter taste. As a salad the roots are dug in the autumn and planted in cellars or under a greenhouse bench, where they produce an abundance of blanched leaves, which are eaten raw. The blanched leaves are also boiled and used as greens.

CHIVE.

This is a small onion-like plant having flat, hollow leaves which are used for flavoring soups. The chive rarely forms seeds, and it is propagated by the bulbs, which grow in clusters. (Fig. 27.) The leaves may be cut freely and are soon replaced by others.

CIBOL. (See ONION.)
CITRON.

The citron is a type of watermelon with solid flesh which is used for preserves and sweetpickles. The rind of the watermelon is frequently substituted for citron. The cultivation of the citron is the same as for the watermelon.

CIVE. (See CHIVE.)
COLLARDS.

The culture and uses of collards are the same as for cabbage and kale. Collards withstand the heat better than either cabbage or kale, and a type known as Georgia collards is highly esteemed in the Southern States. Collards do not form a true head, but instead a loose rosette of leaves, which, when blanched, are very tender and of delicate flavor.

CORN SALAD.

Corn salad is also known as lamb's-lettuce and fetticus. Sow the seed during the early spring in drills 14 to 18 inches apart and cultivate the same as for lettuce or mustard. For an extra early crop the seed may be planted during the autumn and the plants covered lightly during the winter. In the Southern States the covering will not be necessary and the plants will be ready for use during February and March. The leaves are frequently used in their natural green state, but they may be blanched by covering the rows with anything that will exclude the light. Corn salad is used as a salad in place of lettuce, or mixed with lettuce or water cress. The flavor of corn salad is very mild, and it is improved by mixing with some other salad plant for use. It is also boiled with mustard for greens.

FIG. 27.—Chive.

CORN, SWEET.

Plant sweet corn as soon as the soil is warm in the spring, and make successive plantings every two weeks until July, or the same result can be attained to some extent by a careful selection of early, medium, and late varieties. Plant the seeds in drills 3 feet apart and thin to a single stalk every 10 to 14 inches, or plant 5 to 6 seeds in hills 3 feet apart each way, and thin out to 3 to 5 stalks in a hill. Cover the seeds about 2 inches deep. Cultivate frequently and keep down all weeds, removing suckers from around the base of the stalk.

Sweet corn should be planted on rich land, and the method of cultivation is practically the same as for field corn, but should be more thorough. There are a number of good early varieties, and for a midsummer and late sort there is none better than Stowell's Evergreen.

CRESS.

Under the name of cress there are two forms, the water cress and the upland cress. The upland cress, sometimes called peppergrass, is easily grown from seed sown in drills a foot apart. As the plants last but a short time, it will be necessary to make a sowing every few days if a continuous supply is desired.

Water cress can be grown all the year in small open ditches containing running spring water. It is best and most easily produced in water from rather warm springs in limestone regions. A sufficient supply for family use can be grown in a small spring-fed brook, and the plants may be started either from small pieces of plants or from seed. Cress is used in salads, to which it imparts a pleasant pungency.

CUCUMBER

The soil for cucumbers should be a rich sandy loam, rather moist, but not wet. Plant in hills 4 feet apart each way as soon as all danger of frost is past. It is a good plan to work thoroughly a shovelful of well-rotted manure or a small handful of fertilizer into each hill in addition to the regular manuring of the land. The manure in the hill will give the plants a good start. Cucumbers are frequently planted in drills about 7 feet apart and thinned to 12 or 18 inches apart in the row. If it is desirable to secure extra early cucumbers, the plants may be started in a hotbed and transplanted to the garden by means of berry boxes. (Fig. 13.) At the South, cucumbers are planted in the open ground as early as February or March. Cucumber seedlings are easily injured by cold, even where no frost occurs, and throughout the northern part of the country the planting should be deferred until the soil is warm.

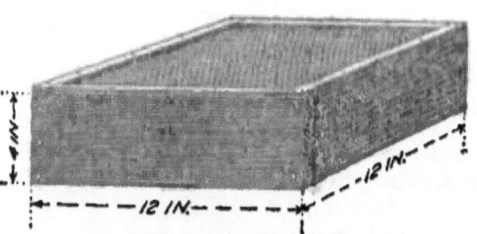

FIG. 28.—Device for protecting young cucumber plants.

While young the cucumber plants are frequently destroyed by a small beetle that attacks the lower part of the stem and the under side of the leaves. To preserve the plants some remedy will be necessary, and, where only a few hills are grown for family use the beetles may be kept off by covering the plants with frames over which fly screen or mosquito netting has been stretched, as shown in figure 28. Another method of protecting the plants is to set an arch of wire or one-half of a barrel hoop over the hill and spread a piece of mosquito netting over this support. The edges of the netting may be held down by covering with earth, and as soon as the plants are beyond danger of attack the netting may be stored for future use.

For further information on the protection of cucumber plants from the striped beetle see Circulars 31 and 59 of the Bureau of Entomology.

Cucumbers should receive frequent shallow cultivation until the vines begin to run freely; after this very little attention is required except to pull out stray weeds as they may appear. In order to keep the vines in good bearing condition, no fruit should be allowed to ripen, and when grown for pickles the fruits should all be removed while quite small.

As cucumbers are subject to several diseases, the old vines and fruits should all be destroyed and the crop should not be planted two years in succession on the same land. As a rule garden cucumbers and melons will not be greatly injured by diseases. Full information on this subject can be secured by consulting Farmers' Bulletin No. 231, entitled "Spraying for Cucumber and Melon Diseases."

DANDELION.

Sow the seed of dandelion in spring in drills 18 inches apart, covering it one-half inch deep. Thin the plants to about 12 inches apart and give good clean cultivation throughout the summer. In the colder parts of the country it may be desirable to mulch slightly during the winter to prevent the plants heaving out of the soil. Early the following spring the plants will be ready for use as greens, but they are greatly improved if blanched by setting two boards in the form of an inverted letter V over the row. The blanching not only makes the leaves more tender but destroys a part of the bitter taste. Dandelion greens should be boiled in two waters to remove the bitterness.

EGGPLANT.

The plants for this crop should be started and handled in the same manner as described for the tomato. After the weather has become settled and the ground quite warm, set the plants in the garden in rows 3 feet apart and 2 feet apart in the row. The soil best adapted to the production of eggplant is a fine, rich sandy loam and should be well drained. Cultivate freely and keep the plants growing rapidly. Many growers believe that fresh stable manure should not be used in connection with the growing of eggplant and that the land should not contain unfermented vegetable matter to any extent.

Eggplant is used in several ways, among which are the following: Peel and cut into slices one-half inch thick, soak in salt water one hour; boil until tender; then coat with rolled crackers or flour and fry in butter or fat. Another method is to steam or bake the eggplant whole and serve in the shell, the pulp being eaten with salt, pepper, and butter.

ENDIVE.

The endive is a form of chicory. Sow the seeds thinly in drills, and when the plants are well established thin to 8 inches. Water and cultivate thoroughly in order that a good growth of leaves may be made. When the leaves are 6 to 8 inches in length draw them together and tie them so the heart will blanch. The leaves should not be tied up while wet or decay will follow. The heads should be used as soon as blanched. For winter use sow the seeds rather late and remove the plants, with a ball of earth adhering to the roots, to a cellar or cold frame, and blanch during the winter as required for use.

Endive is used as a salad at times of the year when lettuce and similar crops are out of season.

FETTICUS. (See CORN SALAD.)

FLAG. (See LEEK.)

FRENCH ARTICHOKE. (See ARTICHOKE, GLOBE.)
GARLIC.

Garlic is closely allied to the onion, but will remain in the ground from one year to another if undisturbed. Garlic is planted by setting the small bulbs, or cloves, either in the autumn or early spring. The culture is practically the same as for the onion. The bulbs are used for flavoring purposes.

GEORGIA COLLARDS. (See COLLARDS.)
GERMAN CELERY. (See CELERIAC.)
GROUND CHERRY. (See PHYSALIS.)
GUMBO. (See OKRA.)
HORSE-RADISH.

Horse-radish will thrive best in a deep, rich soil, where there is plenty of moisture. The rows should be 3 feet apart and the plants 12 to 18 inches apart in the row. Tops cut from large roots or pieces of small roots are used for planting. A comparatively few hills of horse-radish will be sufficient for family use, and the roots required for starting can be secured of seedsmen for 25 or 30 cents a dozen. This crop will require no particular cultivation except to keep down the weeds, and is inclined to become a weed itself if not controlled.

The large fleshy roots are prepared for use by peeling and grating. The grated root is treated with a little salt and vinegar and served as a relish with meats, oysters, etc. The roots should be dug during the winter or early spring before the leaves start. After being treated with salt and vinegar the grated root may be bottled for summer use.

HUSK TOMATO. (See PHYSALIS.)
IRISH POTATO. (See POTATO, IRISH.)
JERUSALEM ARTICHOKE. (See ARTICHOKE, JERUSALEM.)
KALE, OR BORECOLE.

There are a large number of forms of kale, and these are thought by some to be the original type of the cabbage. Kale does not form a head and has convoluted leaves and thick leaf stems. It is cultivated the same as cabbage, but may be set somewhat closer. This crop is very hardy and will live through the winter in the open ground in localities where freezing is not too severe. The flavor of kale is improved by frost.

Kale is used for greens during the winter, and as a substitute for cabbage.

KOHL-RABI.

Kohl-rabi belongs to the same class as cabbage and cauliflower, but presents a marked variation from either. It is, perhaps, half-way between the cabbage and turnip, in that its edible part consists of the swollen stem of the plant, as shown in figure 29. For an early crop, plant and cultivate the same as for early cabbage. For a late crop or for all seasons in the South the seed may be sown in drills where the crop is to be grown and thinned

Fig. 29.—Kohl-rabi.

to about 8 inches apart in the row. The rows should be from 18 to 36 inches apart, according to the kind of cultivation employed. The fleshy stems should be used while they are young and quite tender.

Prepare kohl-rabi for the table in the same manner as turnips, which it very much resembles when cooked.

LAMB'S-LETTUCE. (See CORN SALAD.)

LEEK.

This plant belongs to the same class as does the onion, but requires somewhat different treatment. Leeks can be grown on any good garden soil and are usually sown in a shallow trench. The plants should be thinned to stand about 4 inches apart in the row and the cultivation should be similar to that for onions. After the plants have attained almost full size the earth is drawn around them to the height of 6 or 8 inches to blanch the fleshy stem. The leek does not form a true bulb like the onion, but the stem is uniformly thick throughout. Leeks are marketed in bunches like young onions, and they may be stored the same as celery for winter.

Leeks are used for flavoring purposes and are boiled and served with a cream dressing the same as young onions.

LETTUCE.

This crop attains its best development in a rich sandy loam in which there is plenty of organic matter. Lettuce thrives best during the early spring or late autumn and will not withstand the heat of summer. In order that the leaves may be crisp and tender, it is necessary to force the growth. The usual method of growing lettuce for home use is to sow the seeds broadcast in a bed and remove the leaves from the plants as rapidly as they become large enough for use. A much better method is either to thin or transplant the seedlings and allow the plants to form rather compact heads and then cut the entire plant for use.

In the Southern States the seeds may be sown during the autumn and the plants allowed to remain in the ground over winter. At the North the seeds may be sown in a hotbed or cold frame and the seedlings transplanted to the open ground, or the seeding may be in rows in the garden and the plants thinned to 5 or 6 inches in the row. Lettuce may be grown in rows about 12 inches apart. In order to produce crisp and tender lettuce during the summer months, it may be necessary to provide some form of partial shading.

MELON—MUSKMELON.

A sandy loam with plenty of well-rotted barnyard manure will be found to be adapted to the cultivation of the muskmelon. When commercial fertilizer is used instead of manure, it should be applied at the rate of from 500 to 1,000 pounds of high-grade material to the acre. The muskmelon requires a long season to develop and is easily injured by frost or even by cool weather.

For an early crop in the North, start the hills in a hotbed in berry boxes and plant out after the soil becomes warm. For the main crop throughout the country the seeds are planted in the open ground as soon as the soil is reasonably warm. Place the hills about 6 feet apart each way and 8 or 10 seeds in a hill. After the plants become established, thin out all but the four best ones. Another method is to sow in drills and thin to single plants 18 inches to 2 feet apart. Good cultivation should be maintained until the vines interfere.

Muskmelons are subject to a number of diseases, and while the plants are quite young they are attacked by the cucumber beetle. The same precautionary measures as are recommended in the case of cucumbers should be observed for both troubles.

There are a number of good varieties of muskmelons, and the Rocky Ford, or Netted Gem, is one of the best.

MELON—WATERMELON.

The cultivation of the watermelon is practically the same as for the muskmelon, except that the plants grow larger and require more room for development than those of the muskmelon. Watermelons require that the soil should contain a larger percentage of sand than muskmelons, and that the land should be quite rich. Watermelons should be planted 10 feet each way between the hills, or in drills 10 feet apart and thinned to 3 feet apart in the drills. The watermelon seedlings must be protected from the cucumber beetle until the foliage becomes toughened.

MULTIPLIER ONION. (See ONION.)

MUSKMELON. (See MELON—MUSKMELON.)

MUSTARD.

Almost any good soil will produce a crop of mustard. The basal leaves of mustard are used for greens, and as the plants require but a short time to reach the proper stage for use frequent sowings should be made. Sow the seeds thickly in drills as early as possible in the spring, or for late use sow the seeds in September or October. The forms of white mustard, of which the leaves are often curled and frilled, are generally used. Mustard greens are cooked like spinach.

NEW ZEALAND SPINACH.

The plant known as New Zealand spinach is not a true spinach, but grows much larger and should be planted in rows 3 feet apart, with the plants 12 to 18 inches apart in the row. Some difficulty may be experienced in getting the seeds to germinate, and they should be soaked one or two hours in hot water before planting. New Zealand spinach is satisfactory for growing in warm climates, as it withstands heat better than the ordinary spinach. The fleshy leaves and tender stems are cooked the same as spinach.

OKRA, OR GUMBO.

Sow the seeds of okra in the open after the ground has become quite warm, or start the plants in berry boxes in a hotbed and transplant them to the garden after all danger of frost is past. The rows should be 4 feet apart for the dwarf sorts and 5 feet apart for the tall kinds, with the plants 2 feet apart in the row. Okra does best in rather rich land and requires frequent shallow cultivation until the plants cover the ground.

The young pods are the part used, and these are employed principally in soups, to which they impart a pleasant flavor and mucilaginous consistency. If the pods are removed from the plants and none allowed to ripen, the plants will continue to produce pods until killed by frost, but the best pods are grown on young plants. Okra pods can be dried or canned for winter use.

For further information on okra, see Farmers' Bulletin No. 232, entitled "Okra: Its Culture and Uses."

ONIONS.

A rich sandy loam containing plenty of humus is best suited to the production of onions. This crop has been grown very successfully on the muck beds of the States bordering on the Great Lakes. The usual plan on a small scale is to plant one or two quarts of "sets" in drills 12 to 18 inches apart and 2 to 3 inches apart in the row, covering about an inch deep. When a large acreage is to be grown the soil is made very fine and smooth and the onion seed is sown in drills and then thinned to 2 or 3 inches apart after the plants become established. For the best results from seed, sow in cold frames during the fall or in a hotbed in the early spring and transplant to the open ground as soon as the soil is in good condition to work. Figure 30 shows an ideal stand of onions.

FIG. 30.—Onions.

FIG. 31.—Cross section of Potato or Multiplier onion.

Onions require frequent shallow cultivation and it may be necessary to resort to hand work in order to keep the crop free from weeds. If it is desired to hasten the maturity of the bulbs by preventing continued growth of the tops, this may be accomplished by rolling an empty barrel over the rows and breaking down the tops. After the tops are practically dead the onion bulbs should be removed from the soil and spread in a dry, well ventilated place to cure, after which they may be stored in crates or bags for winter use.

There are several kinds of onions that may remain in the soil over winter. The Multiplier or Potato onion can be planted from sets in the autumn and will produce excellent early green onions. This type of onion is peculiar in that a large onion contains a number of distinct hearts, as shown in

FIG. 32.—Top or Tree onion, producing bulblets on top of stem.

figure 31, and if planted will produce a number of small onions. On the other hand, a small onion contains but one heart and will produce a large onion. A few large onions should be planted each year to produce the sets for the following year's planting.

Another variety is the Top or Tree onion, which produces a large number of bulblets above ground on the top of a stem, as shown in figure 32. The small bulbs can be planted in the autumn and will produce onions the following season.

The small onion known as the shallot is frequently planted in early spring for its small bulbs, or "cloves," which are used in the same manner as onions. The leaves are also used for flavoring.

The cibol or Welsh onion is grown either from seeds or bulbs. Where the climate is not severe, the seed may be sown in the autumn, and the leaves, which are used for flavoring soups, will be ready for use in the spring.

For additional information on the onion, see Farmers' Bulletin No. 39, entitled "Onion Culture."

OYSTER-PLANT. (See SALSIFY.)

PARSLEY.

After soaking the seeds of parsley for a few hours in warm water, they may be sown in the same manner as celery seed and the plants transplanted to the open ground. At the North, parsley will live over winter in a cold frame or pit, and in the South it will thrive in the open ground during the winter, but it can not withstand the heat of summer. The plants should be set in rows 12 inches apart and every 4 inches in the row.

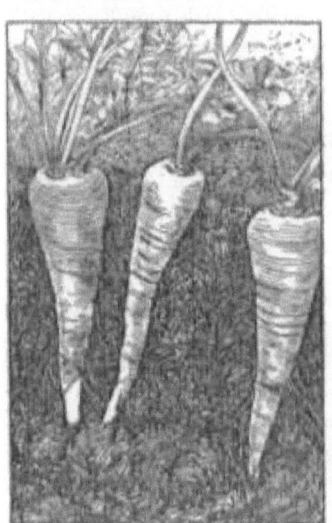

FIG. 33.—Parsnips.

The leaves of parsley are used for garnishings around meats and for flavoring soups.

PARSNIP.

Sow the seeds of parsnip as early as convenient in the spring in drills 18 inches to 3 feet apart. Thin the plants to stand 3 inches apart in the rows. The parsnip requires a rich soil and frequent cultivation. The roots can be dug late in the fall and stored in cellars or pits, or allowed to remain where grown and dug as required for use. (Fig. 33.) It is considered best to allow the roots to become frozen in the ground, as the freezing improves their flavor. As soon as the roots begin to grow the following spring they will no longer be fit for use. All roots not used during the winter should be dug and removed from the garden, as they will produce seed the second season and become of a weedy nature. When the parsnip has been allowed to run wild the root is considered to be poisonous.

To prepare parsnip for the table, boil the roots until tender and then cut in slices and brown in butter. They may also be roasted with meat the same as potatoes.

PEAS.

Garden peas require a rather rich and friable soil with good drainage in order that the first plantings may be made early in the spring. Fertilizers that are high in nitrogenous matter should not be applied to the land immediately before planting, as they will have a tendency to produce too great growth of vines at the expense of pods. Land that has been well manured the previous year will be found satisfactory without additional fertilizer. A sandy loam is to be preferred for growing peas, but a good crop may be produced on clay soils; however, the pods will be a few days later in forming. Peas are easily grown and form one of the most palatable of garden products.

The first plantings should be of such varieties as Alaska or Gradus, which make a small but quick growth, and may or may not be provided with supports. The dwarf sorts like American Wonder come on later, require very little care, and produce peas of fine quality. The tall-growing sorts of the Telephone type are desirable for still later use on account of their large production and excellent quality. Sugar peas have tender pods and if gathered very young the pods may be eaten in the same manner as snap beans. In order to maintain a continuous supply of fresh peas, plantings should be made every ten days or two weeks during the spring months, beginning as soon as the ground can be worked. In the extreme South peas may be grown during the entire winter.

For the best results peas should be planted in the bottom of a furrow 6 inches in depth and the seeds covered with not more than 2 or 3 inches of soil. If the soil is heavy the covering should be less than 2 inches. After the plants attain a height of 4 or 5 inches the soil should be worked in around them until the trench is filled. The rows for peas should be 3 feet apart for the dwarf sorts and 4 feet apart for the tall kinds. A pint of seed will plant about 100 feet of single row. Many growers follow the practice of planting in a double row with a 6-inch space between. The double-row method is especially adapted for the varieties that require some form of support, as a trellis can be placed between the two rows.

Brush stuck in the ground will answer for a support for the peas to climb upon. Three-foot poultry netting makes a desirable trellis. If peas are planted for autumn use, the earliest varieties should be employed.

PEPPERS.

Plant the seed of peppers in a hotbed, and transplant to the open ground as soon as it is warm, or sow the seeds in the garden after all danger of frost is past. When grown in the garden the plants should be in rows 3 feet apart and 15 to 18 inches apart in the row. The plants require about the same treatment as the tomato. There are a large number of varieties of the pepper, including the large sweet sorts used for pickling and the small hot kinds, such as Chili, Tabasco, and Cayenne.

PEPPERGRASS. (See CRESS.)

PHYSALIS.

The physalis is also known as the ground-cherry or husk-tomato. Sow the seed in a hotbed or cold frame and transplant to the garden after danger of frost is past, or the seeds may be sown in the row where the plants are to remain and thinned to 12 or 18 inches. No particular care is required except to keep them free from weeds. There are a large number of varieties of the physalis, and the fruits vary in size and color. The variety commonly used in gardens produces a bright-yellow fruit, which is about the size of an ordinary cherry. Toward fall the fruits will drop to the ground and will be protected for some time by their husks. If gathered and placed in a cool place the fruits will keep for a long time. The physalis will self-sow and may become a weed, but it is easily controlled. A few of the volunteer plants may be lifted in the spring and placed in rows instead of making a special sowing of seed. Ten plants will produce all the husk-tomatoes desired by the average family. The fruits are excellent for making preserves and marmalade.

PIE-PLANT. (See RHUBARB.)

POTATO, IRISH.

A rich, sandy loam is best suited to the production of Irish potatoes, and the fertilizers employed should contain high percentages of potash. The main crop of Irish potatoes for family use should be grown elsewhere, but a small area of early ones properly belongs in the garden. The preparation of the soil should be the same as for general garden crops.

Early potatoes should be planted as early in the spring as it is feasible to work the land, irrespective of locality. This will require planting in January in the extreme Southern States, and as late as May in the extreme Northern States. Late potatoes are extensively grown in the North, and the planting should be done late in May or during June. The rows should be $2\frac{1}{2}$ to 3 feet apart, and the hills 14 to 18 inches apart in the row. Lay off the rows with a one-horse plow or lister, and drop the seed, one or two pieces in a place, in the bottom of the furrow. Cover the seed to a depth of about 4 inches, using a hoe or a one-horse plow for the purpose. One to three weeks will be required for the potatoes to come up, depending entirely upon the temperature of the soil. The ground may freeze slightly after the planting has been done, but so long as the frost does not reach the seed potatoes no harm will result, and growth will begin as soon as the soil becomes sufficiently warm.

As soon as the potatoes appear above the ground and the rows can be followed, the surface soil should be well stirred by means of one of the harrow-toothed cultivators. Good cultivation should be maintained throughout the growing season, with occasional hand hoeing, if necessary, to keep the ground free from weeds. Toward the last the soil may be well worked up around the plants to hold them erect and protect the tubers from the sun after the vines begin to die.

After digging the potatoes they should not be allowed to lie exposed to the sun or to any light while in storage, as they soon become green and unfit for table use. Early potatoes especially should not be stored in a damp place during the heated part of the summer, and will keep best if covered with straw in a cool, shady shed until the autumn weather sets in, after which they can be placed in a dry cellar or buried in the open ground. The ideal temperature for keeping Irish potatoes is between 36° and 40° F., but they will not withstand any freezing.

POTATO ONION. (See ONION.)

POTATO, SWEET.

The sweet potato is of a tropical nature and succeeds best in the warm, sandy loam soils of the Southern States. Sweet potatoes are, however, grown commercially as far north as the southern line of the State of Pennsylvania, and for family use even in southern New York and Michigan. A warm, loose sandy soil is best adapted to the production of sweet potatoes, and good drainage is essential. In order to improve the drainage conditions, it is customary to set the plants on top of ridges which are thrown up by means of a plow, two furrows being turned together. For best results the soil should be well fertilized throughout, but in commercial sweet potato culture the plan is frequently adopted of placing the fertilizer or manure in a furrow and then turning the ridge up over it, as shown in figure 4. The manure should be evenly distributed, and it is advisable to run a cultivator once or twice in the furrow to mix the manure with the soil. Too much manure in one spot under the hill will produce a large growth of vine at the expense of the potatoes.

Toward the northern part of the area over which sweet potatoes are grown it is necessary to start the plants in a hotbed in order that the length of season may be sufficient to mature the crop. The roots that are too small for marketing are used for seed, and these are bedded close together in the hotbed and covered with about 2 inches of sand or fine soil, such as leaf mold. The seed should be bedded about five or six weeks before it will be safe to set the plants in the open ground, which is usually about May 15 or May 20. Toward the last the hotbed should be ventilated very freely in order to harden off the plants.

The ridges for planting sweet potatoes should be 3 to 5 feet apart and the plants about 14 inches apart in the row. Cultivate sufficiently to keep the surface soil loose and free from weeds, and the vines will soon cover the ground, after which no cultivation will be necessary. In the warmer parts of the country the seed is not bedded, but is cut in small pieces and planted in the ridges instead of plants. After the plants come up and begin to make vines freely, pieces of the vines are removed and used as cuttings for planting additional areas, the cuttings taking root and growing the same as plants grown from seed. In this manner 3 and 4 plantings are made, the last being as late as the middle of July. If a rainy spell be selected for making and planting the cuttings, very few will fail to grow, and an excellent crop may be produced.

To the north, sweet potatoes are dug as soon as the vines are nipped by frost. In the South the potatoes are allowed to remain in the ground until a convenient time for handling them, and in Florida or Texas they are frequently left until required for use. Sweet potatoes should be dug on a bright, drying day when the soil is not too wet. On a small scale they may be dug with a spading fork, and great care should be taken that the roots do not become bruised or injured in the process of handling. It is desirable that the roots should lie exposed for two or three hours to dry thoroughly, after which they may be placed in a warm, well ventilated room to cure for several days. The proper temperature for curing sweet potatoes is from 80° to 90° F. and 45° or 55° F. afterwards. A small crop may be cured around the kitchen stove, and later stored in a dry room where there will be no danger of their becoming too cold. Sweet potatoes should be handled as little as possible, especially after they have been cured.

Sweet potatoes are used the same as Irish potatoes, and may also be employed in making pies the same as squash. For further information the reader should obtain Farmers' Bulletin No. 129, entitled "Sweet Potatoes."

PUMPKIN.

The true pumpkin is hardly to be considered as a garden crop, and, as a rule, should be planted among the field corn. Plant where the hills of corn are missing and cultivate with the corn.

RADISH.

The radish is quite hardy and may be grown throughout the winter in hotbeds at the North, in cold frames in the latitude of Washington, and in the open ground in the South. For the home garden the seed should be sown in the open ground as soon as the soil is moderately warm. Plant in drills 12 to 18 inches apart, and as soon as the plants are up thin them slightly to prevent crowding. Radishes require to be grown on a quick, rich soil, and some of the earlier sorts can be matured in two to three weeks after planting. If the radishes grow slowly they will have a pungent flavor and will not be fit for table use. For a constant supply successive plantings should be made every two weeks, as the roots lose their crispness and delicate flavor if allowed to remain long in the open ground. As a rule a large percentage of radish seed will grow, and it is often possible by careful sowing to avoid the necessity of thinning, the first radishes being pulled as soon as they are of sufficient size for table use, thus making room for those that are a little later. Radishes will not endure hot weather and are suited to early spring and late autumn planting.

There are a number of varieties of winter radishes, the seed of which may be planted the latter part of summer and the roots pulled and stored for winter use. These roots should remain in the ground as long as possible without frosting and should then be dug and stored the same as turnips. This type of radish will not compare with the earlier summer varieties, which may be easily grown in a hotbed or cold frame during the winter. One ounce of radish seed is sufficient to plant 100 feet of row, and when grown on a large scale 10 to 12 pounds of seed will be required to the acre.

RHUBARB.

The soil for rhubarb should be deep, and there is little danger of having it too rich. Like asparagus the seedling plants of rhubarb can be grown and transplanted. Ten to twelve good hills are sufficient to produce all the rhubarb required by the average family, and these are most easily established by planting pieces of roots taken from another bed. Good roots may be secured from dealers and seedsmen at about $1.50 a dozen. The old hills may be divided in the early spring or late fall by digging away the earth on one side and cutting the hill in two with a sharp spade, the part removed being used to establish a new hill.

The usual method of planting rhubarb is to set the plants in a single row along the garden fence, and the hills should be about 4 feet apart. If more than one row is planted the hills should be 3½ or 4 feet each way. The thick leaf stems are the part used, and none should be pulled from the plants the first year after setting. Rhubarb should receive the same treatment during winter as asparagus, and the plants should never be allowed to ripen seed. The roots may be brought into the greenhouse, pit, cold frame, or cellar during the winter and forced. Rhubarb does not thrive in warm climates.

The use of rhubarb is principally during the early spring for making pies and sauces, and the stems may be canned for winter use.

RUTA-BAGA.

The culture of the ruta-baga is the same as for the turnip, except that the former requires more room and a longer period for its growth. The roots are quite hardy and will withstand considerable frost. The ruta-baga is used like the turnip, and also for stock feed. Two pounds of seed are required for one acre.

SALAD CHERVIL. (See CHERVIL.)

SALSIFY, OR VEGETABLE OYSTER.

Sow seeds of salsify during the spring in the same manner as for parsnips or carrots. At the South, a sowing may be made in summer to produce roots for winter use. One ounce of seed is required to plant 100 feet of row, and on a large scale 10 pounds to the acre. After the plants are well established they should be thinned sufficiently to prevent their crowding. The cultivation should be the same as for parsnips or carrots, and frequent use of a wheel hoe will avoid the necessity for hand weeding. Salsify may be dug in the autumn and stored or allowed to remain in the ground during the winter, as its treatment is the same as for parsnips. Salsify is a biennial, and if the roots are not dug before the second season they will throw up stems and produce seed. It is of a weedy nature and care should be taken that it does not run wild by seeding freely.

Salsify is deserving of more general cultivation, as it is one of the more desirable of the root crops for the garden. The uses of salsify are similar to those of the parsnip, and when boiled and afterwards coated with rolled crackers and fried in butter it has a decided oyster flavor, from which the name vegetable oyster is derived.

SCALLION. (See ONION.)

SHALLOT. (See ONION.)

SPINACH.

Spinach thrives in a rather cool climate and attains its best development in the Middle South, where it can be grown in the open ground during the winter. Large areas of spinach are grown near Norfolk, Va., cuttings being made at any time during the winter when the fields are not frozen or covered with snow. When the weather moderates in the early spring, the plants make a new growth, and a large crop of early greens is available. (Fig. 34.)

North of the latitude of Norfolk, spinach can be planted in the autumn and carried over winter by mulching with straw or leaves. Sow the seeds of spinach in drills 1 foot apart at the rate of 1 ounce to 100 feet of row, or 10 to 12 pounds to the acre. To produce good spinach, a rich loam which will give the plants a quick growth is required. As ordinarily grown, spinach occupies the land during the autumn and winter only and does not interfere with summer cultivation.

FIG. 34.—Spinach plant in proper condition for cutting.

Spinach is an easily grown garden crop, and there is, perhaps, no other of its kind that will give as good satisfaction. Three or four ounces of seed, planted in the autumn after a summer crop has been harvested from the land, will produce an abundance of greens for the average family during the late autumn and early spring. In gathering spinach the entire plant is removed rather than merely cutting off the leaves. The larger plants are selected first, and the smaller or later ones are thus given room to develop. No thinning is required if this plan of harvesting is practiced.

SQUASH.

There are two types of the squash, the bush varieties, which may be planted in hills 4 or 5 feet apart each way, and the running varieties, which will require from 8 to 16 feet for their development. Squashes may properly be grown in the garden, as 3 or 4 hills will produce all that are required for family use. They require practically the same soil and cultural methods as the muskmelon. A number of varieties are used during the summer in the same manner as vegetable marrow, but squashes are principally used during the winter, in much the same way as pumpkins, to which they are superior in many respects. Squashes are also used extensively for pie purposes. The varieties known as Hubbard and Boston Marrow are most commonly grown.

Squashes, like pumpkins, should be handled carefully to avoid bruising, and should be stored in a moderately warm but well ventilated room.

SWEET POTATO. (See POTATO, SWEET.)
SWEET CORN. (See CORN, SWEET.)
TOMATO.

At the North it is very desirable to start tomato plants in a house or in a hotbed, and transplant once or twice in order to secure strong, vigorous plants by the time all danger from frost has passed. In the South the plants are started in cold frames or in beds in the open ground and protected by cotton cloth during the cool weather. In the southern parts of Florida and Texas large fields of tomatoes are planted in the same manner as corn, by placing five or six seeds in a hill where the plants are to be grown. After the seedlings become established, all but the two best are thinned out, and later but one is left in the hill.

The tomato is one of the crops that can be hastened to maturity by carefully growing the plants indoors and transplanting to the open ground. Pot-grown plants are especially desirable, and they may be brought to the blooming period by the time it is warm enough to safely plant them in the garden. If the plants are not to be trained but allowed to lie on the ground they should be set about 4 feet apart each way. If trimmed and tied to stakes they may be planted in rows 3 feet apart, and 18 inches apart in the row.

The tomato is one of the American vegetables that have come into general use during the past half century, and it now forms one of the most important of our garden crops. The uses of the tomato are too numerous and too well known to require attention here. For complete information regarding this vegetable, read Farmers' Bulletin No. 220, entitled "Tomatoes."

TOP ONION. (See ONION.)
TREE ONION. (See ONION.)
TURNIP.

The turnip requires a rich soil, and may be grown either as an early or a late crop. For an early crop, sow the seeds in drills 12 to 18 inches apart as early in the spring as the condition of the soil will permit. Two pounds of seed are required to plant an acre. After the plants appear, thin to about 3 inches. The roots will be ready for use before hot weather. For late turnips the seeds are usually sown broadcast on land from which some early crop has been removed, generally during July or August, but later in the South. Turnips are quite hardy and the roots need not be gathered until after several frosts. Turnips may be stored in a cellar or buried in a pit outside. Before storing, the tops should be removed.

Turnips are used in pot-boiled preparations with potatoes, cabbage, and meat, or are boiled with pork, or mashed like potatoes.

TURNIP-ROOTED CHERVIL. (See CHERVIL.)
VEGETABLE MARROW.

The so-called vegetable marrows are closely allied to the pumpkin, both as to species and habit of growth, the principal difference being that the vegetable marrows are used while quite young and tender, and may be baked and served very much the same as sweet potatoes. The vegetable marrows should receive thorough cultivation in order that a tender product may be secured, and should be gathered while the outside skin is still so tender that it may easily be broken by the finger nail. The flesh is either boiled and mashed or baked in the oven and served with butter while hot.

VEGETABLE OYSTER. (See SALSIFY.)
WATER CRESS. (See CRESS.)
WATERMELON. (See MELON—WATERMELON.)
WELSH ONION. (See ONION.)
WITLOOF. (See CHICORY.)

GARDENER'S PLANTING TABLE.

Quantity of seeds or number of plants required for a row 100 feet in length, with distances to plant, times for planting, and period required for production of crop.

Brackets indicate that a late or second crop may be planted the same season.

Kind of vegetable.	Seeds or plants required for 100 feet of row.	Distance for plants to stand— Rows apart. Horse cultivation.	Hand cultivation.	Plants apart in rows.	Depth of planting.	Time of planting in open ground. South.	North.	Ready for use after planting.
Artichoke, Globe	½ ounce	3 to 4 ft	2 to 3 ft	2 to 3 ft	1 to 2 in	Spring	Early spring	15 months.
Artichoke, Jerusalem	2 qts. tubers	3 to 4 ft	1 to 2 ft	1 to 2 ft	2 to 3 in	Spring	Early spring	6 to 8 months.
Asparagus, seed	1 ounce	30 to 36 in	1 to 2 ft	3 to 5 in	1 to 2 in	Autumn or early spring	Early spring	3 to 4 years.
Asparagus, plants	60 to 80 plants	3 to 5 ft	12 to 24 in	15 to 20 in	3 to 5 in	Autumn or early spring	Early spring	1 to 3 years.
Beans, bush	1 pint	30 to 36 in	18 to 24 in	5 or 8 to ft	½ to 2 in	February to April. [August to September.]	April to July	40 to 65 days.
Beans, pole	½ pint	3 to 4 ft	3 to 4 ft	3 to 4 ft	1 to 2 in	Late spring	May and June	50 to 80 days.
Beets	2 ounces	24 to 36 in	12 to 18 in	5 or 6 to ft	1 to 2 in	February to April. [August to September.]	April to August	60 to 80 days.
Brussels sprouts	¼ ounce	30 to 36 in	24 to 30 in	16 to 24 in	½ in	January to July	May and June	90 to 120 days.
Cabbage, early	¼ ounce	30 to 36 in	24 to 30 in	12 to 18 in	½ in	October to December	March and April. (Start in hotbed during February.)	90 to 130 days.
Cabbage, late	¼ ounce	30 to 40 in	24 to 36 in	16 to 24 in	½ in	June and July	May and June	90 to 130 days.
Cardoon	½ ounce	3 ft	2 ft	12 to 18 in	1 to 2 in	Early spring	April and May	5 to 6 months.
Carrot	1 ounce	30 to 36 in	18 to 24 in	6 or 7 to ft	½ in	March and April. [September.]	April to June	75 to 110 days.
Cauliflower	¼ ounce	30 to 36 in	24 to 30 in	14 to 18 in	½ in	January and February. [June.]	April to June. (Start in hotbed during February or March.)	100 to 130 days.
Celeriac	¼ ounce	30 to 36 in	18 to 24 in	4 or 5 to ft	¼ in	Late spring	May and June. (Start in cold frame during April.)	100 to 150 days.
Celery	¼ ounce	3 to 6 ft	18 to 36 in	4 to 8 in	¼ in	August to October	May and June. (Start in hotbed or cold frame during March or April.)	120 to 150 days.
Chervil	1 ounce	30 to 36 in	18 to 24 in	3 or 4 to ft	1 in	Autumn	Autumn	1 year.
Chicory	¼ ounce	30 to 36 in	18 to 24 in	4 or 5 to ft	½ in	March and April	May and June	5 to 6 months.
Citron	1 ounce	8 to 10 ft	8 to 10 ft	8 to 10 ft	1 to 2 in	March and April	May and June	100 to 130 days.
Collards	¼ ounce	30 to 36 in	24 to 30 in	14 to 18 in	½ in	May and June	Late spring	100 to 120 days.
Corn salad	2 ounces	30 in	12 to 18 in	5 or 6 to ft	½ to 1 in	January and February. [September and October.]	March to September	60 days.
Corn, sweet	¼ pint	36 to 42 in	30 to 36 in	30 to 36 in	1 to 2 in	February to April	May to July	60 to 100 days.
Cress, upland	½ ounce	30 in	12 to 18 in	4 or 5 to ft	¼ to 1 in	January and February. [Autumn.]	March to May. [September]	30 to 40 days.
Cress, water	¼ ounce	Broadcast			On surface	Early spring	April to September	60 to 70 days.
Cucumber	½ ounce	4 to 6 ft	4 to 6 ft	4 to 6 ft	1 to 2 in	February and March. [September.]	April to July	60 to 80 days.
Dandelion	¼ ounce	30 in	18 to 24 in	8 to 12 in	½ in	Early spring or autumn	Early spring	6 to 12 months.

Eggplant	½ ounce	30 to 36 in	24 to 30 in	18 to 24 in	½ to 1 in	February to April	April and May. (Start in hotbed during March.)	100 to 140 days.
Endive	1 ounce	30 in	18 in	8 to 12 in	¼ to 1 in	February to April	April. [July]	90 to 180 days.
Horse-radish	70 roots	30 to 40 in	24 to 30 in	14 to 20 in	3 to 4 in	Early spring	Early spring	1 to 2 years.
Kale, or borecole	½ ounce	30 to 36 in	18 to 24 in	18 to 24 in	½ in	October to February	August and September. [March and April.]	90 to 120 days.
Kohl-rabi	½ ounce	30 to 36 in	18 to 24 in	4 to 8 in	½ in	September to March	March to May	60 to 80 days.
Leek	½ ounce	30 to 36 in	14 to 20 in	4 to 8 in	1 in	May to September	March to May	120 to 180 days.
Lettuce	¼ ounce	30 in	12 to 18 in	4 to 6 in	¼ in	September to March	March to September	60 to 90 days.
Melon, muskmelon	½ ounce	6 to 8 ft	6 to 8 ft	Hills 6 ft	1 to 2 in	February to April	April to June. (Start early plants in hotbed during March.)	120 to 150 days.
Melon, watermelon	1 ounce	8 to 12 ft	8 to 12 ft	Hills 10 ft	1 to 2 in	March to May	May and June	100 to 120 days.
Mustard	¼ ounce	30 to 36 in	12 to 18 in	4 or 5 to ft	½ in	Autumn or early spring	March to May. [September]	60 to 90 days.
New Zealand spinach	1 ounce	36 in	24 to 36 in	12 to 18 in	1 to 2 in	Early spring	Early spring	60 to 100 days.
Okra, or gumbo	2 ounces	4 to 5 ft	3 to 4 ft	24 to 30 in	1 to 2 in	February to April	May and June	90 to 140 days.
Onion, seed	1 ounce	24 to 36 in	12 to 18 in	4 or 5 to ft	½ to 1 in	October to March	April and May	130 to 150 days.
Onion, sets	1 quart of sets	24 to 36 in	12 to 18 in	4 or 5 to ft	1 to 2 in	Early spring	Autumn and February to May.	90 to 120 days.
Parsley	½ ounce	24 to 36 in	12 to 18 in	3 to 6 in	½ in	September to May	September and early spring	90 to 120 days.
Parsnip	½ ounce	30 to 36 in	18 to 24 in	5 or 6 to ft	½ to 1 in		April and May	125 to 160 days.
Peas	1 to 2 pints	8 to 4 ft	30 to 36 in	15 to ft	2 to 3 in	September to April	March to June	40 to 80 days.
Pepper	½ ounce	30 to 36 in	18 to 24 in	15 to 18 in	¼ in	Early spring	May and June. (Start early plants in hotbed during March.)	100 to 140 days.
Physalis	½ ounce	30 to 36 in	18 to 24 in	18 to 24 in	½ in	March to May	May and June	130 to 160 days.
Potato, Irish	5 lbs. (or 9 bu. per acre).	30 to 36 in	24 to 36 in	14 to 18 in	4 in	January to April	March to June	80 to 140 days.
Potato, sweet	3 lbs. (or 75 slips).	3 to 5 ft	3 to 5 ft	14 in	3 in	April and May	May and June. (Start plants in hotbed during April.)	140 to 160 days.
Pumpkin	¼ ounce	8 to 12 ft	8 to 12 ft	Hills 8 to 12 ft.	1 to 2 in	April and May	May to July	100 to 140 days.
Radish	1 ounce	24 to 36 in	12 to 18 in	8 to 12 to ft	½ to 1 in	September to April	March to September	20 to 40 days.
Rhubarb, seed	½ ounce	36 in	30 to 36 in	6 to 8 in	½ to 1 in		Early spring	2 to 4 years.
Rhubarb, plants	33 plants	3 to 5 ft	3 to 5 ft	3 ft	2 to 3 in		Autumn or early spring	1 to 3 years.
Ruta-baga	¼ ounce	30 to 36 in	18 to 24 in	6 to 8 in	½ to 1 in	August and September	May and June	60 to 80 days.
Salsify	1 ounce	30 to 36 in	18 to 24 in	2 to 4 in	½ to 1 in		Early spring	120 to 180 days.
Spinach	1 ounce	30 to 36 in	12 to 18 in	7 or 8 to ft	1 to 2 in	September to February	September or very early spring.	30 to 60 days.
Squash, bush	½ ounce	3 to 4 ft	3 to 4 ft	Hills 3 to 4 ft.	1 to 2 in	Spring	April to June	60 to 80 days.
Squash, late	¼ ounce	7 to 10 ft	7 to 10 ft	Hills 7 to 9 ft.	1 to 2 in	Spring	April to June	120 to 160 days.
Tomato	½ ounce	3 to 5 ft	3 to 4 ft	3 ft	¼ to 1 in	December to March	May and June. (Start early plants in hotbed during February and March.)	100 to 140 days.
Turnip	¼ ounce	24 to 36 in	18 to 24 in	6 or 7 to ft	¼ to ½ in	August to October	April. [July]	60 to 80 days.
Vegetable marrow	¼ ounce	8 to 12 ft	8 to 12 ft	Hills 8 to 9 ft.	1 to 2 in	Spring	April to June	110 to 140 days.

www.ingramcontent.com/pod-product-compliance
Lightning Source LLC
Chambersburg PA
CBHW021103080526
44587CB00010B/365